For

Not to be taken
from the room.

reference

HIP HOP
CULTURE

HIP HOP CULTURE

EMMETT G. PRICE III

Santa Barbara, California • Denver, Colorado • Oxford, England

Library of Congress Cataloging-in-Publication Data

Price, Emmett George.
  Hip hop culture / Emmett G. Price, III.
      p. cm.
  Includes bibliographical references (p.   ), discography (p.   ), and index.
    ISBN 1-85109-867-4 (hardback : alk. paper) — ISBN 1-85109-868-2 (ebook) 1. Hip-hop. 2. Rap (Music)—History and criticism. 3. Popular culture. 4. Rap musicians. 5. Music--Social aspects. I. Title.

  ML3531.P75 2006
  306.4'84249--dc22

                                    2006007460

09 08 07   10 9 8 7 6 5 4 3 2

ISBN-13: 978-1-85109-867-5   eBook ISBN-13: 978-1-85109-868-2
This book is also available on the World Wide Web as an e-book.
Visit http://www.abc-clio.com for details.

ABC-CLIO, Inc.
130 Cremona Drive, P.O. Box 1911
Santa Barbara, California 93116–1911
This book is printed on acid-free paper. ∞
Manufactured in the United States of America

*This book is respectfully
dedicated to all of the
Hip Hop Generations—
past, present, and future.*

Contents

Preface

rom the gang-ridden, drug-infested streets of Bronx, New York, in the late 1960s and early 1970s, there arose an urban culture that spread like an antidote to a horrible plague. Hip Hop was the solution, the product of self-determination, self-realization, creativity, and pride. Former late sixties gangs evolved into early seventies "posses" and "crews." Former gang territories became prime locations for block parties and outdoor jams. Prior gang warfare turned into aggressive competitions of turntable jousting by DJs, joined by countless male and female street dancers, often called "b-boys" and "b-girls," and the colorful artistic presentations of graffiti artists. Later, the verbal wit of the MCs was added. From the vivid illustration of the Bronx described by Melle Mel (Grandmaster Flash and the Furious Five) in the 1982 release "The Message" to the prosperity jingle presented by B.G. (Cash Money Millionaires) in the 1999 release "Bling Bling," Hip Hop Culture has gone through a number of transitions. It has grown from a local, non-profit-bearing culture to an international, multibillion-dollar industry that is now to many a model of success. *HIP HOP Culture* not only chronicles these changes but also attempts to create a framework through which Hip Hop and its various manifestations can be further explored.

Although this book is an in-depth and multifaceted examination of Hip Hop, it is not exhaustive. It is not an instructive manual on how to accomplish the various elements of Hip Hop; nor is it a concentrated study on rap music. Instead, this handbook is designed to provide the first step to successful research in the various realms of Hip Hop. Written for a wide range of readers, including high school and college students, high school and college instructors, and the general lay reader, this volume offers guidance on the evolution and development of Hip Hop; covers basic terms, concepts, and important issues related to Hip Hop; and provides detailed information on accessible and widely held resources and references.

Aimed at the novice "Hip Hop fan," the longtime "Hip Hop head," and both beginner and intermediate researchers, *HIP HOP Culture* provides the opportunity to explore and better understand this diverse, influential, and rapidly growing culture. From its roots as an inner-city phenomenon to its global appeal, Hip Hop has spawned a continuing economic, political, social, and cultural movement around the world. Originally a means and manner of expression for economically disenfranchised, politically abandoned, and socially repressed youth grounded in Black expressive culture, Hip Hop has become the look and feel of numerous Fortune 500 companies such as Pepsi, Coca-Cola, Nike, and Reebok. Hip Hop's ability to empower, encourage, and embrace young people (and now the middle aged) is alone worthy of study. Surpassing the international acclaim of rock and jazz, Hip Hop has through a unique system of adoption, appropriation, and association become the voice and culture of international youth and young adults regardless of race, class, gender, ethnicity, political affiliation, or economic standing. The narrative within this handbook tackles these topics as well as the effect of technology and a shifting global economy.

The approach to *HIP HOP Culture* is twofold, both narrative and reference. The volume offers a solid overview of Hip Hop, integrating both an experiential and practical approach. Further, it presents the most comprehensive collection of facts and data to date under one cover. It does not discuss or list everyone who has influenced the movement; nor does it list every place, event, major recording, text, documentary, film, and Web site that has ever played a role in its development. Instead, in an attempt to present a wide-angled view of Hip Hop Culture, I have sifted through a great deal of research in order to select the most accessible and widely held resources to annotate. Although all resource contact information, such as Web URLs, phone numbers, and e-mail addresses, were checked, rechecked, and checked again to assure that they were still active and available up to the latest possible moment before the book went to press, such information inevitably will change and become outdated with time.

The book is organized in ten chapters, each operating both as an individual resource that can stand alone and as part of a complete picture. Chapter 1 sets the backdrop for the evolution and emergence of Hip Hop. The second chapter introduces the various elements of Hip Hop as both independent art forms and as segments of the combined culture. Chapter 3 presents an unbiased analysis of numerous issues and challenges in Hip Hop. Chapter

4 offers an analysis of the influence, appropriation, adaptation, and adoption of Hip Hop Culture around the world.

In an extensive chronology, chapter 5 reveals an interesting array of major events, innovations, and recordings in Hip Hop's history. The sixth chapter offers a brief look into the accomplishments of forty-seven highly regarded Hip Hop innovators, and the seventh assembles an assortment of useful figures, tables, and documents. Chapter 8 offers a close look at organizations, associations, agencies, and programs dedicated to the preservation, promulgation, and/or practice of Hip Hop. Finally, chapter 9 provides an annotated bibliography of the most accessible and widely held print resources on Hip Hop, and chapter 10 provides an annotated listing of the most accessible and widely held non-print resources, including documentaries and other films as well as Web sites. The appendices include annotated lists of influential Hip Hop albums and singles. A glossary is provided to define major Hip Hop terms, and an index concludes the handbook.

It is important to note for purposes of continuity and distinction that in this text "Hip Hop" (with capitals) implies Hip Hop Culture. The same term without the capitals ("hip hop") refers to the musical genre also known as rap music, although some people draw a distinction between the two, a topic discussed in chapter 3. Other spellings, such as "hiphop" or "hip-hop," will only be used when citing sources and referencing particular ideological approaches to hip hop or Hip Hop.

It is my hope that this handbook will be a helpful resource that will increase readers' appetite, admiration, and respect for Hip Hop Culture.

Acknowledgments

his reference handbook is the fruit of years of research and teaching on the subject of Hip Hop Culture, yet it would mean nothing without recognition of the thousands of people who inspired the development of this phenomenon over the past few decades. It was through their pain and suffering that what we now refer to as Hip Hop Culture came into existence, and sometimes, it was through their deaths. It is from that dismal reality that this fruitful phenomenon now thrives. I also acknowledge the countless artists who over the past thirty years have given of themselves to keep this culture alive and healthy. I am grateful as well for the numerous scholars, historians, journalists, critics, and archivists who have worked to illuminate the rich legacy of Hip Hop Culture. There are too many to mention by name, but they have given generously of their time and energy to assist in promoting a greater respect for the culture. At the very least, they have exclaimed to the world that from the core of destitution arose a most valuable and rare treasure. This volume stands on their shoulders.

I also extend a huge thank you to all of the students in my courses on Hip Hop Culture at Washington University in St. Louis (Spring 2001) and Northeastern University (Spring 2004 and Spring 2005). Their willingness to explore the intimate terrain of Hip Hop Culture within the classroom encouraged me to undertake this project. One student in particular saw the project through from beginning to end as my lead research assistant: a very special thank you to Jared Reed, whose commitment did not come without sacrifice or growing pains. I believe that Jared learned that his skills go far beyond what he had previously thought. Jared, I am grateful for your contribution of time, energy, and brilliance!

To all of my supporters, encouragers, readers, and critics—you know who you are—thank you! A special shout out to the Northeastern University Hip Hop Studies Collective (Murray Forman, Alan West-Duran, Geoff Ward, Nadine Yaver, and Paul Saucier); the Journal of Popular Music Studies–Boston Collective

(Jeff Melnick, Murray Forman, Patricia Tang, Reebee Garofalo, Deborah Pacini Hernandez, and Rachel Rubin); the Northeastern University Departments of Music and African American Studies; and the Christa Corrigan McAuliffe Branch of the Framingham Public Library, which provided a wonderful ambiance for writing. This project was also made possible through the special assistance of Rob Sherman, Ann Galligan, and the Northeastern University Division of Cooperative Education. This section would not be complete with a special thanks to the ABC-CLIO staff, particularly Mim Vasan, whose steady communication guided the early phases of this work, and to Dayle Dermatis, Elaine Vanater, Giulia Rossi, Laura Esterman, and Cisca Schreefel, each of whom contributed greatly during the final stages. Thank you!

To my wife, Nicole, whose stern and compassionate voice kept me focused amid numerous distractions, thank you for your numerous edits, suggestions, critiques, and countless hours of sacrifice while I completed yet another one of my projects. Last but not least, I thank my sons: Emmett IV, whose birth at the beginning of this project, and funky drumming and wild style illustrations, clearly show that Hip Hop is in his blood, and Nicholas, whose birth at the conclusion of the project symbolizes for me the birth of yet another generation of Hip Hop. Watching Emmett and Nicholas grow while this project was in progress has made it the most exciting and memorable project of all.

The Rise and Spread of Hip Hop Culture

1

ulture is a way of life that combines intellectual, spiritual, and aesthetic pursuits, thereby grounding the daily decisions and activities of its participants. Hip Hop evolved during the 1970s as a liberation movement in the form of a diverse culture; it was a next-generation civil (human) rights movement sparked by ostracized, marginalized, and oppressed inner-city youth. Grounded in the traditions of U.S.-born Blacks and first- and second-generation Latinos and Latinas as well as people of Caribbean origin (primarily Jamaican, Puerto Rican, Cuban, and Bahamian), Hip Hop is a product of the African diaspora and combines music, dance, graphic art, oration, and fashion with a growing aesthetic leaning heavily on material objects and media. It is a means and method of expression thriving on social commentary, political critique, economic analysis, religious exegesis, and street awareness while combating long-standing issues of racial prejudice, cultural persecution, and social, economic, and political disparities. Over the past three decades, Hip Hop Culture has grown to represent urban, rural, suburban, and global communities of all ages, genders, religions, economic classes, and races. From a local phenomenon addressing the needs and desires of poor inner-city youth, Hip Hop has become an international, multibillion-dollar institution that has virtually changed the nature of the music and entertainment industries. This chapter offers a look at the rise and spread of Hip Hop Culture.

The Changing Landscape: 1960s and 1970s

The 1960s and 1970s were extremely transitional years for the cultural landscape of the United States. Compelled by a lack of access to justice, health care, voting rights, employment, and other everyday privileges of citizenship, numerous groups of minorities took to the streets in strategic offense against the racist and highly discriminatory practices of the country.

The civil rights movement, beginning with a bus boycott in Montgomery, Alabama, in 1955, sparked a nationwide struggle to gain full citizenship rights for Blacks and to essentially end the practice of segregation and the prevailing Jim Crow laws. Using protests, marches, boycotts, sit-ins, and other nonviolent means, the civil rights movement accomplished numerous feats, such as passage of the Civil Rights Act to stop racial discrimination (1964) and the Voting Rights Act (1965). Led by Rev. Dr. Martin Luther King, Jr., the movement aimed to continue the battles against racial and economic inequality in the United States, not just for Blacks, but for all who were without basic equal rights. The assassination of Dr. King on April 4, 1968, left the movement without its leader and without much steam to continue.

Primarily a political movement, the Black power movement also arose during the "turbulent sixties" as Blacks sought an alternative to Dr. King's nonviolent methodology. Led by the Black Panther Party (formerly known as the Black Panther Party for Self-Defense) and indirectly by Malcolm X, the movement aimed to challenge Blacks to be self-determined, self-reliant, and proud of their pursuit to attain cultural autonomy. The assassination of Malcolm X on February 21, 1965, was a tremendous setback, but none was greater than the creation of COINTELPRO (counterintelligence program), launched by then FBI director J. Edgar Hoover. Referring to the national Black Panther Party as the "greatest threat to internal security in the country," Hoover used spies, informants, agents, and other willing parties to indict and implicate the party, offering full permission to break various laws in their pursuit (Ciment 2001, 170). By the mid-1970s, many of the Black Panther Party members were either in jail, murdered, in exile, or underground.

The Black arts movement, rarely mentioned in association with Hip Hop Culture, was the artistic and aesthetic complement to the Black power movement. Championed by Larry Neal, Amiri Baraka (b. LeRoi Jones), Ed Bullins, and a host of other poets, playwrights, thespians, artists, musicians, writers, and the like,

A bus carrying civil rights "freedom riders" is fire-bombed during a caravan to advocate Black voting rights in 1961. The freedom riders were civil rights advocates, both black and white, who traveled to the South from the North on buses in 1961 as volunteers for the Congress of Racial Equality. (Library of Congress)

the Black arts movement revisited the ideas of Black pride and Black beauty popularized in the 1920s and 1930s with the Negro Renaissance in Harlem, Chicago, and other metropolises. Sparked by the 1965 assassination of Malcolm X, and continuing through the mid-1970s, the arts activists created, supported, and taught art from the Black perspective, relying on the theoretical principles taught and practiced by the Black power activists.

The Immigration Act of 1965, sparked by the civil rights movement, abolished the nationality prerequisite for immigrant visas and instead allowed for immigration based on skills and professions. Though the act set annual limitations on immigration, it still allowed for an increase in non-European immigration. Numerous Asian and Caribbean populations took advantage of the new opportunity to come to the United States.

Amid the various victories, numerous civil disturbances occurred. In Harlem, a riot arose in July 1964 in response to the killing of a fifteen-year-old Harlem male by a white policeman. Approximately 112 stores were looted or burned, and more than 500 arrests were recorded (ibid., 173). In Watts in 1965, two white police officers were confronted by a mob as they attempted to arrest a Black driver. After six days, 34 were dead, 900 were injured, 4,000 had been arrested, and over $225 million in property damages were tallied (ibid.). The long, hot summer of 1967 witnessed disturbances in Detroit, Newark, and a number of other urban areas.

The entrance of the United States into the Vietnam War in 1961 ushered in a new dilemma as numerous inner-city young men were drafted to serve in the military and sent overseas to fight in the controversial conflict. The social, political, and economic disparities were easily visible: The same young people who were often mistreated and abused by the law and the legal system were sent away to fight for the very laws and legal systems that abused them. Their peers from more affluent areas took advantage of educational and business options. Civil unrest and urban disturbances continued in certain areas as the disparities created a serious decline in neighborhoods around the country. One of the most notable areas of the country in dire straits during this period was the New York borough called the Bronx.

The Bronx

Known affectionately within the Hip Hop nation as the "Boogie Down," the Bronx during the late 1960s and 1970s proved fertile grounds for the birth of the revolutionary cultural movement named Hip Hop. Often called "America's worst slum" or "the epitome of urban failure," the immensely impoverished, crime-ridden, drug-infested streets of the Bronx were not always a symbol of economic demise and social decay (Fernando 1994, 2).

The Bronx is one of New York City's five boroughs. The remaining four are Manhattan, Brooklyn, Queens, and Staten Island. During the 1910s, the advent and rapid growth of the Manhattan-based subway lines created a huge population growth demanding new housing options for inhabitants who worked in the city. The Bronx quickly grew as a desired place of residence for upwardly mobile working- and middle-class families aiming to escape the hustle and bustle of Manhattan yet live within suitable commuting distance. Filled with primarily first- and second-generation immigrants, the Bronx of the 1920s, 1930s, and prewar 1940s was a platform from which the "American Dream" could be realized. The Mott Haven, Melrose, and Highbridge areas were highly populated by Irish. The Morrisania and Belmont areas were Italian. The Jewish populations of Hunt's Point, West Farms, East Tremont,

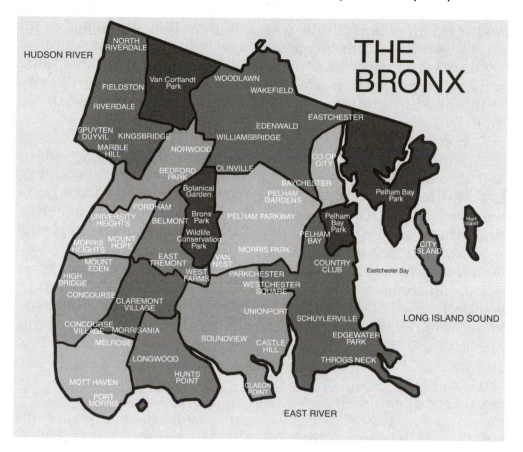

Map of the Bronx, New York. Map is not to scale. (ABC-CLIO from TheAmazingBronx.com)

and the Grand Concourse area made up the majority of the city. Small printing shops and clothing factories, in addition to trucking, warehousing, and wholesale trade businesses, provided a stable economy. Blue-collar civil servants, unionized day laborers, and clerks worked hard, believing their children would benefit from their efforts and eventually rise to wealth.

The post–World War II Bronx was dramatically different from the prewar Bronx, however. As soldiers returned from abroad, many took advantage of new GI-specific housing opportunities in the Queens and Long Island sections of New York and in numerous New Jersey areas. The postwar economy diminished urban industrialization as the rich manufacturing, garment, and printing industries of New York City began to decline, giving rise to a new economy based in information technology. The successes of the burgeoning civil rights movement rang loud in New York as numerous working- and middle-class U.S.-born Blacks and Puerto Ricans moved into Bronx neighborhoods. The new cry of "mandatory busing" enraged many white citizens, and the "white flight" from the Bronx north into Westchester County began. As the predominantly Irish, Italian, and Jewish populations departed, more Black, Latino, and Caribbean families moved in.

The greatest transition of the Bronx, however, occurred from the combined effects of several related phenomena: the actions of the city construction coordinator, Robert Moses; the opening of Co-op City; and an abundance of arsons during the 1970s. These three factors caused the mass exodus of thousands of working- and middle-class families from the Bronx, now deemed "the worst neighborhood in America" (Grogan and Proscio 2000, 15).

In 1944, Moses announced plans for a major thoroughfare that would connect Long Island (through Queens) to Manhattan and New Jersey. This 7-mile-long, six-lane highway, called the Cross-Bronx Expressway, would cater to the needs of suburban commuters. By the 1970s, the construction of the expressway had interrupted "113 streets, avenues and boulevards; sewers and water and utility mains numbering in the hundreds; one subway and three railroads, five elevated rapid transit lines, and seven other expressways or parkways, some of which were being built by Moses simultaneously" (quoted in Jonnes 2002 [1986], 120–121). The construction devastated the once stable community, pummeling some 60,000 homes, though, through the Title I Slum Clearance program, affected families had the opportunity to relocate, and some 170,000 people took advantage of it (Rose 1994, 31). Part of Moses' plans included the removal of single-family homes in exchange for large high-rise apartments. These apartments quickly became public housing as the demographics of the inhabitants changed. Property owners sold their rapidly depreciating real estate, most often to slumlords, who in turn thrived by taking advantage of those who were unable to relocate. Migrants fled to northern areas of the Bronx as well as into the suburbs of Westchester County. In addition, Moses' 1961 Urban Renewal Project, an effort to clean and clear the areas of Chinatown, Soho, Greenwich Village, and Little Italy in order to create office lofts and high-rise apartments, and to make room for the lower Manhattan Expressway, further relocated folks—this time into the Bronx.

The opening in 1968 of Co-op City, a massive offering of 15,000 new subsidized apartments in massive towers in the northeast corner of the Bronx, created a cost-effective safe haven for fleeing working- and middle-class families who could secure the highly competitive housing. Working- and middle-class Blacks, Latinos and Latinas, and people of Caribbean descent were amongst those seeking to capitalize on the new opportunity. The mass departure of economically stable families from the central and lower Bronx, and the influx of more impoverished families into the Bronx, transformed the formerly thriving area into a "city of despair" (Fernando 1994, 2).

With the realities of rent control—a practice that had been in place since 1943 nationwide, and since 1950 specifically in New York—and the steady flight of working- and middle-class families—who were discouraged by the lack of safety in the Bronx and the diminishing property values—the majority of property fell into the hands of slumlords. By 1969, the fate of the Bronx was sealed for years to come when slumlords and others began setting blaze to the buildings. From 1973 to 1977, more than 12,000 fires were reported every year, and over 5,000 apartment buildings, holding more than 100,000 units of housing, were destroyed (Jonnes 2002 [1986], 8).

On July 13, 1977, at 9:35 p.m., all of New York City went dark from the effects of a citywide electrical power outage. The hours of civil unrest, looting, vandalism, theft, and destruction had their greatest effect on the Bronx, as news cameras from all over the nation came to the borough to witness the results of years of decline and demise. In an effort to separate the "good" Bronx (the northeastern areas, such as the newly constructed Co-op City) from the "bad" Bronx (the southern, western, and central areas), the term "South Bronx" became popularized all over the country and subsequently the world. Thus, everywhere that a large population of impoverished people (whether Black, Latino, Caribbean, Irish, Italian, Jewish, or other) lived was now deemed "the South Bronx." At first the term was used to describe just 1 square mile in the southeast corner of the Mott Haven neighborhood, but by 1980, the South Bronx included parts of Melrose, Hunt's Point, Morrisania, West Farms, Tremont, the Grand Concourse area, Highbridge, and Morris Heights. The South Bronx had grown to cover a whopping 20 square miles encapsulating pretty much everything south of Fordham Road. The concentration of welfare households showed no sign of having any working- or middle-class inhabitants, and the abandoned and arson-ridden shells of buildings, mixed with the overwhelming signs of urban decay and political disenfranchisement, made a fertile territory for crime, drugs, and gangs.

From Gangs to Crews

The presence of gangs in the United States dates back to the 1800s. Gangs serve to fulfill the needs of youth and some adults who have unmet social and emotional needs. Often created within an ethnic- or class-oriented enclave, gangs provide a "family" to young people who find their present family structures either insufficient or unpromising. These newly created families rely on extremely organized hierarchies, loyalty, and most significantly, respect.

Historically, gangs have been male dominated, although numerous women also participate in gangs and gang activity. During the 1940s and 1950s, gangs often protected the neighborhood—elders and children in particular—from vandals and drug dealers. Drug-addicted streetwalkers and "junkies" were prime targets for gangbangers, as they were often unable to take revenge or defend themselves, but in that era, the junkies' fate upon encountering a gang was most often a beating, rarely anything more. By the 1970s, gangs in metropolises around the country had evolved into extremely violent organizations known for undertaking life-threatening actions, including those featured at their own initiations.

Within the Bronx, initiations occurred at early ages and most often included rituals such as the "Apache line," "running the mill," "Russian roulette," and other violent and often criminal activities. Young initiates, often including the siblings of older members, would be inducted into the baby or young crews (for example, Baby Kings or Young Samurais). As the demise of the Bronx occurred, displaced and ostracized youth took to the streets amid the "urban decay" in order to forge a life of their own. Many of these youths were affected by the changing nature of society, and in particular, the redefinition of family. They traded in their realities as latchkey kids, children of depressed, alcoholic, or drug-addicted parents, or children disinherited by neglect or abuse for the enjoyment of local celebrity status. Gang affiliation offered the social status that money could not buy. As gang leaders surrounded themselves with devout and loyal members, gang affiliation further offered street credibility, instant respect by rival gang members, and prestige in the community. Upon successful initiation, a new member was permitted to wear gang insignias and other indicators of induction into the family, such as tattoos, colors associated with the gang, and certain fashions.

A Latin Kings gang leader in the Bronx wears a crown as he holds his baby. As with most gang origins, the Latin Kings claimed as their intention to protect their members, but are reputed to be a street gang involved in criminal activities. (Andrew Lichtenstein/Corbis)

As territorial associations, gangs identified their turf by "tagging," that is, by leaving written identifiers (usually on public property) demarking the perimeter of their geographical space. Turf dens or meeting chambers were usually held in abandoned buildings taken custody by the gang, often with eventual renovations. Many gangbangers dropped out of high school and then had more time on their hands to strategize, recruit, commit crimes, engage in war with rival gangs, and, most important, get in trouble with the law.

By 1968, gang warfare in the Bronx was extremely high. Numerous young people had been murdered, families had been destroyed, and the streets were in utter chaos. When Black Benjie (Cornell Benjamin), a member of the Ghetto Brothers, was killed, a historic truce was called on December 8, 1971, at the Bronx Boys Club. Hundreds of gang members met to discuss the possibilities for finding a better way to handle their aggression and for having peace on the streets of their city. Many prominent gang leaders were present, including fourteen-year-old Afrika Bambaataa (Kevin Donovan), who would quickly rise as a leader of the Black

Some Prevailing Gangs in the Bronx and Surrounding Areas	
Arthur Ave Boys	Minister
Bachelors	Mongols
Black Assassins	Peacemakers
Black Cats	P.O.W.E.R.
Black Falcons	Reapers
Black Spades	Roman Kings
Blue Diamonds	Royal Charmers
Ching-a-Lings	Royal Javelins
Cofon Cats	Savage Nomads
Dirty Dozen	Savage Samurais
Flying Dutchmen	Savage Skulls
Ghetto Brothers	Seven Crowns
Ghetto Warriors	Seven Immortals
Glory Stompers	Spanish Kings
Golden Guineas	Supreme Bachelors
Grateful Dead	Turbans
Inter Crime	Uptown Organization
King Cobras	War Pigs
Latin Aces	Young Sinners
Majestic Warlocks	

Spades. Although the truce did not end gangs, it did offer alternatives to the continuing bloodshed. Gangbangers began to use dance and other expressive means to rid themselves of their frustrations.

Although these highly competitive public demonstrations did reroute some of the aggressively violent behavior, the bloodshed did continue. Shortly after the truce meeting, the New York Police Department (NYPD) launched a ninety-two-member squad called the Bronx Youth Gang Task Force. Under the command of Deputy Inspector William Lakeman, the task force was given the responsibility of profiling, infiltrating, and containing the gang pandemic. Meanwhile, gangs were spreading to surrounding states, particularly New Jersey and Connecticut. Even with the effects of the 1971 truce and the creation of the NYPD task force, gang activity peaked in 1973. Estimates place more than 300 gangs in the Bronx and surrounding areas at that time with over 19,500 members (Hager 2002, 40). Yet, by the mid-1970s, the tide was beginning to turn as the sounds, dances, looks, and feels of the burgeoning Hip Hop Culture revealed a new reality for these disenfranchised, ostracized, marginalized, and oppressed young people, who were seen by outsiders as social, political, and economic misfits.

The saga of gangs in the Bronx and surrounding areas could be told of any major urban area in the United States. By 1995, national statistics showed that "gang activity existed in all fifty states, including rural, urban, and suburban communities" (Kitwana 2002, 20). Through the 1980s and 1990s, gang culture became imbedded into urban (and in many cases, rural and suburban) culture. Yet, it is the story of the gangs of the Bronx and surrounding areas that creates the intriguing backdrop that led to the birth of Hip Hop Culture.

In the Beginning

Prior to the rise of recorded rap music via Sugar Hill Gang's highly influential and highly controversial 1979 recording "Rapper's Delight," Hip Hop had already been created as a burgeoning culture driven by self-determination, a love for life, and a desire to have fun. When Kool Herc (Clive Campbell) arrived in the Bronx, bringing with him his passion for music and an extensive record collection, he also brought with him a youthful edge. As he walked the streets with some of the gangs and involved himself in some of the tagging cliques and dancing crews, his desire to be different and to infuse all of his diverse experiences with that edge propelled him to be a unique DJ who understood not only the importance of music but also the role that music played in healing the lives of the oppressed youths who made up his audience, even if only for a brief moment.

Born in the Kingston area of Jamaica, as a child Campbell heard the sounds of the DJs toasting over instrumental tracks played through their massive dub systems. These memories, along with the house parties that Campbell attended after relocating to the Bronx with his mother in 1967, inspired the new style of DJing that he promulgated. Focused on expanding the breakdown section of the record, Campbell, now called Herc, brought forth the break beat, which not only gave dancers a new canvas on which to present their fancy footwork and moves, but also offered a clean palette from which the DJ or an MC might motivate others to come to the dance floor and "get down." With his collective, which included MCs, dancers (b-boys/b-girls), security, and roadies to help him transport his massive sound system, he created the first Hip Hop crew: Kool Herc and the Herculords (also referenced as Herculoids).

A DJ displays his skills on the twin turntables also known by some as the "wheels of steel." (Mika/Zefa/Corbis)

Although Kool Herc's crew did not rid the Bronx of the tremendous gang crisis, it did contribute to changing the nature of gangs. By the mid-1970s, as Herc's sound and idea were distributed around town and adapted by other innovative DJs, it appeared that each former turf area now had its own DJ and discothèque. Herc played the West Bronx neighborhood and the East Bronx nightclubs; Grandmaster Flash (Joseph Saddler) played the South Bronx (from 138th Street to 163rd Street). Afrika Bambaataa held the southeast, and in the north, DJ Breakout and DJ Baron held court (Chang 2005, 83). Offering "shout-outs" to local gang leaders and members while also motivating them to dance, have fun, and leave crime and violent acts behind, early Hip Hop changed the nature of the times—temporarily. Kool Herc ignited the spark that created what would later be called rap music and Hip Hop Culture, yet it was Afrika Bambaataa who institutionalized it and served as its first ambassador.

During the mid-1970s, former gang warlord Afrika Bambaataa built the house from which Hip Hop would be introduced to the nation and world through the creation of the Universal Zulu Nation. Headquartered at the Bronx River Center, the Universal Zulu Nation brought together DJs, dancers (b-boys/b-girls), graffiti artists, MCs, and rap enthusiasts to party, providing a venue where they might express themselves via the four foundational elements (DJing, graffiti, b-boying/b-girling, and MCing). Former and present gangbangers and drug dealers would lay down their weapons and drug paraphernalia for a time at Zulu Nation functions and join the burgeoning Hip Hop community. Armed with the motto "Peace, Love, Unity, and Having Fun," Bambaataa, through his "Infinity Lessons," not only aimed to offer an expressive outlet but also encouraged intellectual pursuit via study, affirmations, and a systematic process of getting to know one's self (ibid., 105). Zulu Nation events drew folks from as far as New Jersey and Connecticut who came to be involved in the new movement created by Herc and spread by Bambaataa. By the summer of 1976, Hip Hop was on the radar of many young people and establishing itself as a prominent force for change.

Hip Hop Spreads across the Country

In 1979, the independent label Sugar Hill Records released "Rapper's Delight," a lengthy group rhyme by the label's signature group, Sugar Hill Gang. Although the record was preceded by the Fatback Band's "King Tim III (Personality Jock)," "Rapper's Delight" gained notoriety through radio play, achieving instant acclaim and recognition as the characteristic sound of the new music and its subsequent culture. Inspired by the public display of affection awarded to the Sugar Hill Gang, numerous Bronx-, Harlem-, and Brooklyn-based practitioners soon made their way to the office of Sylvia and Joe Robinson hoping to sign a record contract. Noted artists, such as Afrika Bambaataa, Grandmaster Flash, the Cold Crush Brothers, and many other local innovators who had prestige and instant name recognition in their local neighborhoods, were all seeking to sign with fledgling record labels such as Sugar Hill Records, Paul Winley, and subsequently Tommy Boy Records and Def Jam Records, among others. The record contract quickly elevated the MC to prominence, allowing for the greatest platform for exposure and the greatest chance for making money. DJs, graffiti artists, and b-boys/b-girls became less visible and were often given a subordinate role in the mainstream media presentation of this rich, expressive culture.

Kurtis Blow (Kurtis Walker) earned rap music's first certified gold record for posting more than 500,000 sales of "The Breaks" in 1980. This success not only earned him a record deal with Mercury Records but also validated rap music and Hip Hop Culture's appeal as money makers. Major record labels now knew that rap music and Hip Hop Culture were worth the investment. This sent new adrenaline and motivation to hundreds of rhyming youth nationwide who began to hear the new sounds of rap music over the airwaves of their local urban radio stations.

During the early 1980s, numerous college radio stations around the country began to schedule isolated time for rap music programming, playing many of the recent releases of the independent and major record labels. In January 1982, the first commercial radio all–hip hop mix show was featured on New Jersey's WHBI by Afrika Islam. Named *Zulu Beats,* the show began a trend. Playing rap music caught on across the country, even in the Northeast. Yet it was on the West Coast where the first twenty-four-hour station dedicated to broadcasting hip hop, 1580 AM KDAY, would launch in 1984. The broadcast of released singles, as well as "live," in-studio performances and "on the air" interviews with popular artists, offered a unique appeal to young people, who were fascinated by the liberal approach to expression. The music often included street metaphors, foul language, and extensive discussion of rather taboo yet intriguing subjects such as sex, gangs, drugs, and the pursuit of the rich lifestyle. The radio shows often allowed young consumers to preview entire albums prior to purchase, serving as a reliable source of information about when new releases would be available and which ones would be worth purchasing. By the mid-1980s, urban radio was a major form of entertainment within the country's metropolises. Although the urban sounds of hip hop might not have vibed well in southern or midwestern areas, live performances in concert settings would eventually catch on and capture a larger audience.

Although the 1982 Kitchen Tour, featuring Rock Steady Crew, FAB 5 FREDDY, Crazy Legs, DJ Spy, and others, was one of the first publicized national excursions, performing in Washington, D.C., Pennsylvania, New York, Minnesota, Iowa, Illinois, Michigan, and Toronto, Canada, the Fresh Fest Tour was the first major tour earning big money and wide recognition. The 1984 schedule of twenty-seven dates, featuring Run-DMC, Kurtis Blow, Whodini, Fat Boys, and Nucleus, grossed $3.5 million and spread rap music and Hip Hop Culture across the country, filling arenas and catering to a wide spectrum of soon-to-be rap fans and Hip Hop headz. The Fresh Fest Tour became an annually scheduled event, most often featuring Def Jam artists. Audiences were mesmerized by the personal appeal of the artists and identified with much of the lyrical content and musical context. Once thousands of young people experienced the raw sounds and presentation of hip hop, they were afflicted with passion for the new genre. They purchased not only musical recordings but also T-shirts, bandanas, and other merchandise portraying their favorite artists. With the help of managers such as Russell Simmons, the artists received invitations to television variety and talk shows, gaining even wider exposure across the country. As exposure reached unprecedented levels and entertainment industry executives began noticing changes in the public interest in rap music and Hip Hop Culture, numerous motion pictures, documentaries, and featured sequences highlighting the new phenomenon began to appear.

The first major motion picture presentation of Hip Hop Culture was the 1982 movie *Wild Style* (Wild Style Productions). Filmed on the very scene where Hip Hop Culture was born and brewing, the film portrayed the actual innovators living their lives. The main stars of the film were practitioners of the foundational elements and not hired actors, which added an extra zest of realness to the captured experience. At the time of the launch of the film, the major participants embarked on a national tour showcasing the various expressions of Hip Hop in person from city to city in hopes of not only promoting the film but also enticing the viewer to engage in this form of expression. The popularity and prominence of *Wild Style* was quickly supported by the release of *Style Wars* (New Day Films) in 1983. This film focused on the graffiti movement within Hip Hop Culture, offering an insightful approach to exposing the urban realities of the country. The film was broadcast on PBS, instigating a new generation of young taggers who dared to emulate the dangerous and honorable lifestyle, from their perspectives, exhibited in the documentary.

By the mid-1980s, numerous motion pictures featuring choreographed segments highlighting aspects of Hip Hop had appeared, including the 1983 *Flashdance* (Polygram Filmed Entertainment), which showcased the fancy foot and floor work of Rock Steady Crew members. This film, in particular, reached a new audience, as did films such as *Beat Street* (MGM/UZ Home Entertainment, 1984); *Body Rock* (New World Pictures, 1984); *Breakin'* (Cannon Group, 1984); *Breakin' 2: Electric Boogaloo* (Cannon Film Distributors, 1984); *Krush Groove* (Film Development Fund and Visual Eyes Productions, 1984); and *Rappin'* (Cannon Pictures, 1985), each of which prominently featured elements of Hip Hop and showcased the culture. When these films hit the national movie theaters, they spread the culture to places not previously on the tour routes or within the bandwidth of popular radio stations broadcasting the urban sounds of rap music.

As artists earned unprecedented recording contracts, competed for prime-time radio play, traveled the nation on tours, and awaited opportunities to showcase their skills on film, television appearances on variety shows such as *Soul Train* and *Showtime at the Apollo* would take a backseat. This trend continued with the rise of BET and MTV, television stations launched in 1980 and 1981, respectively, that catered to the very clientele identified as potential Hip Hop consumers. With programming such as *Yo! MTV Raps* and *The Basement,* Hip Hop found a home on television. The images and sounds were sent into households across the nation, becoming readily accessible for all who were willing and able to watch. The rise of Hip Hop–oriented trade magazines, such as *Source* in 1988 and *VIBE* in 1993, provided another opportunity for the spread of Hip Hop. As interested consumers purchased the publications in search of feature stories and opinion essays, they were also exposed to a wealth of advertisements. The magazines informed the entire nation of the fashion trends, the hot records, the touring schedules of various artists, and a host of additional information.

By the 1990s, Hip Hop was the dominant force in popular culture as numerous Hip Hop artists rose in prominence as popular-culture icons. Widely acclaimed Hip Hop artists distinguished themselves from among the Hip Hop fold as businessmen/women and moguls. Soaring above the media coverage of the rising gangsta rap and the ensuing East Coast versus West Coast rivalry, as well as above the acclaim of MC Hammer and Vanilla Ice and the inflated commercialized rap, Russell Simmons, P. Diddy, Jay-Z, Master P, and Queen Latifah mastered numerous elements of Hip Hop and moved forward to master the business side of Hip Hop as well. These innovators created multimillion-dollar-earning record labels (for example, Def Jam Records, Bad Boy Records, Roc-A-Fella Records, No Limit Records, and Flava Unit Records). They also entered the fashion world with tremendous success (for example, Phat Farm, Sean John, Roca Wear, and No Limit Clothing). In addition, these artists have controlled the emergence of Hip Hop into media realms previously inaccessible. Jay-Z's purchase of a share of the New Jersey Nets franchise, Queen Latifah and P. Diddy's entrance onto the Broadway stage, and numerous other innovative, pioneering events symbolized the very empowering nature of Hip Hop from its foundations in the 1970s. The realization of the Hip Hop movement occurred during the 1990s as the culture spread into all facets of society within the United States and abroad.

The Future of Hip Hop

As Hip Hop Culture embarks on its future as a thirty-plus-year-old expression and cultural movement, its future is as bright as it is dark. Following the path of its predecessors—jazz and rock 'n' roll—Hip Hop's vibrant ebbs and flows of creative ingenuity may never stop, but they will no doubt eventually lose their captive audience to a lesser known tributary. As a new generation of youth rise in search of their own unique manner and method of expression and aim to challenge various issues from generations past, their creativity will spark a new genre and perhaps a new cultural movement. Although it may be grounded and based in the urgent and accessible sounds, language, graphic depictions, and movement of Hip Hop, it certainly will be different.

One of Hip Hop's greatest strengths is that it has ignited conversation around the development of new cultural aesthetics and renewed approaches to the formation and expression of artistic endeavors as a culture. Jazz, rock 'n' roll, and numerous highly popular and tremendously significant genres from the past all had characteristics and elements through which they could have been expressed and presented as cultures. They all possessed uniquely stylized approaches to performance practice and instrumental (including vocal) presentation as well as complementary variations on dance, dress, language, and graphic presentation. Hip Hop and its innovators pressed the envelope by presenting the vibrant compilation of expressions as one cultural movement, a practice that will more likely than not continue as new forms of expression evolve and begin to seek their place within the rough terrain of popular culture.

Hip Hop's dominant claim on the music industry will forever be felt. Numerous aspects of the industry, including its relationship with artists and with other forms of media and entertainment, were sparked and developed through the rise of Hip Hop. The proliferation of home-based studios by self-acclaimed, technically skilled MCs and producers has revolutionized the music industry. For example, the number of development record deals has greatly diminished owing to the increased number of talented artists pitching their work to the major labels already polished in the use of technology. Furthermore, the timely development of MP3 technology and digital file sharing has offered some artists an opportunity to bypass the major record label altogether and distribute their music online through various Internet-based venues.

Although past jazz and rock 'n' roll artists worked in the film industry prior to the rise of Hip Hop, their roles were often predisposed to that of performance and/or in some way related to the expression on screen of their musical talent. Hip Hop has sparked the new action hero, the Hip Hop artist, who, through prominence and wide appeal, draws a substantial audience previously untapped. The rise in Hip Hop–oriented comedies and romance pictures reflects the motion-picture industry's attempt to capture the multibillion-dollar consumer profile of the Hip Hop audience. Similarly, big and small businesses alike have been inspired to formulate relationships with the Hip Hop community through the appropriation of hip hop music and the presence of Hip Hop–oriented aesthetics in numerous commercials, advertisements, and the like in order to cater to the Hip Hop dollar. The focus and presentation of the importance of material culture within Hip Hop will maintain this and other examples of these types of relationships into the next century.

Hip Hop's greatest potential, though, is to be a catalyst for racial and social-class healing and reconciliation. As an expression catering to a variety of communities both around the country and around the world, Hip Hop is positioned to begin conversations addressing ways to mend both racial tensions and social-class disparities. Although these conversations are already prevalent in lyrics, more steps can be taken to address these and other issues more directly as young and impressionable generations come of age listening to, comprehending, and analyzing Hip Hop and becoming actively engaged in these discussions.

Although the future of any artistic form is extremely difficult to predict, one thing is certain, Hip Hop Culture will remain a dominant force within mainstream popular culture for quite some time. It may sound different, the art may look different, the dancing may seem different, and the MCs may rhyme differently, but as living expressions, these foundational elements will continue to push forward as a cultural movement grounded in social, political, and economic liberation for disenfranchised, ostracized, and oppressed youth who have been systematically removed from access to what, in their own perspective, equates to full citizenship.

Summary

In order to better understand Hip Hop Culture, it is imperative to revisit the political, social, economic, and cultural developments that the early innovators faced. Through this panoramic view of life via the eyes of the innovators, we are more equipped to contextualize the need and the desire for something such as Hip Hop, a cultural movement with the aim of empowering disenfranchised, ostracized, and oppressed youth.

As a product of urban neglect and a descendant of the civil rights, Black power, and Black arts movements, Hip Hop arose as a unifying force for young people of all races and ethnicities who had two major things in common: an experience with Black expressive culture (whether through birthright or adaptation) and an experience with the brutal clutches of poverty. With these two experiences in place, U.S.-born Blacks, first- and second-generation Latin-born folks, first- and second-generation people of Caribbean descent, and whites united under the rubric of the Universal Zulu Nation to breed Hip Hop Culture. Arising from the street culture of the Bronx, Afrika Bambaataa and the Universal Zulu Nation built on the early achievements of DJ Kool Herc and the Herculords, spreading the Hip Hop message through music and other expressive forms via the foundational elements of DJing, graffiti, b-boying/b-girling, and MCing.

By the 1980s, the local expression spread nationwide as numerous artists followed in the wake of the success of the Sugar Hill Gang and Kurtis Blow. Rap records sold nationwide as the music was broadcast over numerous radio stations, artists traveled the country touring, and an abundance of Hip Hop–oriented films and documentaries helped the expressive culture rise in popularity even in remote places within the country. Subsequently, Hip Hop–influenced magazines continued the proliferation of Hip Hop Culture across the country.

As artists began to achieve visibility and prestige as influential members of society, they launched a variety of entrepreneurial endeavors that showcased the empowering aspect of Hip Hop that had led to its development during the early 1970s.

Although it is difficult to speculate, Hip Hop Culture and Hip Hop's dominance in the entertainment industry will likely be strong for many years to come as more artists seek to explore new avenues of expression beyond the foundational elements.

References

Chang, Jeff. 2005. *Can't Stop Won't Stop: A History of the Hip-Hop Generation.* New York: St. Martin's Press.

Ciment, James. 2001. *Atlas of African-American History.* New York: Checkmark.

Fernando, S. H., Jr. 1994. *New Beats: Exploring the Music, Culture, and Attitudes of Hip-Hop.* New York: Anchor/Doubleday.

Fricke, Jim, and Charlie Ahearn. 2002. *Yes, Yes, Y'all: The Experience Music Project Oral History of Hip-Hop's Decade.* Cambridge, MA: Da Capo.

Grogan, Paul S., and Tony Proscio. 2000. *Comeback Cities: A Blueprint for Urban Neighborhood Revival.* Boulder: Westview.

Hager, Steven. 2002. *Adventures in the Counterculture: From Hip Hop to High Times.* New York: High Times Books.

Jonnes, Jill. 2002. *South Bronx Rising: The Rise, Fall, and Resurrection of an American City,* 2d ed. New York: Fordham University Press.

Kitwana, Bakari. 2002. *The Hip Hop Generation: Young Blacks and the Crisis in African-American Culture.* New York: BasicCivitas.

Light, Alan, ed. 1999. *The VIBE History of Hip Hop.* New York: Three Rivers.

Rose, Tricia. 1994. *Black Noise: Rap Music and Black Culture in Contemporary America.* Hanover, CT: Wesleyan University Press.

Thompson, Robert Farris. 1996. "Hip Hop 101." In *Droppin' Science: Critical Essays on Rap Music and Hip Hop Culture,* ed. William Eric Perkins. Philadelphia: Temple University Press.

Toop, David. 2000. *Rap Attack 3: African Rap to Global Hip Hop,* 3d ed. London: Serpent's Tail.

The
Elements

Z

ip Hop Culture is most commonly defined as the combination of four foundational elements: DJing, graffiti, b-boying/b-girling, and MCing. Each element serves as a method of self-expression relying on individual creativity and highly personalized modes of performance. Each has roots in urban metropolises and arose from the socially dim, economically dire, and politically hopeless inner cities. And each somehow intersects with the prevalence of gangs and the gang lifestyle during the 1960s. The rise in popularity of Hip Hop Culture during the 1980s offered numerous opportunities for continued innovation, giving rise to additional elements: beat boxing/vocal percussion, fashion, language, and numerous others, including the acceptance of a Hip Hop aesthetic. This chapter offers an in-depth look at each of these elements and discovers how they work together to construct Hip Hop Culture.

The DJ

The DJ, or disc jockey, presents prerecorded music or sound to an audience. The first DJs were radio disc jockeys who presented music over the radio airwaves to audiences of dedicated listeners.

The first radio broadcast of any kind of music was on Christmas Eve of 1906, when Reginald A. Fessenden, an engineer in Boston, attempted to send uncoded signals of music and speech to Scotland. By the mid-1920s, the radio was very popular, as was the DJ, broadcasting hours of music in a program format. As the recording industry continued to grow through the 1930s and 1940s, broadcasting more and more popular music, radio DJs continued to rise in notability and popularity, particularly in major cities such as New York, Pittsburgh, Hollywood, Memphis, and

Cleveland. During the 1950s, DJs began performing "live" at "platter parties" and "sock hops," local dances for high-school and college-age young adults. Television shows such as Dick Clark's *American Bandstand* and Don Cornelius's *Soul Train* sprang forth as byproducts of these collective gatherings where young, passionate music lovers enjoyed dancing to the latest hits as played by local bands and eventually DJs. The emergence of rock 'n' roll in the 1950s was popularized by DJs who had a subtle way of making formerly Black or "race music" accessible to white kids. During the 1970s, the DJs broadcasted a new style of music called "disco" all across the nation. Yet not every DJ wanted to play the up-tempo, energetic, dance-oriented music.

With the 1970s came a very energetic and aggressive style of dancing associated with funk and eventually disco. A young DJ, Kool Herc (Clive Campbell), decided to give the dancers what it appeared they were looking for as they waited anxiously for the break of the records to hit in order to crowd the dance floor in joust, or competition, against one another. Kool Herc decided to mix the break sections of a few choice records together in sequence without playing the beginning or ending of each corresponding song, fading one song directly into the next. This soon became known as "mixing breaks" or "creating break beats." Previously DJs would use the microphone to talk and inspire the crowd between songs. The reaction to this new style of DJing was immediate and so well-liked by the dancers that they soon became known as b-boys and b-girls, or break boys and break girls. Numerous b-boys/b-girls sought out parties and clubs where Kool Herc was scheduled to DJ in anticipation of these clever break beats. B-boys such as Grandmixer DXT (formerly known as D.ST), Kurtis Blow, Grandwizard Theodore, and Jazzy Jay were so influenced by Kool Herc that they themselves became DJs.

With two turntables, numerous speakers, and an extraordinary collection of records, Kool Herc created the backdrop for rap music and the subsequent Hip Hop Culture. Herc's first party was in 1971 at the Sedgwick Avenue Community Center, where he performed to a community plagued with gang violence and political and economic demise. His desire to provide an escape through the music profoundly influenced more than the graffiti artists with whom he ran or the b-boys/b-girls and DJs who now held him in high regard. He further influenced gangbangers, who subsequently dropped their violent weapons and criminal acts to participate in the rising culture of Hip Hop.

"The Father of Hip Hop," DJ Kool Herc, appears as a special guest on Channel V's "What U Want" in Sydney, Australia, 2004. (David Bebber/Reuters/Corbis)

Adding to his accomplishments, Herc included MCs (masters of ceremony) to assist in keeping the crowd engaged as well as to help him cover the silence as he mixed from one track to another's break. Herc's innovation, however, was his massive mobile sound system. He understood how to wire up more speakers than other DJs and how to create enough electrical power to drive a louder sound. Kool Herc named his mobile sound system of amplifiers, turntables, speakers, and other equipment "the Herculords." By all accounts, Herc's mobile sound system was the biggest, best, and loudest system on this side of the Atlantic. No other DJ with a mobile sound system could compete with the size and volume of the Herculords. Herc's Jamaican upbringing served as an influence in the creation of this mobile sound system, as he modeled his setup after the Jamaican dub system.

If Kool Herc was the architect, then Grandmaster Flash (Joseph Saddler) was the contractor who served as rap music's developer. Flash took Herc's idea of break beats and perfected the art of mixing two records by developing what he called a "quick mix theory." His system leaned on learning how to mark records and use a headset so that he might hear the second record being merged into the first before it played over the loudspeaker and make a smooth transition from one record to another. Whereas Herc was not concerned about making sure the beat and the pulse from one record to another was seamless, Flash was. His techniques earned him the rank of Grandmaster, a term used in the Bruce Lee movies of the day, symbolizing the highest level of accomplishment. Flash was influenced by Herc as well as by disco DJs Maboya, Ron Plumber, Pete DJ Jones, and Grandmaster Flowers. Like Herc, Flash surrounded himself with talented MCs who could keep the crowd pumped and encourage the b-boys/b-girls to do their thing to the break beats.

Grandwizard Theodore (Theodore Livingston), one of Flash's main pupils, was responsible for creating the "scratch." He apparently discovered the technique by accident. Once, when he was practicing his DJing techniques in the family home, his mother asked him to turn down the volume to his turntables. Not listening, Theodore continued to perform his mixes while she entered the room banging on the door and reprimanding him. Startled, he attempted to stop the music by putting pressure on the actual record to stop its rotation. Gently rocking it back and forth, attempting to keep the record muted while tending to his mother's scolding, he noticed that the recurring rocking movement produced a unique sound. Theodore continued to perfect

Legendary DJ and inventor of the quick mix, Grandmaster Flash, 1981. (S.I.N./Corbis)

the technique at local parties, where he displayed how to use the sound to accent and punctuate different rhythmic phrases.

Theodore's innovation would become a household sound by the time Grandmixer D.ST collaborated with Herbie Hancock on the influential and extremely prominent recording "Rockit" in 1984. When "Rockit" was performed at the 1984 Grammy Awards, it changed the reception of DJs everywhere. Hip Hop was suddenly viewed by a wider audience as an influential and relevant art form. The recording and subsequent performance of "Rockit" has been documented as the single most notable influence on the Hip Hop DJ. Previous to the performance and to the inclusion of a DJ in a travel band of a major recording artist, DJs worked only at small venues, on the radio, and at private functions and public jams, in addition to creating mix tapes. They played their local area, establishing credibility and a following in their own neighborhoods and local clubs. DJ Kool Herc was well known within the west Bronx, Afrika Bambaataa in the Bronx River area, DJ Breakout in the uptown area past Gunn Hill, and

Select Venues Showcasing Early Hip Hop Culture

123rd St. P.A.L.	Harlem World
Audubon	Hevalo
Back Door	The Latin Quarter
Blue Lagoon	Negril
Cedar Park	PS22
Celebrity Club	PS123
Charles' Gallery	Renaissance
Danceteria	The Rooftop
Devil's Nest	The Roxy
Diplomat Hotel Ballroom	Small's Paradise
Disco Fever	Sparkle
The Dixie	T-Connection
Echo Park	Twilight Zone
Ectasy Garage	Union Square's Underground
Executive Playhouse	Webster Park

Grandmaster Flash in the area between 138th Street and Cyprus Avenue on up into Gunn Hill. But by the mid-1980s, clubs such as Disco Fever, Michael Holman's Negril, and particularly the Roxy were the major scenes for Hip Hop DJs.

Thriving on competition as they battled one another for respect within the profession and for the admiration of partygoers, DJs were greatly affected by rap's first great hit, "Rapper's Delight" (Sugar Hill Records, 1979), as it featured a "live" band and no DJ. Capturing the hearts of passionate music lovers, especially dancers, as well as of industry executives looking for the next opportunity, "Rapper's Delight" ushered in the next stage of Hip Hop, turning many DJs into behind-the-scenes producers. Hip Hop began to transition from a "live" expression to one mediated and regulated by recorded sound and the recording industry. Utilizing new recording technologies, many DJs left their crates of records in exchange for album credits as producers. They learned to use synthesizers such as the Yamaha DX7 to create futuristic and electronic sounds and effects; samplers such as the Ensoniq ASR-10 to record snippets of sounds and prerecorded material for instant manipulation and playback; sequencers such as the Akai MPC 60 to cut and paste various previously created or sampled sounds and thus compose entire songs over which the MC could record his or her rhyme; and beat boxes such as the legendary

Roland TR-808 Rhythm Composer to create drum and percussion patterns recreating the sound and feel of the funk genre.

Although some DJs did remain behind the turntables on stage as parts of groups such as Grandmaster Flash and the Furious Five and Grandwizard Theodore's Fantastic Five Freaks, the prominence of the DJ as an essential element of Hip Hop would not return until the rise of the turntablism movement in the mid-1990s. Drawing inspiration from the early experiments of Grandmaster Flash, Grandwizard Theodore, and Grandmixer D.ST, a new generation of aspiring DJs set forth to reclaim the dominance of the DJ within the culture and to restore the turntable to its role as a musical instrument. Returning to the ideas and sentiments of Grandmaster Flash's innovative recording "The Adventures of Grandmaster Flash on the Wheels of Steel" single (Sugar Hill Records, 1981), and of D.ST on "Rockit" (Columbia, 1983), groups such as the Invisibl Skratch Piklz, the X-ecutioners, and the Beat Junkies evolved as DJ ensembles using the unique capabilities of the turntable to produce sound collages and extraordinary music.

Led by DJ Babu, who is often credited with the discovery of the term "turntablism," the movement revived the practice and competitive nature of DJing as many of the members of these and other DJ ensembles competed regularly at international competitions, such as those hosted by the Disco Mix Club (DMC) and the International Turntablist Federation (ITF). Although the DMC has been in existence since 1987, it has catered almost exclusively to Hip Hop and its diverse offshoots since the mid-1990s, the same time that the ITF emerged. By the twenty-first century, advances in technology had enabled DJs to expand their terrain and to push the envelope in creation. Digital DJ technology allows DJs to play digital music files stored on laptops or other sources through analog turntables or CD players. Software such as Final Scratch Pro (Scanton Magnetics) and Serato Scratch (Serato Audio Research and Serato Corporation) provide additional opportunities to expand the realm of digital DJ technology. DJs use digital vinyl turntable CD players for scratching, mixing, and the like. Offered by companies that also specialize in turntables, such as Pioneer, Numark, Gemini, and others, these technological advances make DJing more accessible to many without an extensive record collection and without huge areas for storage. With all of these technical advances, though, it is important to mention that the industry's standard turntable remains the Technics SL-1200, a model dating back some thirty years in Hip Hop. From mixing to scratching to producing and on into an abyss of experimentation, however, it is the DJ who began it all and who certainly stands to remain one of the leading innovators of the continuing developments in Hip Hop.

Graffiti

Archeologists first used the term "graffiti" to describe the system of communication and expression depicted by writings, drawings, and scribbling on surfaces. Examples stem from numerous periods and locales, from ancient Kemetic excavations to World War II ships. The well-known saying "Kilroy was here" that appeared on the latter, accompanied by a drawing of a man with a long nose peeking over a wall, may have its origin in the story of a welding inspector named James J. Kilroy, who upon inspection of ships at Bethlehem Steel would apparently leave his signature as his mark of approval. Whether the story is fact or urban legend is unknown, since some say that examples of the phrase predate the war itself, but the drawing was popularly picked up and copied by servicemen and others in the years that followed.

By the twentieth century, graffiti was the product of urban revolutionaries who formed subcultures to rebel against parents, police, and other social authorities for personal satisfaction. Often facing immense danger and breaking the law, these self-acclaimed outlaws displayed their writings on walls, freeway overpasses, buildings, trains, public mailboxes, telephone poles, underground passages, and many other public, visible areas. During the 1950s, street gangs used graffiti to promote their gang, mark their territory, and intimidate others. Numerous tags along a wall exhibiting gang names and affiliations served to identify turf and warn opposing gangs or unaware persons that the territory was claimed and therefore off-limits to those who did not belong. Graffiti was prominent on the East Coast as well as the West Coast. In the west, two Latin/Hispanic gangs, the Cholos and Bachutos, were known for elaborate tags and paintings done in black and white. The style of graffiti associated with Hip Hop Culture, however, originated on the East Coast. During the 1960s, tags featuring the names "CORNBREAD" and "COOL EARL" surfaced around streets of Philadelphia. Influenced by this Philadelphia style, TOP CAT 126, an early tagger in the New York boroughs, developed the style called "platform letters," also known as "Broadway Elegant." This innovation featured long, slim letters, often drawn with thin felt pens. During the early years of graffiti in New York, the tags were primarily created by inner-city Black and Latino youth.

A subway car covered in graffiti travels New York City above ground. August 1975. (John Stanton/Getty Images)

Graffiti artists found that the Magic Marker, a felt tip pen with a wide surface area, allowed them to create large, visible tags. The use of spray paint cans allowed for even more surface area to be covered in a variety of colors, leading to the creation of "pieces," short for "masterpieces," or works of graffiti that are larger than tags and often accomplished in multiple colors. Most pieces had an underlying context conveying a social or political statement or criticism by the artists. By 1969, many authorities and others considered tagging or "bombing" as vandalism. Entire sides of buildings and of New York City Transit trains were full of ink. Transit authorities and the NYPD attempted to apprehend taggers and bombers, which only made the practice even more popular among the young participants. Entire crews would sketch a piece and accomplish it on a set target, often during the late hours of the night. Trains became the coveted target since they traveled from one borough to another, allowing for the writer's piece, tag, "throw-up" (a quick execution of graffiti of any size often using more than one color), or "burner" (a large work of graffiti art produced with a competitive spirit that often

A graffiti-covered subway car travels under ground in New York City. (Charles E. Rotkin/Corbis)

uses bright colors and technical and stylistic expertise) to be seen all across the city. This was known as going "all-city."

As bombers went all-city, the bombs brought fame and respect to the artists from some and tremendous disdain from others. The city trains traveled all across the boroughs. As soon as Transit workers painted over a train, graffiti artists sought it out to create more graffiti on it. The freshly painted cars, called "white trains" by the artists, were the most coveted canvases of all the urban surfaces, and graffiti artists were willing to risk their lives to gain access to them, breaking into the train yards and facing the threat of the high-voltage third rail.

A 1971 *New York Times* article on writer TAKI 183 created widespread media exposure and spread the art and practice of graffiti into the suburbs and beyond. Following TAKI 183's example, graffiti artists in these areas chose pseudonyms that had some connection to their neighborhood or their identity while allowing them the anonymity to avoid prosecution from either the law or their parents.

Although graffiti was prominent within the local gang scene, it was actually not gangbangers who spread graffiti into the burgeoning Hip Hop ranks. Instead, it was the average individuals who were not affiliated with any organization but eager to express themselves in a visible way. During the early 1970s, inspired by the popularity of TAKI 183, young taggers began to draw and then paint small throw-ups and pieces, moving from Magic Markers and other felt pens to spray paint. LEE 163rd and PHASE 2, and then SUPER KOOL 223, were influential. Their bombs, strategically placed along Metropolitan Transit Authority (MTA) railcars, were immensely popular, and the artists garnered prestige among their peers. Guilds of graffiti artists formed during the mid-1970s, including the United Graffiti Artists (UGA) and the Nation of Graffiti Artists (NOGA). Artists such as FAB 5 FREDDY (Frederick Braithwaite), SAMO (Jean-Michel Basquiat), and Keith Haring moved the artistic expression into the art galleries during this period, helping to validate graffiti as an art form and creating the potential to earn a living from its pursuits.

During the late 1970s, escalated run-ins with the MTA and the New York City Mayor's Office led some artists to pursue gallery opportunities exclusively; others continued to use the urban landscape as their canvas because they found graffiti to be a fitting way to raise awareness of social, political, and economic disparities in certain parts of the city. Militant, graphic images represented a form of renewed warfare from disenfranchised and underprivileged youth against the very agencies they felt denied them access to opportunity. Politicians and bureaucrats launched their first of numerous antigraffiti campaigns in 1972, and in November 1973 they spearheaded the complete repainting of 6,800 MTA cars (Chang 2005, 122). Artists such as CAINE 1, MAD 103, and FLAME ONE, and collectives such as the FABULOUS 5, would retaliate against the cleanup plan by painting cars top to bottom in elaborate, colorful, wild styles.

Under the leadership of Mayor Edward Koch, politicians then resorted to a stricter and more aggressive tactic and began to secure the train lay-ups with barbed-wire gates and wolves to deter the committed expressionists. It was thought that wolves would make for better enemies to the daring artists than dogs because they could not be tamed or disciplined. The constant need to repaint cars, hire security forces, and punish caught offenders made the authorities less tolerant of the graffiti and certainly less amiable toward the youth using the defacement of public property as the medium for the message of the movement. By the mid-1980s, graffiti as a movement subsided. Though it remained a frequent theme on T-shirts, posters, album jacket covers, and the like, it never returned to the heights it had reached during the mid-1970s, and it never regained prominence within Hip Hop Culture. On May 12, 1989, the MTA officially declared that it had solved the problem and boasted a graffiti-free environment.

The b-boy/b-girl

Dancing was the essence of early Hip Hop Culture. It was the local dancers who inspired the DJs, including Kool Herc, to expand their arsenal of sound in order to motivate new kinesthetic creation. Each gang during the early 1970s had a group of dancers, and gangs were captivated by the energetic sounds of disco, but Herc's creation and innovation and Afrika Bambaataa's ability to bring opposing forces together gave local youth a chance to gather in a safe location removed from the violence of gang-related warfare with the sole goal of having a good time. During these local parties or outdoor jams, crowds of dancers would respond to prodding by the DJ to engage in creative forms of dancing. Herc, utilizing his innovation, the break beat, would set the crowd up to hear the ambient sounds of the often heavy drum and bass concoction, encouraging a crew of onlookers to engage in amicable competitive dancing. These dancers, self-trained, adapting old moves and creating new ones, learned to wait for strategic moments in Herc's break beats to debut their goods. The combination of fancy footwork, floorspins, and acrobatic gestures combined the look of 1960s and 1970s martial arts flix with the reality of individual and unique urban expression, fused by the ongoing competitive nature of the vibrant communities and the neighborhood representatives.

By the mid- to late 1970s, crews of dancers had formed by soliciting members from the pool of local competitors. Examples of such crews included the Zulu Kings (an affiliate of Afrika Bambaataa's Universal Zulu Nation), Starchild La Rock, the Nigger Twins, the Rockwell Association, the Bronx Boys, and the Crazy Commanders. Yet the most prominent crew of innovators was Rock Steady Crew, formed in 1977 by JoJo (Joe Torres) and Jimmy D. in the Bronx. These crew members became the most prominent ambassadors of Hip Hop and exemplars of b-boying. Although b-boying and Hip Hop in general were male dominated, numerous females participated, including Headspin Janet, Lady Doze, and Baby Love (Daisy Castro). Rock Steady rose as the most challenged competitor and the most sought-out group of spokespersons. They eventually received invitations for television

Breakdancers perform on a stage. (Bettmann/Corbis)

performances, film roles, featured spots in documentaries, and even a record deal.

Although Hip Hop was born on the East Coast, and the b-boy/b-girl element of the movement hailed from the same Bronx-, Harlem-, and Brooklyn-based communities, a throbbing street-dance movement in Los Angeles and Fresno would literally shake things up. The introduction of the "Campbell-lock" by competitive street "funk" dancer Don Campbell and his Lockers added an entirely new flare to the street dance–based expression of b-boying. When Campbell and his crew debuted the dance on Don Cornelious's nationally syndicated television show *Soul Train,* the dance and its offshoots hit the New York City Hip Hop scene, adding extra nuances and variations. Inspired by Campbell, Fresno resident Sam Solomon developed yet another West Coast variation in the form of his "Boog style," later called boogaloo, which also added to the arsenal of dance styles within breakdancing. These two main styles gave birth to numerous other offshoots developed through individual and often independent innovation.

By the mid-1980s, as music videos increased in popularity and the visual enticement of sexuality engaged a new audience of young adolescent viewers, the previous forms of b-boying/b-girling

Selected West Coast Dance Styles Incorporated into Hip Hop Culture	
Air Posing	Locker Hand Shake
Animation	Oil Well (a.k.a. Alpha)
Backsliding	Pales
Boogaloo	Pogo
Bopping	Points
Bump	Popping
Bustin'	Puppet
Campbell Walk	Robot
Centipede	Saccin
Chinese Strut	Scare Crow
Crazy Legs	Scoobops
Creepin'	Scooby Doos
Cobra	Skeeter Rabbit
Dime Stopping	Skeeters
Earth Quake	Sleepy Style
ET	Snaking
Fancies	Spiderman
Filmore	Splits
Floating/Gliding	Sticking
Floor Slaps	Stop 'N' Go
Flying Tuts	Strobing
Funky Air Guitar	Strutting
Hand Chops	Ticking
Hitting	Tutting
Iron Horse (a.k.a. Which-A-Way)	Uncle Sam Points
Knee Drops	Waving
Lock	Wrist Twirls

took a back seat to background singers and dancers who were able to offer a definitive stage presence while not upstaging the MC who was in the limelight. Although b-boying/b-girling remained a vibrant practice below the radar, it would never again have the prominence that it did in its days at the early Hip Hop jams.

The MC

Short for master of ceremonies, the term "MC" predates Hip Hop. The role of the MC also predates its incorporation into the Hip Hop Culture. Like the DJ and graffiti artist, the MC played a practical role in the urban community, although the title itself was adapted from elite high society.

Within the tradition of urban "griots," a name most often associated with the West African poet/musician who carries and reveals the local history of a community through oral tradition, who used the microphone to taunt, tease, testify, and please, Gil Scott-Heron, Pigmeat Markham, Rev. Jesse Jackson, Muhammad Ali, and countless others set the stage for the rise of the MC. While DJing for his indoor and outdoor jams, Kool Herc desired assistance keeping the crowd excited, entertained, and motivated to participate. After trying out techniques perfected by DJ Hollywood and Disco King Mario, he passed the microphone to Coke La Rock (also known as A-1 Coke and Nasty Coke), who became Hip Hop's first noted MC. He was later joined by Timmy Tim and the original Clark Kent. During this early phase, the MC's sole

Promotional photo of the Hip Hop group Salt-n-Pepa, 1992. (Bettmann/Corbis)

responsibility was to keep the crowd engaged and to assist the DJ; over time, they developed intermittent party rhymes, sparking the interest of numerous partygoers, who would follow the MC around as they set the party off. By the mid-1970s, MCs had gained value, becoming partners with, not just helpers for, the DJ. Numerous groups evolved featuring an MC. "Rapper's Delight" offered an alternative: The "live" band took over the DJ's role, providing a sonic backboard from which the MCs could spring forth with their verbal wit. Increased technology also endangered the MC/DJ relationship. As the cassette and DAT (digital audiotape) became available, MCs could perform without a band or DJ because they had the aid of a tape-playing device. Although pioneer MCs such as Melle Mel, Busy Bee, Spoonie Gee, the Cold Crush Brothers, and the Funky Four + 1 More would not dare use a tape, MCs in the 1980s had the option.

By then, MCs dominated the Hip Hop landscape. Record labels sought them out, attempting to capitalize on the rising culture. They paid special attention to notable and unique MCs such as Kurtis Blow, Rakim, Big Daddy Kane, Kool Moe Dee, KRS-One, Salt-n-Pepa, and Queen Latifah. Elevated by the verbal eloquence of Rakim and the content-heavy rhymes of Latifah, MCs rose as Hip Hop superstars and popular-culture icons. Groups such as Public Enemy launched an entire generation into socially conscious political activity while enjoying the onstage eccentric behavior—including his unique style of fashion and dance—and comedic antics of Flava Flav. The inclusive urban flare of the early 1970s dissipated for a highly charged and widely marketable sound, look, and feel. This new look was also led by the likes of Run-DMC and LL Cool J. The MC literally earned all the money and took all the spoils.

The rise of "gangsta rap" in the late 1980s and early 1990s again changed the sound, look, and feel of Hip Hop as the rising gang warfare on the West Coast revisited the early scene from which early Hip Hop was vehemently opposed. Yet, groups such as Niggaz With Attitude (NWA) promulgated the violence through there graphic lyrics and representation of gang culture in their language, dress, and demeanor. NWA did not follow the footsteps of Afrika Bambaataa and the Universal Zulu Nation in the promotion of unity and peace. To capture the interest of suburban kids who were out of harm's way but extremely interested in gangs, guns, and violence, the recording industry ditched the socially conscious and politically active acts in exchange for more gang-oriented, gun-waving, violence-oriented artists whose rhymes were clever, colorful, and captivating. Dr. Dre, Ice Cube, Tupac Shakur, and eventually affiliates Eminem, 50 Cent, and The Game would rise on the West, whereas Notorious B.I.G., Nas, Jay-Z, and the Wu-Tang Clan, among others, would reclaim the East as the stronghold of Hip Hop. But the rising innovations in technology during the 1980s and 1990s allowed for other players to enter the game as well, including Master P in Louisiana, Missy Elliott in Virginia, Outkast in Georgia, the Geto Boys in Texas, and Bone Thugs-n-Harmony in Ohio. According to legendary MC Kool Moe Dee, the best MCs have a high degree of originality and versatility; attain a high level of mastery over substance, flow, and "battle skills"; have a significant social impact; and possess outstanding live performance abilities. The importance of these criteria increased as the underground MCs began to take center stage, attaining a new stature and a new level of name recognition in the American public and becoming potential spokespersons for major corporations and their products. Artists such as Common (formerly known as Common Sense), Talib Kweli, Mos Def, the Roots, and Lauryn Hill are just a few of the many artists who have changed the nature and identity of the Hip Hop MC during the late 1990s and the 2000s.

"The Fifth Element"

During the 1980s, as Hip Hop expanded in territory and in prominence, it also expanded in content. Additional elements were added not as replacements, but as complementary expansions of the growing Hip Hop cultural movement. Afrika Bambaataa and his Universal Zulu Nation advocated for the fifth element: "Knowledge, Culture and Overstanding." Basing his ideas in the principle of understanding the groundwork laid by the pioneers and the conceptual history of the previous elements, especially the social, political, and economic aspirations at their core, Bambaataa attempted to revitalize the collective consciousness that had created the culture to begin with. The numerous individual compromises that had taken place, in his opinion, subverted the initial intent of the culture, creating a breeding ground for artists in pursuit of financial opportunity instead of activism. Though he did not cast the pursuit of money as evil, he advanced the notion that the co-optation of Hip Hop by the music and entertainment industry during the 1980s and 1990s had left it virtually devoid of its original context and content. Perhaps the changes he observed were a sign of the changing times and an evolving new generation. In any case, Bambaataa's ideas themselves led to new ways of seeing the movement. His notion of "overstanding," for example, as opposed to "understanding," applied a positivist ideological framework borrowed from Rastafarianism to the realm of Hip Hop. This notion emphasized connection to a higher positive power rather than a negative lower power.

Other groups considered vocal percussion, otherwise known as human "beat boxing," as the fifth element. Although beat boxing evolved as a human imitation of the increasingly popular electronic drum machines, or beat boxes, the practice of using the human voice to produce rhythmic phrases and other sounds is an extremely ancient practice in many of the world's oldest cultures. As a matter of fact, the human voice is the basis of nearly every musical instrument, the model that other instruments imitate (some mimic the sounds of nature and animals). Yet during the 1980s, Doug E. Fresh, an MC, popularized the art of beat boxing as part of his live performance, using his voice to produce drum beats, imitations of record samples, and other sound effects. Buffy of the Fat Boys and Biz Markie further popularized this practice. Although beat boxing was not extremely popular during the 1990s, Rahzel M. Brown, known simply as Rahzel, repopularized it through his performances with the Roots as well as via his own recordings. Although this form of expression continues to be heard on local street corners as the backdrop to young MCs engaged in freestyle ciphers, it remains an underground phenomenon with few widely known performers to showcase it.

Additional Elements

Fashion

As the 1980s evolved and Hip Hop Culture went national, youth across the country began to identify with one another through their selections in fashion. In accordance with Hip Hop's emphasis on the importance of self-expression, the collective identity maintained an overall look and feel while allowing for individual nuances. Clothing lines such as Karl Kani, FUBU, Sean John, Phat Farm, and a host of others offered youth and young adults the opportunity to participate in this distinctive look and feel of the culture. Adidas, Nike, Reebok, and other shoe manufacturers, including Lugz and Timberland, offered footwear options that, whether consciously or through sheer luck, attracted Hip Hop practitioners and fans. Hairstyles offered an additional opportunity for Hip

Hip Hop artist Pharrell Williams answers questions at a news conference in London to launch his clothing label Billionaire Boys Club. (Young Russell/Corbis Sygma)

Hop followers to express their wild, nationalistic, or creative side. Even within the realm of the gangsta rap craze, sagging pants, multiple white T-shirts, and certain colors were in vogue. The western part of the country added flannel oversized shirts to this mix, and the South brought gold and porcelain capped teeth. The East contributed hooded coats and Timberland boots. Hip Hop has always been fashionable.

Language

Hip Hop was a street-produced and a street-evolved culture, and the language of the streets certainly has always been and remains the lingua franca of Hip Hop. Even as Hip Hop became commercialized and industry based, its ear remained tuned to the street, and in many instances Hip Hop Culture has created the popular slang of the era. Though the music has often been criticized for the foul and often obscene jargon, phrases, and colloquialisms that it uses, many of its expressions and idioms have made it into mainstream society, and some even into contemporary dictionaries. The noted *Oxford English Dictionary* includes entries such as "jiggy," "dope," "phat,"and "bling bling" in its most recent updated online and print editions.

Street Knowledge

In the inner-city context, "street knowledge" refers to one's knowledge of events, people, and inter-personal skills associated with life on the streets and the ability to stay in touch with what is happening. It also refers to having the skills it takes to survive in the metropolitan city. In order to achieve street credibility, a sign of localized power and esteem, one has to be validated by the local urban leader, who, by his stature in the community and exemplary display of wisdom, offers insight and a connection to the past. These elders attain a circle of influence and are often revered as street legends.

Entrepreneurialism

As Hip Hop's appeal grew, the opportunity to create grassroots business ventures materialized. This is only natural, considering the capitalistic nature of the country's economy. These businesses took the form of independent record labels, recording studios, T-shirt design companies, concert promotion entities, booking agents, and the like. An entrepreneurial spirit prevailed in these companies that recognized the importance of being self-employed, providing innovative goods or services, and attaining self-reliance and self-determination. Examples of extremely successful, self-motivated Hip Hop entrepreneurs include Karl Kani, Ice Cube, P. Diddy, Master P, Russell Simmons, and Jay-Z. These participants in the music, motion picture, publishing, clothing, and production industries were essential to the success of Hip Hop. Hip Hop needs active, major players in each industry in order to continue to exist and thrive.

Hip Hop Aesthetic

Perhaps the glue that holds all of the elements of Hip Hop together, the "Hip Hop aesthetic" encompasses all of the styles, concepts, opinions, and ideas that are well liked and accepted by the general populace of Hip Hoppers. These things reflect the general sentiments of the Hip Hop community and the changing attitudes within it. Hip Hop has not only spawned specific works of art in many genres but has also influenced fictional novels, Broadway choreography, paintings, and motion pictures not dedicated specifically to Hip Hop. This aesthetic disseminates Hip Hop to a wider audience through many creative and expressive venues.

Summary

Hip Hop Culture is generally defined by the combination of four foundational elements: DJing, graffiti, b-boying/b-girling, and MCing. Sparked by the creative ingenuity of Bronx-based DJ Kool Herc and his creation, the break beats, Hip Hop assembled energetic music, passionate graffiti artists, acrobatic dancers, and skilled wordsmiths into a unified aesthetic, each in its own way representing a passion for life and a commitment to individual and collective expression. Although each of the foundational elements previously existed as independent movements, it was the dire social, political, and economic situations of the inner-city Bronx, Brooklyn, and Harlem areas that initiated their strategic merger.

Known for the ability to produce sound collages from previously recorded or sampled materials, the DJ was the lead voice in the collective creation of Hip Hop. He/she reminded the crowd that it was okay to have a good time while subtly interjecting messages through music and over the microphone. A long line of DJs has inspired the creation of Hip Hop Culture, and many even moved into the realm of production at a time when the recording industry was unwilling to cater to the demands of this central force.

The graffiti movement, perhaps the most engaged in direct combat with the system as artists confronted the MTA, the Mayor's Office, and others who felt their artistic contributions as displayed on public property were criminal, served as the arms and legs of Hip Hop. Starting by "bombing" trains, walls, and the like, they later moved into creating album jackets, flyers, and various other modes of advertisement for the DJs and MCs.

The b-boys/b-girls served as the inspiration of the movement. If there had been no dancers or "party people," Hip Hop would not have existed. There would have been no audience of enthusiastic participants to interact with the DJs' creative innovations. More important, the b-boys/b-girls showed how violent gang warfare could be turned into competitive street fighting via dance.

It is the MC, however, who has the last word as the most visible symbol of Hip Hop Culture. Serving as the voice of Hip Hop, the MC has been best positioned to create change, whether for good or bad. The recording industry has put the MC into the spotlight, often ignoring the other foundational elements of Hip Hop, and thus, the MC's role has become primary while the role of the DJs, graffiti artists, and b-boys/b-girls has diminished.

The fifth element is often debated, but ultimately it simply does not matter which element is the fifth or which is the fifteenth. One contender, Afrika Bambaataa's notion of "Knowledge, Culture and Overstanding," has had a significant impact on the movement, but so has beat boxing and other additional elements. What is important is that Hip Hop participants take pride in understanding the history of the movement and the lineage of these forms of expression in an effort to acknowledge past and present innovators and recognize the value that Hip Hop Culture has had both for its participants and society at large. As this positive aspect of what began as inner-city life is celebrated, perhaps some of the negative aspects that have occurred in the past can be avoided in the future. This is the primary sentiment of Bambaataa's fifth element and the rationale for the numerous extensions that allow the culture to remain alive, vibrant, timely, and, in the truest sense of the word, fun.

References

Books

Brewster, Bill, and Frank Broughton. 1999. *Last Night a DJ Saved My Life: The History of the Disc Jockey.* New York: Grove.

Chang, Jeff. 2005. *Can't Stop Won't Stop: A History of the Hip-Hop Generation.* New York: St. Martin's.

Dee, Kool Moe. 2003. *There's a God on the Mic: The True 50 Greatest MCs.* New York: Thunder's Mouth.

Fricke, Jim, and Charlie Ahearn. 2002. *Yes Yes Y'all: Oral History of Hip-Hop's First Decade.* New York: Da Capo.

George, Nelson. 1998. *Hip Hop America.* New York: Viking.

Hager, Steven. 1984. *Hip Hop: The Illustrated History of Break Dancing, Rap Music, and Graffiti.* New York: St. Martin's.

Light, Alan, ed. 1999. *The Vibe History of Hip Hop.* New York: Three Rivers.

Ogg, Alex, with David Upshal. 2001. *The Hip Hop Years: A History of Rap.* New York: Fromm International.

Reighley, Kurt B. 2000. *Looking for the Perfect Beat: The Art and Culture of the DJ.* New York: Pocket Books.

Rose, Tricia. 1994. *Black Noise: Rap Music and Black Culture in Contemporary America.* Hanover, NH: Wesleyan University Press.

Toop, David. 2000. *Rap Attack 3: African Rap to Global Hip Hop,* 3d ed. London: Serpent's Tail.

Documentaries

Rhyme & Reason. 1997. Directed by Peter Spirer. City Block Productions. Distributed by Miramax Films.

Scratch. 2001. Directed by Doug Pray. Firewalks Film. Distributed by Palm Pictures.

Style Wars. 1983. Directed by Tony Silver and Henry Chalfant. VHS. New Day Films. Distributed by Public Broadcasting Service (PBS).

Wild Style. 1982. Directed by Charlie Ahearn. Wild Style Productions. Distributed by First Run Features.

Websites

Art Crimes: http://www.artcrimes.com/

Mrwiggles.biz: http://www.mrwiggleshiphop.net/index.htm

Rock Steady Crew: http://www.rocksteadycrew.com/

Temple of Hiphop: http://www.templeofhiphop.org/

The Universal Zulu Nation: http://www.zulunation.com/

Issues in Hip Hop

his chapter offers an unbiased, objective view of some of the major challenges and controversies of Hip Hop Culture. The aim is not to provide solutions to the problems that are introduced, but to offer a grounding that readers and serious researchers may use as a launching pad for their own discovery. These topics are presented as responses to some of the most "Frequently Asked Questions" in the study of Hip Hop Culture.

Who Is Hip Hop?

Questions of authenticity, membership, and ownership have plagued the Hip Hop community since Hip Hop's transition from a local South Bronx, regional, and New York–based phenomenon to a national and subsequently international one. During the evolving days of the culture in the mid-1970s, questions of authenticity were irrelevant. Artists were simply motivated to articulate their despair and celebrate their self-determination through the foundational elements of DJing, graffiti tagging, b-boying/b-girling, MCing, and later beat-boxing and producing. There was a sense of urgency and immediacy about what was happening, with the DJs providing the soundscapes, the graffiti artists painting the landscapes, the b-boys/b-girls aggressively challenging their competition in an all-out yet nonviolent manner, and the MCs offering the critical analyses to tie it all together. The latter spoke for an entire community faced with a common reality, and that was the only authenticity that was necessary.

Yet when the early inner-city expression spread beyond its local epicenter, the lack of commonality among enclaves of Hip Hop communities across the country led to a search for the "real

Hip Hop." The deviations in sound, sentiment, and even dialect provided the backdrop for some to challenge the notion of the authenticity of Hip Hop groups outside of New York City. Funk-influenced street dancers from California moved in manners different from the original New York City b-boys/b-girls, yet both styles of dance became fused under the name "breakdancing." MCs from the South had no experience with the hustle and bustle of northern city living, nor did they have any experience with the high-rise apartments of inner cities such as the Bronx, but they could identify with the urgency of the need to remove the systematic oppression mentioned in much of the early music, regardless of where it came from.

During the 1980s, as Hip Hop spread throughout the country, and into the 1990s, the question of membership continued to open a Pandora's box of mischief. The notion of membership is one of the most challenging and confrontational questions of youth popular culture, and Hip Hop was not spared from this vexing issue. Simply stated, "Who is Hip Hop?" Do practitioners have more rights and privileges within the community than the fans or onlookers, who are inspired and affected by this uniquely intimate and often accessible form of expression? Is inclusion into the realm of Hip Hop based on participation as an artist, or can participation as a consumer offer the same entitlement to claim Hip Hop affiliation? Is Hip Hop only for Blacks? Latinos and Latinas? Is the culture only for the poor and downtrodden? For those who are broken and forgotten?

Although no quick study of Hip Hop history could reveal any definitive answers to these questions, the sentiment of the question remains valid. Any simple answer would most likely be due to frantic stereotyping on the basis of race or class or the denial of the extremely inclusive nature of youth culture and its various musical and subcultural manifestations. Do women have as much access and opportunity to dictate the path of Hip Hop as men, or are they simply along for the ride? Might gay, lesbian, bisexual, and/or transgender individuals participate and receive full-fledged membership? What of liberal whites and racist Blacks? Do suburban enclaves of Hip Hop activity receive the same acknowledgment and its participants the same recognition as their inner-city equivalents? Are any of these examples any less authentic? These questions complicate the idea of Hip Hop Culture because they reveal the lack of infrastructure

Melle Mel of the Sugar Hill Gang at VH1 Hip Hop Honors held at the Hammerstein Ballroom. New York, NY, October 3, 2004. (Steven Tackeff/ZUMA/Corbis)

and the possibility of numerous Hip Hop communities, each with its own unwritten rules, that are all connected for the sole reason that they showcase one or more of the foundational or additional elements.

Questions of authenticity and membership quickly lead to the discussion of ownership. During the early developmental phases of the culture, the decade of the 1970s, predating the two legendary recordings by the Fatback Band and the Sugar Hill Gang, the expression of Hip Hop was so urgent and immediate that there was no desire to capture the performances on tape, film, or any other available medium. The expressions changed daily and often were based on daily activities, community occurrences, and personal interactions. TAKI 183's instant fame after the 1971 *New York Times* article; the graffiti showcase at the Razor Gallery in Soho, New York, in 1973; the success of the Sugar Hill Gang's "Rappers Delight" in 1979; and Kurtis Blow's successful contract with Mercury Records in 1981 all offered new opportunities to view Hip Hop and its various elements as a possible marketable commodity.

Through the 1980s, as artists were signed to major record label deals, publishing contracts, television appearances, cameos, and feature appearances in documentaries and motion pictures, the question of ownership formed a large gray cloud floating above every major stride or stumble of the growing culture. Is it the artists whose creativity spawned the multibillion-dollar entertainment industry anchored by Hip Hop Culture who "own" Hip Hop, or is it the industry machine that quickly altered its former rock-based ego to cater to a newer, fresher face offering more return on the investment? Some say that it is the Hip Hop consumer whose allegiance offers the greatest validation, and that it is their continued participation, through the expenditure of money, that offers Hip Hop Culture its best chance of longevity; others consider the constant creative innovation of the practitioners to be the driving force because it is the artists who expand the notion of expression and offer ever more captivating, more intriguing, and more entertaining experiences. Still others question whether Hip Hop benefits at all from the commercial acceptance of Hip Hop, noting that although Russell Simmons, P. Diddy, Master P, and Jay-Z are seen as Hip Hop moguls, surely they can't be the only faces able to claim Hip Hop. Whether it is the artist/practitioner, the industry executive, or the consumer, these challenges of authenticity, membership, and ownership are likely to continue to plague the conversation around who is Hip Hop.

Which Is the Real Hip Hop:
Underground or Mainstream?

One of the most prevalent disputes confronting Hip Hop is the quarrel between those who deem underground Hip Hop as the true essence and real expression of Hip Hop and those who participate in the mainstream music and entertainment industry signed to major record labels with national and international distribution, major television appearances, book deals with major publishing houses, and the like. The debate began during the mid- to late 1980s as major record labels diminished the role of the DJs, graffiti artists, and b-boys/b-girls, choosing instead to invest their resources in the MCs. The MCs were often the only Hip Hop practitioners heard on the recordings, the only ones seen in the music videos, and the ones spotlighted as the focus of attention during live concerts. This situation was exacerbated by the rise of gangsta rap, a subgenre that showcased very little b-boying/b-girling, and even less of graffiti's wild styles, yet popularized the DJ-turned-producer. This transformation moved the DJ, graffiti artist, and b-boy/b-girl into the localized underground scene far removed from the economic opportunities and wide visibility of the mainstream. The rise of two extremely innovative, dancing MCs, MC Hammer (later known as Hammer) and Vanilla Ice, who remain two of the best-selling artists of all time within the culture, also signaled the diminishing presence of the missing foundational elements of Hip Hop.

In response to the rapid proliferation and promulgation of rap music on radio and television, and the increased mainstream popularity of the MC, numerous passionate practitioners instituted local Hip Hop enclaves committed not only to the retention of the foundational elements but also to the performance and training of interested individuals. This underground community resides below the radar in locations accessible only to those who know where to look for them. Guided by a foundational and fundamental consciousness, with variations from one enclave to another yet always beginning with an articulated and endearing passion for Hip Hop Culture, the various local undergrounds are often guided by a loose hierarchy of practitioners. Offering equal opportunity for DJs, graffiti artists, b-boys/b-girls, and MCs in the local spotlight, these enclaves counter the high media exposure of the MC and reverse the demise of the other elements by consistently and strategically presenting opportunities for members to grow as practitioners, as knowledgeable patrons, and as committed Hip Hop headz. The membership of most underground communities is often widely diverse in age, gender, class, race, and ethnicity. Members are often committed to open-minded respect of personal similarities and differences and most often rely on the tradition of "battling," the act of competing in a battle, to settle disputes.

Guided by the preferences and desires of the consumer base, the mainstream is extremely accessible and available to all via urban radio, network and cable television, and local, national, and international music stores. Mainstream rappers often enjoy celebrity status and even intermittent popular-culture iconic status, as well as the assumed benefits that accompany such designation. With the rising prominence of controversial material within mainstream rap recordings and performances, the mainstream population of fans has come to be composed mainly of youth and young adults; many of the thirty-and-over Hip Hoppers respond more to the underground artists. Unlike the underground, the mainstream in general is not necessarily focused on the preservation of Hip Hop Culture; nor is there any desire in the mainstream to risk compromising the needs and desires of the record label or the demands of the financial bottom line with personal objectives. These two realms, the mainstream and the underground, lie diametrically opposed on many issues.

Yet attempts to bridge the two occurred in the late 1990s and early 2000s via experiments by KRS-One, Missy Elliott, and other notable artists, who have attempted to reunite the foundational elements on stage, on recordings, and in videos, offering a revised yet retrospective presentation of present Hip Hop close to its original state. The rise of technology has also played a role in bridging the two sides. The increase in digital downloading, file sharing, and the use of MP3 converters allow for local and nonmainstream music to be shared beyond the immediate physical audience, in effect allowing musicians a form of distribution previously reserved for mainstream products, but without the connection to the major record labels or the demands to compromise associated with such a union.

Whether underground or mainstream, the name does not change what people deem as good and worthwhile expression. This realization has allowed underground MCs and groups, such as Talib Kweli, Mos Def, Common (formerly known as Common Sense), the Roots, the Coup, dead prez, and a host of others, to gain recognition and financial rewards and to actually achieve a level of popularity previously enjoyed solely by self-acclaimed mainstream artists.

Can East Coast Hip Hop and West Coast Hip Hop Coexist?

Known as the two media capitals of the nation, New York City and Los Angeles have a lot in common, but they certainly also have a lot of differences. Although they are both economic and social capitals of the country, they are dramatically different in character and aesthetic. Often considered polar opposites in terms of weather, architecture, scenery, city planning, and an extensive list of other recognizable and often subtle features, both have made major contributions to the entertainment industry.

During the 1940s and 1950s, the East Coast–based bebop was compared and contrasted with the progressive jazz styles of the West Coast by critics and journalists. Seen as more aggressive, abrasive, and explosive, bebop was juxtaposed with the soft, sultry sounds of cool jazz and "third stream." These musical differences and alternate methods of expression were often treated more as a product of the environment than as individual variations in approach. Bebop found a passionate and loyal audience among hometown and regional patrons, as did the progressive styles of the West. The fashion world, likewise, has segmented the population according to those who wear New York–based styles versus those who find the California-based aesthetic more appealing—an instant storyboard theme for critics and journalists, and by the late 1990s, reality TV.

The ongoing personal bragging of super-machismo and hyper-ego competitiveness within Hip Hop, by both men and women, is an inherited aspect of the culture often misdiagnosed and misunderstood by some professionals outside the culture. The ritual of "playing the dozens," "baggin'," "cappin'," or "jonesin'"—all terms for diminishing an opponent's importance and raising one's own by exposing a weakness or character flaw in the opponent—is an aspect of Hip Hop warfare in which DJs, graffiti artists, b-boys/b-girls, MCs, and others all may participate. These battles, often between two individuals or crews, developed as expanded turf competitions. It was no longer enough to be the best b-boy/b-girl, for example; instead, one gained merit by being the best b-boy/b-girl representing the Flatbush section of Brooklyn as opposed to the South Bronx, and certainly as opposed to Inglewood, California.

The highly publicized 1991 single by Bronx-based rapper "Tim Dog" (Timothy Blair) entitled "F—k Compton" (Ruffhouse Records) ignited a frenzy of responses, most notably one by Compton-based Tweedy Bird Loc, whose "F—k South-Bronx" (Par Records) was the only battle call needed to ignite a frenzy of inter-coastal warfare, leading to numerous deaths. Although rap battles occurred on the local scene, such as between KRS-One and MC Shan via the rap classics "The Bridge," "South Bronx," "(South Bronx) Kill That Noise," and "The Bridge Is Over," this string of lyrical warfare was not the subject of popular media and certainly did not lead to the type of pandemonium created by the coast-to-coast battles. And though gangsta rap drew attention to the inter-coastal feuds, the grumblings of warfare had already existed in the Bronx and other New York City areas, since the mid- to late 1980s.

The rift would explode when Death Row Records, owned by Dr. Dre and Suge Knight, began to dominate Hip Hop in both sales and prominence, especially with Dr. Dre's debut solo album *The Chronic* (1992) and Snoop Doggy Dogg's debut *Doggystyle* (1993). For the first time in the history of the genre and culture, the epicenter moved to the West Coast from its East Coast birthplace. The voice of Notorious B.I.G. (Christopher Wallace) a few years later would return New York to prominence via Puff Daddy's Bad Boy Records, but the feud took a turn for the worse when Tupac Shakur accused Notorious B.I.G. of plotting against him. The former best friends became archenemies, and the New York–born, yet West Coast–affiliated, MC/actor Tupac Shakur signed with Death Row Records, heightening the East Coast–West Coast rivalry. He offered insult after insult on subsequent recordings. The media picked up on this outspoken and public feud, as well as on one between Puffy and Suge Knight, and then provided frequent coverage of the rivalries in print, on television, and online. Unfortunately all of this culminated in the deaths of numerous fans and artists, including Tupac Shakur (September 13, 1996) and Notorious B.I.G. (March 9, 1997). After all the dust settled, the question still remains: Was there ever truly an inter-coastal war, or were these just personal feuds gone awry that were depicted as such by the media?

Can Hip Hop and Religion Coexist?

Many commentators have remarked that Hip Hop connects with religion only in times of sorrow or celebration. Numerous hardcore gangsta rappers have offered their commitments to prayer for a slain friend or associate, and many begin award acceptance speeches by thanking God or Allah for His contribution to their successes. Although neither example provides real evidence of religious fervor or belief, the notions of prayer and praise are significant to some practitioners of Hip Hop. From the early party calls and Hip Hop chanting of Afrika Bambaataa to the revision of biblical details by Kanye West, Hip Hop has acknowledged its religious influences even when critics, journalists, and media representatives do not. Largely influenced by either the Nation of Gods and Earths (also known as the Five Percent Nation, an offshoot of the Nation of Islam) or Christianity, many of Hip Hop Culture's DJs, graffiti artists, b-boys/b-girls, and MCs are guided by their religious convictions and attempt to balance these convictions with their personal pursuits in and through Hip Hop Culture. This influence is evident in their lyrics, aesthetics, and ideologies.

The most noted and acclaimed international collective of Hip Hop practitioners, the Universal Zulu Nation, acknowledges one God who is called by many names (Allah, God, Jah, and so on). Notable groups and artists such as Rakim, Brand Nubian, Poor Righteous Teachers, Lakim Shabazz, and members of Wu-Tang have at one time or another been believers in the Five Percent Nation founded by Clarence 13X, who defected from the Nation of Islam in 1964. Although their lyrics do not always resound as clearly as those in Brand Nubian's "Allah and Justice" on *In God We Trust* (Time Warner, 1992), the sentiments, commentaries, symbolism, metaphors, and illustrations often allow for some of their religious identity and ideology to seep through. Within Wu-Tang's "We Revolution" on the *Wu-Tang Forever* album (RCA, 1997), embedded within what appears to be a tirade on the effects of slavery on the Black man, for example, one finds a perfect example of an exegetical analysis of the Nation of Gods and Earths. DMX displays his belief in God in numerous recorded lyrical revelations, including his 1998 release "Ready to Meet Him" on the album *Flesh of My Flesh, Blood of My Blood* (Def Jam). KRS-One's 2002 album *Spiritual Minded*, recorded in collaboration with his Temple of Hiphop, a Christian album full of Hip Hop, was a dynamic change in mood and style.

KRS-One's confessions of faith may have shocked many, but many more have been shocked by the various religious communities that are using the medium and method of Hip Hop as a tool of catechism. Christian rappers who have removed themselves from the mainstream realm of Hip Hop have created underground enclaves with the goal of uniting a community of Holy Hip Hoppers or Christian Hip Hoppers (for example, T-Bone, Grits, and Cross Movement). Enticed by the urgency, passion, and dedication to convictions evident in such works, enclaves of Jewish (e.g., Hip Hop Hoodíos, Solomon & Socalled, and Sagol 59), Catholic (e.g., Father Stan, Dr. D., and mayd by God), Muslim (e.g., Mujahideen Team, Captain D., and Native Deen), and other religious communities across the country and around the world are imitating, adopting, and in many ways appropriating Hip Hop's authentic performance practice for the purpose of religious worship.

Is Graffiti an Art Form or a Nuisance?

Kool Herc began Hip Hop. Yet prior to his days as the pioneering DJ with the legendary sound system, Herc was an associate of the Ex-Vandals, a graffiti crew. Armed with Magic Markers and aerosol cans, the crew painted the town in colorful splendor, offering creative illustrations grounded in revolutionary thought. As the first foot soldiers of the Hip Hop movement, the graffiti artists often contextualized the sentiments of the party music played, performed, and danced to at the jams. Their open depictions of often satirical and cynical commentary on local public policy challenged viewers to imagine the untapped potential of their decaying urban terrain. Often presented on public and widely visible property, the graffiti served as a tool for social expression and a call to social, political, and economic action.

Often criticized for their obnoxious and rebellious lifestyle, the graffiti artists aimed to reclaim the possession of their community by one means or another. Stymied by the failure of local and state politicians to address the concerns of their communities, the graffiti artists took to the streets, claiming partial ownership of public walls of numerous city- and state-owned venues and facilities, and most notably the state transportation system. In this way, Hip Hop–oriented graffiti differed from gang graffiti—which served to mark the boundaries of gang territory as well as to signify the actions and attributes of individual members—and from random graffiti appearing in public bathrooms (particularly in neighborhood high schools, parks, and college campuses). Hip Hop–oriented graffiti most often appeared outdoors.

In some cases, graffiti artists have offered unique monuments to slain heroes, such as a host of depictions around the country honoring Tupac Shakur and Notorious B.I.G. and major works on icons such as John Coltrane and Rev. Dr. Martin Luther King Jr. Artists such as FAB 5 FREDDY (Frederick Braithwaite), SAMO (Jean-Michel Basquiat), and Keith Haring achieved great recognition as major gallery artists, taking their individual styles of graffiti from walls to canvas and from public local walls to private international galleries.

Nevertheless, graffiti did not always end up on public property. Numerous private business owners and homeowners were routinely plagued with unwanted paintings and murals on the sides of their property. The unwanted artists were charged as trespassers and their graffiti was considered vandalism. Graffiti quickly achieved a negative reputation within numerous civic circles. Local politicians and government officials used their own attacks on graffiti to earn favor from the local businesspeople and homeowners. Many cities around the country initiated antigraffiti campaigns, issuing brochures to local citizens alerting them to their rights and informing them of the proper procedure by which to notify authorities when catching graffiti artists in the act of criminal activity. Local and state government agencies spent an immense amount of money to remove and prevent graffiti. The Metropolitan Transit Authority (MTA) spent in excess of $1,500 per car painting over graffiti during the 1970s, in many cases painting particular cars numerous times. In addition, the MTA spent over 1 million dollars retrofitting train lay-ups with security systems and onsite security patrols.

Although the prominence of Hip Hop–related graffiti has diminished since the early to mid-1980s, the presence of graffiti has not, creating yet another opportunity for Hip Hop to receive the lion's share of blame for something for which it may or may not be fully or solely responsible. Nevertheless, the debate over whether graffiti is an art form or a nuisance continues.

Can Hip Hop Serve as a Tool in Healing Racial Tension?

Hip Hop is most often described as a product of African American or Black culture within the United States. In his monumental book *The Hip Hop Generation: Young Blacks and the Crisis in African-American Culture* (Basic Civitas, 2002), Bakari Kitwana suggested that the term "hip hop generation" is synonymous with Black youth culture and further argued that this postsegregation and post-civil rights generation is composed of African Americans born between 1965 and 1984. Prior to Kitwana's text, the issue of racial tension plagued the very perception and reception of Hip Hop Culture, as DJs were characterized as all Black and graffiti artists were characterized as Latinos in the east and Hispanics in the west. The b-boys and b-girls were loosely described as Black in the beginning and later, as Blacks defected, as Latin and Hispanic. MCs have predominantly been Black as well, with numerous disputable exceptions, including the Beastie Boys, 3rd Bass, Vanilla Ice, and, most recently, Eminem.

Yet how do these racially based, stereotypical groupings work in light of the fact that numerous Hip Hop innovators and pioneers who were often assumed to be African Americans or U.S.-born natives were, in fact, not? What happens when we acknowledge that the father of Hip Hop, DJ Kool Herc, was not born in the United States but was in fact born in Kingston, Jamaica, as was Sandra "Pepa" Denton, legendary member of one of the most noted female MC groups, Salt-n-Pepa? Might we have a similarly difficult time acknowledging that the greatest Hip Hop entertainer and original human beat box, Doug E. Fresh, was not born in the United States but in Barbados? Famed storytelling MC and legendary pioneer Richard "Slick Rick" Walters (also known as MC Ricky D), although Black, hails from London, England. Even though the Godfather of Hip Hop, Afrika Bambaataa, was born in the United States, his mother was born and raised in Barbados. Pioneering DJ Grandmaster Flash was also born in the United States to parents hailing from Barbados, where his father was a record collector. These different examples show the variety in global influence on Hip Hop. Although Hip Hop was not present in Jamaica, London, or Barbados, the prevalence of Black expressive culture, whether by birth or cultural adaptation, created a common experience through which Hip Hop was born in the United States. Its innovators may have been from different geographical locations, but they were united by the fact that they were impoverished and lived in locations where they felt marginalized.

These facts are only further complicated by the numerous Latin/Caribbean contributors to the framework and popularity of Hip Hop Culture, including DJ O.C. (Oscar Rodriguez) of the Fearless Four, and various b-boys (Mr. Wiggles [Steve Clemente], Fabel [Jorge Pabon], and Crazy Legs [Richard Colon of Rock Steady Crew]); graffiti artists (LEE Quiñones and LADY PINK [Sandra Fabara], the main stars of *Wild Style*); and MCs (Charlie Chase of the Cold Crush Brothers, "Devastating Tito" Dones of the Fearless Four, and Prince Markie Dee [Mark Morales of the Fat Boys]). Perhaps Rick Rubin, the white cofounder of Def Jam Records with Russell Simmons, might deserve some praise for his contribution to Hip Hop, as well as David Mays and Jon Shecter, cofounders of

The Source: The Magazine of Hip-Hop Music Culture and Politics while students at Harvard University.

During the 1990s, Hammer (MC Hammer) and Will Smith (then the Fresh Prince) were two of the most notable artists within Hip Hop, catering to audiences of all races. These two artists at their height showed that the artistic expression could bring diverse people from all walks of life together, united by their passion for the music of these artists and not necessarily the color of their skin. Interracial groups such as the Beat Junkies, the FABULOUS 5, Rock Steady Crew, and the Black Eyed Peas serve as examples of the colorless power of the multifaceted Hip Hop expression.

Yet artists like Vanilla Ice, Marky Mark (and the Funky Bunch), and most recently Eminem have received much criticism due more to the color of their skin than to any lack of artistic talent or ability to perform. Charged as cultural pirates and criticized for infringing on Black culture, these artists and others have felt the bitter sting of the unresolved racial tension of the broader society. In the cases of Vanilla Ice and Eminem, the list of awards and tally of earnings show that they have been able to achieve great fame and financial success in spite of, or perhaps because of, the controversy.

Nevertheless, the rise of gangsta rap and the use of the highly racialized term *nigga* created an immense tension between Blacks and all other races as the term became an insider term used only by Blacks while speaking to and about one another. Charged as an insider term of affection by proponents of its use, the term offered a subtle position of power (some would propose empowerment) to Blacks, who claimed to transform the term from a degrading racist moniker to an intimate exchange between both friends and enemies. By the 2000s, adding more controversy, numerous non-Black communities began using the term, and it became prominent in the lyrics of top-selling artists. Asian American, Latin, and numerous other non-Black practitioners and fans began to call one another by the term, careful not to cross the unwritten rule against referring to a Black peer by the term. The creation of the term *wigger*—a white nigger—further complicated things as white practitioners and participants, feeling empowered to transform the term to allow equal and appropriate use, put a new spin on the old racist epithet. These terms continue to challenge the potential for the use of Hip Hop as a healing tool.

The negative racial politics of the United States has greatly affected the perspectives of numerous citizens who might deem Hip Hop Culture as Black, just as rock is deemed by many as white, neglecting the innovations of Jimi Hendrix (James Marshall Hendrix) or those who came before him, such as Little Richard (Richard Wayne Penniman) or Chuck Berry (Charles Edward Anderson Berry). The list of contributors to various genres, styles, and forms of expression who are disregarded, deleted, or diminished as a result of their racial noncompliance returns to the notion of Hip Hop and race relations in the form of a question: With Hip Hop's unique and uncelebrated racial diversity, could Hip Hop be the catalyst for social, political, and economic change, just as it has already succeeded in helping to bring about cultural change? Might Hip Hop be the perfect catalyst to begin to acknowledge, reflect, and heal this country's cloudy racial past, allowing for greater peace and, above all, harmony? Have we missed the moment of opportunity to focus more on similarities than differences, recognizing that Hip Hop has no race or ethnicity and is created and kept alive by practitioners and patrons of all genders, ages, races, and ethnicities and from all corners of the world?

Is Gangsta Rap a Part of Hip Hop Culture?

During the late 1980s and into the early 1990s, the rising popularity of NWA and its various members sparked a heated debate on whether the violent lyrics of gangsta rap were indeed a part of Hip Hop Culture. Challenged by the criminal acts perpetuated within the storylines of the raps, the sexist and amplified misogynistic viewpoints, and the often violent demeanor of the artists themselves, critics and Hip Hop fundamentalists urged a distinction between hip hop and rap music. Rap music, the term used to designate the commercial-based idioms as opposed to hip hop, became the home for gangsta rap. Arguments continued to unfold charging that the music incited violence and strayed from the practice and presentation of the foundational elements, focusing on MCs and producers to the exclusion of DJs, graffiti artists, and b-boys/b-girls.

Although gangsta rap's prominence and popularity were achieved through the efforts and exploits of NWA, earlier figures played a significant role in its development. Schoolly D (Jesse B. Weaver Jr.), a west Philadelphia native and gangbanger whose 1984 singles "C.I.A." and "Gangster Boogie" paved the way for his monumental 1987 album *The Adventures of Schoolly D* (Rykodisc), featuring "P.S.K. What Does It Mean?," was one of the earliest innovators of gangsta rap. Referencing his crew, the Parkside Killers, a Philadelphia gang whose members frequented the area surrounding Parkside Avenue and 52nd Street, Schoolly D brought the gang culture into rap music.

However, he did not reach the acclaim that Newark, New Jersey–born Ice-T (Tracy Morrow) enjoyed. After moving to California as an adolescent, Morrow became fascinated with the Los Angeles gang and hustling scene. After roles in the early Hip Hop films *Rappin'* (MGM, 1985), *Breakin'* (Cannon Group, 1984), and *Breakin' II: Electric Boogaloo* (Cannon Film Distributors, 1984), he landed a record deal with Sire Records, launching his recording career. His experiments with the fusion of rock and Hip Hop, and his numerous commentaries on police brutality, political and economic injustice for Blacks, and battles against censorship, offered him as a double target on top of his gangsta-based lyrical tales and exploits.

The East Coast also had its share of hard-core gangsta rap in the form of the early KRS-One, Rakim, Notorious B.I.G., and a host of others. However, the group NWA, led by Easy-E (Eric Wright), CEO of Ruthless Records based in Compton, California, popularized the dope dealing, hustling, and gangbanging reality of some inner-city youth. Their tales offered a vivid fantasy for other inner-city and suburban youth and an opportunity for these outsiders to become vicarious onlookers in these mysteriously gruesome yet very appealing affairs.

Gangsta rap's largest population of fans, judging by concert attendance and record sales, has always been white suburban youth, whose interests in the inner-city underworld was appeased by the graphic exploits recorded on the albums. Gangsta rap's ability to cater to multiple audiences enhanced its appeal to outsiders, causing record sales to rise. The industry sought more artists to record, and the opportunity was accepted by numerous artists who, though not familiar with the harsh and brutal reality of the gangsta story, were eager to make money by exploiting the music industry, perhaps not aware they were endangering their own lives. Gangsta rap, which neither boasts equal treatment of the four foundational elements nor makes any attempt to stand on high moral ground, was responsible for an entire generation's entrance into the Hip Hop fold. For those born in the early to mid-1970s and coming of age in the late 1980s and early 1990s, NWA was the soundscape of their time. It was accessible and of interest, catering to a unique yet common perspective of social, political, economic, religious, and cultural commentary that many in this age group identified with. They considered gangsta rap the epitome of Hip Hop because it offered an uncensored social commentary, a charged political critique, and an economic potential that

Rappers Snoop Doggy Dogg (left) and Tupac Shakur attend the 1996 MTV Video Music Awards at Radio City Music Hall in New York City, NY. Both were prominent figures in West Coast gangsta rap during the mid-1990s. (Reuters/Corbis)

early Hip Hop only dreamed about. In a strange way, it even offered the religious and cultural sentiments considered missing by opponents: notions of a heaven for thugs and various symbolic and metaphoric representations of Christian and Muslim theological perspectives, as well as references to classic cultural characters such as Iceberg Slim, Superfly, and other widely celebrated figures from films of the 1960s and 1970s.

Gangsta rap, amid its numerous negative overtones, has many positive attributes, including the fact that it presents the real crisis of inner-city living from the inside out, offering an intimate portrayal of the failure of many social service and governmental aid programs and bringing to the forefront the persistent problems of police brutality, racial profiling, and a broken legal system. From this perspective, gangsta rap retains the raw and passionate charges for equality and justice offered by early innovators. Yet for many others, including a large population of white suburban youth, it offers the same kind of transcendental experience created by a science-fiction film or book: The life depicted, so distant from their personal reality that it seems as if it could not possibly be true, is simply an extremely appealing experiment.

Nonetheless, gangsta rap and its effect on society are real. Numerous artists have been sued, with claims that their violent lyrics influenced murders and other extremely violent acts. Such was the case for Tupac Shakur, who was sued because his music allegedly influenced the murder of a Texas police officer by a young Hip Hop fan (the civil suit against Tupac was later dropped). Numerous politicians and parental advisory groups have questioned the merits of gangsta rap. Interestingly enough, though, the same effort has not been made to limit or remove violent action movies, gruesome horror flicks, or the mob and Mafia films widely popular among these same impressionable youth. To some, gangsta rap has become the scapegoat for a diminishing society with weakened values and depreciating morals, while to others it is simply great entertainment, nothing more, nothing less. Regardless of where the balance falls, the debate will continue as a hot topic of discussion as long as gangsta rap remains popular and influential.

Can Hip Hop and the Academy Coexist?

In 1985, Tricia Rose, an employee of a local housing authority in Connecticut, decided to pursue her interests in rap music by tracing its rich lineage at the local library. A year later, her pursuits led to Brown University, where she enrolled as a graduate student in the American Studies program, destined to produce in 1994 one of the first critically acclaimed intellectual works on rap music and Hip Hop Culture. Rose's *Black Noise: Rap Music and Black Culture in Contemporary America* (Wesleyan University Press) was not the first text written on rap music or Hip Hop Culture; however, it was the first widely heralded text on the subject within academe. Rose's ability to use culture-based theories and modes of analysis to unravel the multiple layers and flows of rap music and Hip Hop Culture inspired many to follow her path. As a female scholar approaching a male-dominated expression, her ability to wade through the deep gender politics as well as the murky historical and cultural baggage relative to gender, sexism, misogyny, and the like continues to maintain model status among other female and male scholars. Her chapter "Bad Sistas: Black Women Rappers and Sexual Politics in Rap Music" remains an influential examination of this very topic. Rose's work also launched an instant yet quiet voice of validation to academic presses as well as academic institutions, as journal articles, book chapters, and, eventually, dedicated books and courses focusing on Hip Hop sprang forth over the next decade.

Other scholarly treatments of Hip Hop appeared in the years following the publication of *Black Noise,* including Russell A. Potter's *Spectacular Vernaculars: Hip Hop and the Politics of Postmodernism* (State University of New York, 1995), William Eric Perkins's *Droppin' Science: Critical Essays on Rap Music and Hip Hop Culture* (Temple University Press, 1996), and S. Craig Watkins's *Representing: Hip Hop Culture and the Production of Black Cinema* (University of Chicago Press, 1998). Numerous professors, lecturers, and instructors used them as course textbooks or suggested reading. During the late 1990s, beyond the addition of Hip Hop within course curricula, Hip Hop Culture clubs began to spring forth on hundreds of college and high school campuses. Dedicated to the preservation, promotion, and, in some cases, the practice of Hip Hop's elements, these groups brought the street-based sounds, fashions, language, and aesthetic onto campus.

The greatest sign of Hip Hop's intersection with academia, however, was the establishment of the Hiphop Archive in 2002 under the direction of Dr. Marcyliena Morgan at the W. E. B. Du Bois Institute of African and African American Research at Harvard University. Aimed at providing students, faculty, artists, and community members access to a wealth of reference materials, the archive symbolized a tremendous validation of Hip Hop not only as a subject of intellectual pursuit but as a culture relevant and stable enough for study. The archive's debut "Hiphop Community Activism and Educational Roundtable" in 2002 brought national activists and educators to Harvard in order to discuss and organize frameworks to achieve similar goals in different local and regional communities. The archive's "All Eyez on Me: Tupac Shakur and the Search for a Modern Folk Hero" conference in 2003 drew Hip Hop scholars from around the globe to discuss the influence and international appeal of the slain Hip Hop and popular-culture icon.

Harvard University is not the only institution hosting conferences on or related to Hip Hop. Since the late 1990s, the University of Wisconsin–Madison has hosted an annual three-day Hip Hop conference. Aimed at national student activists, Hip Hop headz, and other interested participants, the conference, which draws a slate of top-notch artists and scholars, has aided in the recognition of Hip Hop as a topic of interest within the academic community. By 2003, more than 70 courses prominently featuring Hip Hop Culture were being taught at the university level, and this number grew to slightly more than 100 for the 2005–2006 academic year. By the spring of 2005, an accumulation of over 100 Hip Hop–oriented conferences had been hosted on college campuses.

The movement of Hip Hop into the twenty-first century ushered in new treatments of Hip Hop with Murray Forman's *The 'Hood Comes First: Race, Space and Place in Rap and Hip-Hop* (Wesleyan University Press, 2002), Cheryl L. Keyes's *Rap Music and Street Consciousness* (University of Illinois Press, 2004), Imani Perry's *Prophets of the Hood: Politics and Poetics in Hip Hop* (Duke University Press, 2004), and Gwendolyn D. Pugh's *Check It While I Wreck It: Black Womanhood, Hip-Hop Culture, and the Public Sphere* (Northeastern University Press, 2004), among others. Even among the faculty corps, groups such as the Northeastern University Hip Hop Studies Collective sprang forth in 2004, identifying like-minded faculty who collaborate with students and staff to preserve, promulgate, and practice Hip Hop on campus and in the greater Boston metropolitan area.

The most recent and perhaps greatest advancement toward the intersection of Hip Hop Culture and academia is the 2004 release of the monumental *That's the Joint!: The Hip-Hop Studies Reader* (Routledge, 2004) by Murray Forman and Mark Anthony Neal, with a foreword by Michael Eric Dyson. Single-handedly introducing the notion of the intellectual study of Hip Hop Culture to millions, this seminal text is perhaps a sign of things to come.

Can Hip Hop and Activism Coexist?

The 1981 recording "The Message" (Sugar Hill) by Grandmaster Flash and the Furious Five offered an early glimpse of the relationship between Hip Hop and activism. Many pioneers hasten to remark that Hip Hop in its very essence is activism, as it was the early Hip Hop movement that transformed the gang-infested neighborhoods of the New York City boroughs into thriving nests for sonic, colorful, animated, and verbal expression. From the reflective yet empowering lyrics of "The Message" to the 2004 slogan "Vote or die," led by P. Diddy's Citizen Change Organization and amplified by thousands, if not millions, of youth, young adults, and middle-aged adults who challenged the nation, and specifically the Hip Hop community, to vote, Hip Hop from its very inception had a purpose. Hip Hop has always had an activist edge to it, whether through Chuck D's influential presence fronting Public Enemy or the more recent work of Boots Wiley and the Coup, dead prez, Black Star, Common, or Talib Kweli. All these groups have infused in their lyrics and presentation critical social analysis, economic critique, a call for economic justice, and a cultural consciousness grounded in the original intent of DJ Kool Herc and the collective spirit of Afrika Bambaataa and the Universal Zulu Nation. Even the gangsta rap of NWA had a quasi-activist aspect as it brought national attention to police brutality and racial profiling, and in many ways offered an introspective look at the effects of drugs and gangs in major metropolises. Indirectly, this form of activism may be quite effective, as the music certainly received the attention of local, state, regional, and federal civil servants as well as mention by the White House and Supreme Court.

Activism in Hip Hop has taken many shapes and stances, from Rap Coalition's Wendy Day, who has advocated on behalf of numerous Hip Hop artists who were either mistreated by the music industry or on the verge of entering a nonbeneficial contract, to Kevin Powell, a journalist and curator of national tours on Hip Hop history. Day, committed to overturning decades of mistreatment of artists, founded Rap Coalition in 1992 as a nonprofit company dedicated to protecting the rights of artists, who are often exploited by the industry they dreamed of joining. She later expanded her business to also serve as a clearinghouse of information, training young Hip Hop practitioners in business savvy, legal awareness, and general best practices of negotiating a contract. Powell, a Hip Hop historian, author, and widely sought-after lecturer on the topic, offers discussions on race and gender relations and serves as a nationally ranked speaker to audiences at high schools, colleges, community centers, churches, and the like.

Like Day and Powell, many others have committed themselves to Hip Hop activism. Rock Steady Crew member and vice president Fabel Pabon and his wife, Christie Z-Pabon (organizer of DMC competitions, and the Zulu Nation Anniversary), for example, through their Tools of War company, organize, promote, and consult on socially conscious Hip Hop and non–Hip Hop events. Activists such as Ras Baraka and Toni Blackman come in the form of Hip Hop politicians. Baraka is a poet, educator, and deputy mayor of the city of Newark, New Jersey. Born into a family of activists (Amiri and Amina Baraka), Baraka committed his life to his passion for music, education, and people. He has worked with a prominent list of artists on numerous important issues, including cofounding and hosting the National Hip-Hop Political Convention, held on May 19–22, 2004, with the goal of unifying the Hip Hop generation through the creation and ratification of a Hip Hop political agenda. Blackman, a poet, educator, and performance artist, is the U.S. "Hip Hop ambassador." She is the first person to hold the prestigious U.S. Department of State (DOS) post and has traveled on behalf of the DOS to Senegal, Ghana, and Nigeria. She has performed around the world and has been curator for the International Hip Hop Festival. Advocating for the use of Hip Hop as an agent of healing and peace, Blackman is not only a Hip Hop head but also an international leader. Hip Hop has truly crossed social, political, economic, and cultural boundaries, implementing change at every juncture.

The most effective and perhaps most revealing activist projects within Hip Hop may be those bringing artists together, often for the first time, to offer creative works for public consumption in order to raise money and resources for particular causes. These "compilation projects," which include recordings such as the single "Self-Destruction" and the albums *America Is Dying Slowly* and *Hip Hop for Respect,* offer a unique approach to activism.

"Self-Destruction" was sparked by a conversation at the 1987 Unity Summit held at the Latin Quarter nightclub and hosted by Universal Zulu Nation leader Afrika Bambaataa. Following this conversation, KRS-One and a few friends were led to form the Stop the Violence Coalition in 1988 with two main goals: serving as a positive force within Hip Hop and helping to remove the growing association between violence and the Hip Hop movement. Together with "Tokyo Rose" (Ann Carli) and Nelson George, the coalition assembled the talents of Stetsasonic, Kool Moe Dee, MC Lyte, Just-Ice, Doug E. Fresh, Heavy D., and Public Enemy along with KRS-One. Calling themselves the Stop the Violence All-Stars, they collaborated and recorded the track in 1989. The song, a strong and powerful decree against Black-on-Black violence, raised over $600,000, which was donated to the National Urban League to assist with the ongoing struggle to end gang violence.

In 1996, the AIDS awareness group Red Hot Organization sponsored a recording of AIDS awareness tracks by numerous Hip Hop superstars, including Wu-Tang Clan, Coolio, De La Soul, Mac Mall, and Goodie Mob, as a fund-raising effort. The album, *America Is Dying Slowly* (Eastwest Records America), assisted the organization, which has donated over $7 million for AIDS relief worldwide, in reaching a new audience, with all proceeds adding to their global efforts.

The 2000 compilation project *Hip Hop for Respect* (Rawkus) featured the voices of Ras Kass, Nonchalant, dead prez, Parrish Smith, Kool G Rap, Rah Digga, Common, Pharoahe Monche, and numerous other notables, including executive producers and project organizers Mos Def and Talib Kweli. The album served as a fundraiser for the Hip-Hop for Respect Foundation, a nonprofit organization aimed at combating police brutality.

Have Women Played a Prominent Role in Hip Hop?

Hip Hop is dominated by male participants, but that does not mean that women were not involved from the very beginning. A year prior to Sugar Hill Gang's monumental 1979 record "Rapper's Delight," Paulette Tee and Sweet Tee recorded "Vicious Rap" on their father's record label (Paul Winley Records). In the ensuing years, a host of talented female DJs, graffiti artists, dancers, and MCs made substantial contributions to the culture of Hip Hop. Important female DJs included DJ Wanda Dee and DJ Jazzy Joyce, who earned wide recognition early on in Hip Hop's history. Graffiti artists such as LADY PINK (Sandra Fabara) achieved great acclaim from both the women and the men involved in the artistic movement. B-girls such as Baby Love and Pebblee Poo were dominant forces on the early scene. Although they competed primarily against men, they held their own, earning respect and recognition while paving the way for women such as Asia One of No Easy Props and Rock Steady Crew. MCs such as Lady B, Lisa Lee, Sequence (Cheryl the Pearl, MC Blondie, and MC Angie B

Missy "Misdemeanor" Elliott rose as one of the most notable MCs and producers during the late 1990s and early 2000s. Here she performs at Motorola's annual Holiday Party at The Lot in West Hollywood, CA. December 5, 2002. (Corbis)

[a.k.a. Angie Stone]), Debbie Dee, and Sha Rock all debuted well before the rise of Salt-n-Pepa and Queen Latifah in the mid-1980s. Even K Love, who is touted as the first female beat box on record with the 1985 "Bad Boys" (a.k.a. Inspector Gadget) on the Starlite label, was a legend in her own right. Behind the scenes, it was Sylvia Robinson's Sugar Hill empire that launched Hip Hop not only nationally but globally, creating the foundation for the present multibillion-dollar industry.

These highly talented and widely influential ladies were followed by numerous other women who left a lasting impression on Hip Hop Culture. Led by the Salt and Pepper MCs, later known as Salt-n-Pepa, they presented their femininity in a nonpornographic yet sensual manner that complemented their feminist rhymes. Others of the period, such as Queen Latifah and MC Lyte, literally hid their feminine splendor in exchange for the tomboy persona, allowing for no distractions as they battled both men and other women with their superior rhyming skills. Plagued by the growing number of sexually explicit and sexist competitors, they battled the rising challenge of "sex sells" championed by their contemporaries Lil' Kim, Foxy Brown, and Trina, whose exotic dress and graphically explicit lyrics earned them both great acclaim and tremendous critique.

Even though Roxanne Shanté, Yo Yo, Da Brat, Eve, and other influential MCs have all taken their turns as queens of the microphone, women have played a huge role behind the scenes as well. Record executives Sylvia Rhone, former chief executive of East West Records (Yo Yo, MC Lyte, and Das EFX); Monica Lynch, former president of Tommy Boy Records (De La Soul, Naughty By Nature, Digital Underground, House of Pain, and Queen Latifah); and Carmen Ashhurst-Woodard, former president of Def Jam Records (one of the most important Hip Hop record labels after the demise of Sugar Hill Records during the 1980s) all had influential decision-making roles in hip hop music and helped to shape its future.

Media stars, such as radio personalities Angie Martinez (New York City's WQHT "Hot 97" FM) and Wendy Williams (New York City's Hot 97 FM and Philadelphia's WUSL 98.9 FM), and pioneering Hip Hop television host Dee Barnes (*Pump It Up* and *Sisters in the Name of Rap*), ushered Hip Hop into the living rooms, bedrooms, and automobiles of an entire generation. Indie film director Rachel Raimist offered the film *Nobody Knows My Name,* showcasing women practitioners of Hip Hop (2000), and music video directors Sanaa Hamri (Jadakiss's song, "Why"; "Fast Lane-Remix" by Bilal featuring Dr. Dre and Jadakiss; and "Come Close" by Common featuring Mary J. Blige), Diane Martel (Nas's "Bridging the Gap"; Snoop Dogg's "From the Chuuch to da Palace"; and Mobb Deep's "Burn" featuring Noyd), and Nzingha Stewart (Eve's "Satisfaction"; Twista's "Sunshine"; and Ol' Dirty Bastard's "I Got Cha Money") have each established themselves as award-winning creative talents with extraordinary reputations in the industry.

One could not speak of women contributions to the framework of Hip Hop without mention of Wendy Day, founder of the Rap Coalition, an organization that has established a reputation as a protective force within Hip Hop, negotiating numerous contracts and deals to the benefit of the artists, who are predominantly male. Women have played a crucial and critical role in the establishment and development of Hip Hop Culture both in front of the spotlight and behind it.

Has Hip Hop Misrepresented Women?

During the late 1980s and early 1990s, Luther Campbell's 2 Live Crew and Easy-E's NWA were just two of the major groups in the middle of heated debate surrounding their graphically explicit and verbally pornographic representations of women. During the 1990s and into the 2000s, the trend continued, as men boasting hyper-masculine personas referred to one another as "pimps" in recognition of superficial and unrecognized sexual prowess. Often championed by rappers such as Snoop Dogg, Ice-T, 50 Cent, and numerous others, the terms "pimp," as well as "mack" and "playa," served as indirect references to their position of power or control over women. Music videos and lyrics from these rappers offered misogynistic and derogatory images of women similar to those championed by 2 Live Crew and NWA, revealing women as sexual and sensual objects dressed in bikinis, thongs, high-heeled stilettos, and lingerie and often dancing in ways simulating sexual acts. As producers and musicians took advantage of the Hollywood mantra "sex sells," these video vixens were often placed in starring roles as the centerpiece of videos and stage performances, perhaps in an attempt to compensate for the limited physical appeal of the rappers. Young females began to aspire to play these roles, daring to be seen in the spotlight. For some, the role offers more prestige and immediate exposure than being a supermodel.

In the fight over these misogynist aspects of Hip Hop and its various manifestations via images, lyrics, and other presentations, some argue that women who participate should receive the blame for allowing themselves to be portrayed and depicted in this manner. These participants, say some, enjoy the opportunity these roles give them to control male and female viewers by means of sensuality in addition to taking the empowering position of dictating new standards of sexiness to eager male and female viewers. According to this view, it is also empowering to the vixens to know that female viewers are comparing and contrasting their own

Portrait of members of the rap group NWA, including DJ Yella, MC Ren, Eazy-E (2nd from right), and Dr. Dre (right), standing in front of an abandoned convenience store. (Mitchell Gerber/Corbis)

appeal against the portrayed depictions. The women who play these starring roles often feel they are simply taking advantage of their femininity for the pursuit of fame, fortune, and a career in entertainment; they understand that sex is marketable and accepted in mainstream society and the media.

It is nevertheless difficult for some to accept the sensual and sexual dimensions of Hip Hop, whether it might be in terms of deciphering phallic symbolism within a graffiti piece, watching the b-boy end his move holding his crotch and making an explicit motion, or seeing a tremendously talented MC come on stage wearing little more than underwear and leaving wearing even less, while shouting obscenities. Such actions and images have greatly affected how gender is perceived. Many viewers who are not in the Hip Hop generation have commented on the effect these presentations may have on youth as they emulate and celebrate their iconic role models, complaining that the portrayals show unhealthy, unrealistic relationships. For some who portray women in this light, being a real man involves subjecting women to all levels of mischief in order to teach them their place. To some of the women, being a real woman means revealing to men that they can beat them at their own game.

Has Hip Hop Been Misrepresented by the Media?

Hip Hop evolved from the gang-infested, inner-city neighborhoods of New York City's boroughs, bringing with it all of the charismatic charm, passionate expression, and undying dedication toward realizing social, political, and economic equality while having a good time. In a localized or even a regional area, and under the same radar, this might have worked, yet the widely appealing release of "Rapper's Delight" in 1979 by the Sugar Hill Gang, the major recording contract by Kurtis Blow in 1981, the various documentaries and other films of 1984, and the innovative marketing endorsement deal between Run-DMC (brokered by manager Russell Simmons) and Adidas in 1986 changed the local, intimate essence of Hip Hop forever. As Hip Hop developed a financial profile and grew as a profitable stakeholder in American popular culture, and ultimately American culture in general, numerous artists turned their focus from making art to making money while making art.

By the 1980s, Hip Hop had emerged as an opportunity for artists to financially thrive. DJs moved into the production seat at various recording studios and record labels, graffiti artists displayed their works at major art galleries, b-boys/b-girls made the transition from performing on the street to performing on television shows and in motion pictures, and numerous MCs became national, and in many cases international, spokesmen and women for merchandise, achieving superstar status in the popular culture. Driven by the rising material culture craze of the 1980s and feeling empowered to attain the unattainable, many Hip Hop practitioners became agents of material desire flaunting the various symbols of social mobility: money, jewelry, cars, access to informal sex, and drugs, among other things. Yet the question arises: Were these the actual desires of the artists, or were they false perceptions created through media representations of the financially enticing culture?

As the notion of "keepin' it real" began to cascade over the growing Hip Hop landscape, even those artists who did not lyrically or artistically subscribe to the commercialized identities were either pushed into the Hip Hop pool, excommunicated into the abyss of unsuccessful no-hit wonders, or categorized as part of the underground. Throughout the 1980s, the media presented gangs, crime, the abuse of narcotics and alcohol, sex, and the passion for money and materialism as the major images of Hip Hop. By 1999, "bling bling" was the code word for the desire for possession of material things, and the more material things an individual acquired, the more successful he or she appeared. In the twenty-first century, Hip Hop serves as the major marketing tool for Fortune 500 companies and other firms catering to middle-class and wealthy audiences. As a result, Hip Hop appears to be financially successful, yet the culture at times feels broke.

As the culture participates with companies such as Nike, Reebok, Adidas, Mercedes, BMW, Juicy Couture, Versace, Burberry, Vitamin Water, Gatorade, and Motorola, providing a major draw in their advertising, who attracts the consumers and who benefits from their money? For the most part, it is the wealthy corporate world. Recent exceptions sparked by the success of Russell Simmons's Def Jam Records and Phat Farm clothing line; P. Diddy's Bad Boy Records and Sean John clothing line; Jay-Z's Roc-A-Fella Records and Rocawear; and Master P's No Limit empire, as well as other initiatives, have begun to slightly turn the tide. However, these four names make up a tiny percentage of the thousands of young and middle-aged people who turn to Hip Hop every day in pursuit of the gold mine perpetuated by the media portrayal of its participants. Hip hop music videos, Hip Hop–oriented television shows, and even shows that are not specifically in the genre but occasionally feature a Hip Hop artist, such as MTV's *Cribs* or *Punk'd,* like other media entities, present Hip Hop artists flaunting their riches and luxurious lifestyles, enticing millions of youth to follow their lead. These shows subtly—or not so subtly—imply that the outcome will be just as financially rewarding for them as it has been for the major stars.

In media portrayals, Hip Hop also carries the stigma of violence; overindulgence in materialism, sex, narcotics, and alcohol; severe addiction to the pursuit of money; and the pursuit of an unashamed, irresponsible, careless lifestyle. These media presentations, driven by media companies' desire to attain and retain

Reggeaton singer Daddy Yankee, originally from Puerto Rico, appears backstage at the MTV Awards at the American Airlines Arena on Sunday, Aug. 28, 2005. (Alan Diaz/AP Photo)

viewers and ratings, are sensationalized stereotypes, but they are nevertheless the only images of Hip Hop that many people ever see. In many ways, the underground is a safe haven away from the media more than it is a collective of artists in rebellion against the mainstream.

Because of the media spotlight on particular artists, hip hop works that could have had a positive impact, and that spoke to the survival and urgency of the Hip Hop community, such as the anti-cocaine song "White Lines (Don't Do It)" by Grandmaster Flash and the Furious Five, "World Peace" by KRS-One, and a host of other influential, informative, and important tracks, were hidden behind nonsense expressions appealing to the entertainment of outside parties. With some 70 to 80 percent of the consumers of Hip Hop in white middle-class and upper-class suburbs, the goal of the media companies is no secret: ratings, ratings, ratings . . . sales, sales, sales. Millions of suburban white youth flock to Hip Hop, with the help of the media, in their revolt against parents,

teachers, and the law and in an attempt to glimpse the mysteri-
ous, intriguing, and captivating sagas of inner-city life.

From its images of gold teeth or porcelain crowns encrusted
with precious jewels to its stories of an East Coast–West Coast battle staged between two individuals and their respective record labels, media companies have used their power of illusion to create
perceptions of reality based in sensationalism and entertainment.
Although not all of Hip Hop has fallen prey, those who remain
"true" to the essence and collective consciousness of the original
intent of the expression are often castigated to the back of the
room, left with little resources and limited opportunity to reach
the mass audience. From early newspaper articles to motion-picture deals, fashion lines, major endorsements, and beyond, however, one thing is certain—without the influence of the media and
their ability to disseminate information and spread images, Hip
Hop would still be a localized, inner-city expression waiting for
recognition.

Should Hip Hop Be Censored?

During the early stages of prerecorded Hip Hop, the collection of
expressions at its core (DJing, graffiti, b-boying/b-girling, and
MCing) were based on inner-city life—a life and lifestyle that contained, in many cases, gangs and violence, narcotics and alcohol,
crime and poverty, and hustling and the desire to attain riches.
The language of the streets was slang. It was full of graphic imagery and explicit words, phrases, and metaphors that were often
unknown to folks from outside the inner-city perimeter. This was
the situation from which the expressions of Hip Hop grew, and
these were the realities of which Hip Hop spoke. During the early
period, it was the rawness and urgent appeal for equality that
captured the hearts and minds of both artists and fans, revealing
to the world the next tool of global revolution as countries across
the globe imitated, adopted, and appropriated Hip Hop as a
method and manner of communication against local, regional,
national, and global oppression.

During the mid-1980s, as Hip Hop spread nationally and globally, a collective of wealthy mothers, challenged by the addition
of Hip Hop to their children's taste palate, gathered to form a
strategy to contain the "negative" music and to remove it from
their children's reach. Several wives of congressmen, cabinet officials, and notable businessmen founded the Parent's Music Resource Center (PMRC) in May 1985 for the purpose of educating

and informing other parents of the growing trends in popular culture, particularly in recorded music. Aimed at banning explicitly graphic, sexually provocative, and utterly vile material on recordings, the PMRC set out on a course that led to the greater discussion of censorship. With rap music, rock, and heavy metal as the targets, the group spent five years advocating for a change in public policy, seeking to remove questionable music from general circulation and specifically to remove it from the reach of minors. After staging numerous events, from public and highly visible televised appearances and protests to Senate hearings, the PMRC finally reached a level of success in 1990, when the Recording Industry Association of America (RIAA) introduced a uniform labeling system, marking recordings deemed to have questionable material with a sticker reading "Parental Advisory—Explicit Lyrics." These recordings were not to be sold to minors and were to be confiscated upon sight in schools and other public areas such as libraries, parks, and the like.

Interestingly enough, only rap, heavy metal, and rock music were tagged. Country music, some of which also contains sexual overtones and an occasional taste of questionable language, was exempt, as was opera, musical comedy, and other genres not associated with popular youth culture yet containing ample examples of questionable material. In fact, although the RIAA, at the beckoning of the PMRC and other adversarial groups, implemented the labeling system, they never released the criteria by which certain recordings would be labeled. In addition, the Federal Communications Commission (FCC), the governmental agency that regulates interstate and international communications by radio, television, wire, satellite, and cable, began issuing severe fines to radio stations as well as television and cable stations that aired or broadcast tracks from these labeled recordings. Although the laws were clear regarding the fines, they were infrequently policed, and the sudden and strategic policing only of certain genres and certain artists created chaos, drawing numerous complaints from members of the Hip Hop and rock communities, who felt that their artistic endeavors were being unjustly censored.

The cries, though, did not last long, as the system basically backfired. The presence of the sticker did not reduce sales as the PMRC had hoped, nor did it remove the targeted material from circulation. In fact, it increased sales, particularly among white suburban kids, who flocked to record stores to purchase what they were forbidden to purchase: the most graphic, violent, misogynistic, and sexually explicit recordings they could find. The rise of gangsta rap may in fact be due to the "parental advisory" sticker. Although artists and record companies were forced to record two versions of songs (the original and a clean version) for radio and television broadcast, this was an investment that paid off well for numerous artists who were able to sell twice as many records as they might have otherwise because of their reputation for crude lyrics. Artists such as Notorious B.I.G., Tupac Shakur, and Snoop Dogg are a few of the many examples. Others, such as Too Short, established lengthy careers and sold millions of albums without any radio or television assistance. Known for some of the most explicit, derogatory, and misogynistic lyrics, Too Short relied on word of mouth and the presence of the sticker to sell his albums.

The debate and the effects of censorship relative to Hip Hop are perhaps best explored through two very major and widely noted examples dealing with the 1989 double album by Luther Campbell and the 2 Live Crew, *As Nasty as They Want to Be* (Luke Records) and Ice-T's 1992 recording of "Cop Killer" with his band Body Count. Campbell, one of the leaders in the Hip Hop controversy (along with NWA), formed the group 2 Live Crew in California in 1985. Known for outrageously explicit lyrics, pornographic album and CD covers, and X-rated stage performances, Campbell and the group received worldwide recognition with the release of the double album. The momentum of the PMRC and other groups within the nation's courts earned the album a nationwide ban. Additionally, legislation was passed in Florida and Massachusetts insisting on prison time for anyone caught offering the album for sale. Florida retailer Charles Freeman was unlucky: He sold a copy of the double album to an undercover police officer and was arrested, found guilty, and sentenced to a prison term (his sentence was overturned on appeal). Campbell and 2 Live Crew were arrested on obscenity charges stemming from lyrics on the album. They were eventually acquitted with the assistance of expert testimony from then Duke University professor Henry Louis "Skip" Gates, Jr. The album, however, earned multiplatinum status, selling millions of copies as an illegal and controversial album. Some consumers purchased the album and left it unopened in hopes that it might one day serve as a valuable collector's item or at least a valuable souvenir from an interesting time period in American popular culture.

The more famous situation, though, involved Ice-T and Body Count's 1992 single "Cop Killer," which landed criticism from the White House. Sparked by the April 29, 1992, acquittal of four white police officers charged with violently brutalizing Rodney

King, who was Black, while recorded on videotape, Ice-T and Body Count offered the protest record targeting the Los Angeles Police Department, and police in general, for their misuse of power and illegal conduct toward Blacks, their racial profiling, and their brutality. The explicitly violent and threatening lyrics were not well received by the nation's fraternity of police and other civil servants. On June 11, 1992, the Dallas Police Association and Combined Law Enforcement Association of Texas filed action calling for the nationwide banning of the album from circulation and the withdrawal of present units of the album from retail stores. Numerous claims were also filed with the California state attorney general. Vice President Dan Quayle chimed in, calling the record obscene. President George H. W. Bush issued a charge denouncing any record label that would release such a record. Strong-armed by local, state, regional, and federal authorities as well as by statements from the White House, Ice-T personally announced the removal of the single from the album on July 28, 1992. Ice-T and Body Count were subsequently dropped from the Warner Brothers record label.

In both cases and in many more, the political interests of those in power outweighed artists' First Amendment rights to freedom of speech. This very violation is reminiscent of the early scenes of New York City's boroughs and the events that led to the creation of the expressions of Hip Hop in the first place. These expressions united youth under the rubric of Hip Hop Culture to secure social, political, and economic equality, including the right to express oneself freely. Essentially, freedom costs a price that some are not willing to pay, and that others are not given access and opportunity to pay.

Is Hip Hop Plagued with Violence?

In many ways and by numerous accounts, Hip Hop began as a response to social, political, and economic inequities in New York's inner cities. Among the manifestations of these inequities was the presence of violence, via murders and other violent crimes, especially among the gangbanger inhabitants of the communities. Sparked by the murder of "Black Benjie" (Cornell Benjamin), a member of the Ghetto Brothers, and the subsequent December 8, 1971, gang truce meeting at the Bronx Boys Club, Hip Hop Godfather, pioneering DJ, and former Black Spade gang leader Afrika Bambaataa began a long journey toward implementing a method of stopping the violence witnessed in the borough ghettos.

A large poster and video screen promoting the new video game "50 Cent Bulletproof," featuring rapper 50 Cent, is displayed at the Vivendi Universal Games exhibit during the first day the exhibit floor was open at the Electronic Entertainment Expo E3 in Los Angeles, May 18, 2005. The show, one of the largest gatherings of game companies and hardware providers, draws gamers from around the world to see new games and products. (Fred Prouser/Reuters/Corbis)

Thus began his Universal Zulu Nation. Yet by the mid-1980s and into the 1990s, the effects of urban decay and the realities of class-based disparities led youth to engage in urgent, emotionally charged, yet mindless acts of violence against one another. Born of the inner-city cries for assistance and equity, Hip Hop was unable to escape the brutal clutches of these violent acts and violent crimes, even though Bambaataa, the Universal Zulu Nation, and numerous other artists and collectives have stood against the promulgation of violence, whether it be domestic, race-based, gang-related, or any other form.

Selling more than 2.5 million copies of *Straight Outta Compton* (Ruthless Records, 1988), NWA led the early fold of artists who promoted and used violent portraits within their often outrageously graphic storylines. Ice-T, Schoolly D, Kool G. Rap, early KRS-One, and even some early Public Enemy also offered violence as a main ingredient of their particular stylistic approaches to the music. More recent artists, including Mobb Deep, Cam'ron, Capone-N-Noreaga, 50 Cent, The Game, and numerous others, continue to claim that to reveal the plight of the streets and to remain true to the fact that Hip Hop began in the streets, they need to offer the raw, uncut, uncensored truth in the language and sentiments of the street. As the self-acclaimed urban reporters and storytellers, they offer that they are not encouraging violence; they are merely reminding everyone that it is still present.

The media offer an entirely different perspective, using the presence and residue of violence as an opportunity for high ratings, increased viewers, and attention in order to compete with the growing shock-drama and reality-television era. Often spinning the coverage to focus on the violent acts without providing all the facts or the full context, the media often present half-truths and insufficient, biased accounts cloaked as fact. Because the violent lyrics of Hip Hop are so well known, Hip Hop lands as the scapegoat for violent acts that are not perpetrated by Hip Hop practitioners or fans or even associated with the Hip Hop community. The media certainly are not likely to assist in putting any stop to the unbalanced coverage, and neither Hip Hop nor the inner-city communities overwhelmed by the violence have the political or economic power to counter the often negative images and portrayals of the culture and its participants.

From the very beginning of Hip Hop, violence has plagued the community. Gang-infested neighborhood discotheques converted into neighborhood Hip Hop hot spots still reeking of occasional violent acts; personal fights that took place during Hip Hop concerts were blamed on the oblivious performing artists; and notable Hip Hop artists have lost their lives through senseless, violent acts (most notably Tupac Shakur and Notorious B.I.G). If only some of these artists, such as Stretch (Randy Walker), Big L (Lamont Coleman), Freaky Tah (Raymond Rogers), Jam Master Jay (Jason Mizell), Kenneth Walker, Soulja Slim (James Tapp), DJ Scott La Rock (Scott Sterling), Karizma, JoJo White, DJ Cee, Kadafi (Yafeu Fula), Seagram, Black Dynasty, and Young Lay, could return from the grave to offer their opinion, what might they say?

Hip Hop Goes Global

The October 1979 release of "Rapper's Delight" by the Sugar Hill Gang on the fledgling indie label Sugar Hill Records ignited a new musical and cultural movement with a style and flavor all its own. Other musical movements had paved the way, however, showing that innovations in music could be the catalyst for unique cultural trends. During the 1893 Chicago World's Fair, the late nineteenth-century sounds of ragtime debuted before an international audience, launching a trend that would inspire concert music composers around the world as they imitated, adopted, and appropriated the sounds and sentiments of the genre within their own compositions. A similar pattern occurred as jazz traveled the world during the 1920s and 1930s, championed by some of the same countries that became enemies of the United States in vicious war. The 1950s ushered in the rock 'n' roll craze, which would create a pseudo-international youth popular culture based on the sounds and sonic experiments of U.S. and UK superstars. Yet "Rapper's Delight"—perhaps not exactly the best example of Hip Hop, as it omitted the DJ and the b-boys and b-girls, and was not even recorded on a label based in Bronx, Harlem, or Brooklyn—was the catalyst for the dominant international musical and cultural movement of the late twentieth and early twenty-first centuries.

When Hip Hop's first official boy-band and their Englewood, New Jersey–based label, Sugar Hill Records, named after the prestigious section of Harlem, released the first rap hit record, they earned enormous recognition. "Rapper's Delight" became the best-selling twelve-inch single of all time, at one point selling 75,000 copies a week (Chang 2005, 131). The single won the coveted "Record of the Year" award from the National Association of Record Merchandisers and peaked at #4 on the R&B charts

Alums of Sugar Hill Records amongst others pose for a photo as they arrive at the VH1 Hip Hop Honors held on October 3, 2004, in New York City, NY. (Peter Kramer/Getty Images)

(Heibutzki 1997, 14). On the Top 40 chart the record peaked at #36, a rare feat for a small-budget record with limited radio play from a small, family-run, independent label competing against major record labels and rising music-industry conglomerates (Ro 1997, 7). The domestic success of "Rapper's Delight" was quickly matched by its reception on popular music radio stations in France, Japan, Holland, the United Kingdom, and around the globe, igniting a concentric ring of fire that would spread with intensity and power. During the 1980s, small enclaves of Hip Hop activity grew into a monumental, globally relevant culture, unified, in some cases, solely by the presence and expressions of the DJs, graffiti artists, b-boys/b-girls, and MCs. From the local artistic expression based in the Bronx to the imitations, adoptions, and appropriations found in German Hip Hop, Australian Hip Hop, Pinoy rap (Philippines), Azeri rap (Azerbaijan), and rap Nigerien (Niger), to mention a few variations, rap music and Hip Hop Culture have transformed the musical and cultural landscape of the globe. This chapter reveals the various ways that Hip Hop Culture was transmitted from the United States to the world.

Three Early Global Hits

In November 1980, the group Blondie, led by singer Deborah Harry, released its fifth album, *Autoamerican* (Chrysalis, 1980). Blondie already had a number of U.S. and UK Top Ten successes, but *Autoamerican* included two gold-selling, chart-topping singles. The second of these, released in January 1981, was the rap-influenced "Rapture." Prior to recording this single, Harry was a punk rock/New Wave star traveling in the same circles as graffiti artist and MC FAB 5 FREDDY and many other rising artists who frequented The Mudd Club in downtown New York City. The Mudd Club was one of numerous locations where the Hip Hop crowd mingled with the punk rock crowd, where street-based artists mingled with gallery artists, and where, most important, the only membership card was creative, artistic talent. The artists also often possessed an eccentric flair, something both Harry and FAB 5 had in plenty. Their friendship, as well as Harry's passion for the popular New York–based rap music of the late 1970s, and specifically her admiration for the work of pioneering Hip Hop DJ Grandmaster Flash, earned FAB 5 and Flash shout-outs in "Rapture" as Harry rapped her lyrics. The hit, which reached #1 on the U.S. pop charts and made the Top Ten in the United Kingdom, offered a unique and unprecedented validation for these innovators, not only boosting their name recognition but also serving as a preface for the acceptance of Hip Hop among a global audience (Strauss 1999, 244).

"Master of Records" and seminal Bronx DJ Afrika Bambaataa quickly established himself as a quiet yet powerful force in Hip Hop during its infant years. In 1980, as a producer, he led Soul Sonic Force in their anthem, "Zulu Nation Throwdown." But it was not until 1982, when he signed a contract with Tommy Boy Records, that the world would begin to realize what the Bronx had known for a long time—that Bambaataa had a new sound for our times. Following the release of "Jazzy Sensation" by a few months, the release of "Planet Rock" confirmed Bambaataa as the Godfather of Hip Hop, the Father of electro-funk, and one of the most noted international DJs of the decade. Influenced by the melodic approach of Kraftwerk's "Trans-Europe Express," Bambaataa used synthesizers and the Roland TR-808 drum machine as Hip Hop instruments to create sounds that would later be described by critics as a mélange of global music. The gold record sold more than 650,000 copies, rose to #4 on the R&B charts, and transcended national boundaries, rising as an international hit with huge influence in France and England (Chang 2005, 170–173). The record would later rise as one of the most sampled tracks in Hip Hop history both domestically and globally.

Malcolm McLaren's contribution rode on the coattails of these successes, sending the sounds, flare, and sentiments of Hip Hop around the world. Heavily influenced by Bambaataa and the Soul Sonic Force's "Planet Rock," McLaren, the former manager of the Sex Pistols, Adam & the Ants, and Bow Wow Wow, entered the studio in 1982 determined to release an album that would challenge and inspire future innovation. *Duck Rock* (Island Records, 1983) featured the work of the World Famous Supreme Team, Just Allah the Superstar, and Cee Divine the Mastermind. The two late-night-show DJs on New York's WHBI and members of the Five Percent Nation offered their unique style of radio commentary in between tracks as interludes. They were also featured within some tracks as Hip Hop DJs scratching on the record, a feat previously accomplished on Grandmaster Flash's 1981 single "The Adventures of Grandmaster Flash on the Wheels of Steel." McLaren added a band of exceptional musicians (later known as Art of Noise) who experimented with sounds influenced by cultures around the world through the use of synthesizers and other electronic instruments. The album also featured a chorus of singers. The album was launched by the late 1982 release of the lead single "Buffalo Gals," which landed in the #9 slot on the UK charts (Brewster and Broughton 2000, 261). More important, though, was the accompanying music video, which featured Rock Steady Crew breakin', DONDI bombin', and clips of Double Dutch jump roping, offering the world visual images of the New York–based culture that many of Hip Hop's far-flung fans had only heard about. By packaging b-boys and b-girls breakin', graffiti reminiscent of the scene at the Negril nightclub, DJing reminiscent of New York urban radio, the double-dutch jump roping of the urban inner-city landscape, and the fashion of the times, McLaren's contribution finally gave the world a visual of what Hip Hop looked like, setting the stage for the first international Hip Hop tour.

The Roxy Tour

When Ruza Blue came to the United States in 1981 for a two-week sojourn in New York City, the English twenty-something punk rocker had no idea what was in store for her, and certainly had no idea that her trip would last longer than two weeks. Mesmerized

Dancing at The Roxy nightclub in New York. (Kevin Fleming/Corbis)

by the burgeoning culture of Hip Hop that she experienced at the Bronx's Disco Fever, the enthusiastic young mover-and-shaker secured a job with Malcolm McLaren and began plotting a life as a club promoter. Committed to her passion for punk rock and her new-found love for Hip Hop, she sought a downtown location where she could bring the excitement and energy of Disco Fever into town. She quickly persuaded Michael Holman to try the idea of merging the punk rock and Hip Hop scenes at his East Village club, Negril. Blue, now known as Kool Lady Blue, solicited Bambaataa and the Zulu Nation DJs, Rock Steady Crew, the Dynamic Rockers, the Floormasters, numerous graffiti artists, and MCs, along with a host of punk rockers, who would all join in making Negril the happening spot in New York.

When Negril was closed because of overcrowding and failure to comply with the fire code, Blue temporarily moved the Friday night jam to Danceteria, a trendy new wave club. However, she would find a more permanent home for the blossoming Friday night event in June 1982, when she converted a former 3,000-capacity roller-skating rink in Chelsea on West 18th Street and Tenth Avenue into the hottest club with the most-talked-about weekly event in the New York area. Kool Lady Blue's "Wheels of

Steel Night" landed top-of-the-line talent, celebrities, and artists from around the world at the in-spot known as The Roxy. Catering to the youth-driven Hip Hop and punk-rock crowds, and hiring DJs such as Bambaataa and other members of the Zulu Nation, artists such as DONDI, rock stars such as Madonna, and a lengthy list of others, including Run-DMC and New Edition, who had their first professional gigs there, The Roxy became the center of the multigenre, multicultural youth popular culture (Brewster and Broughton 2000, 250–251).

Not only were folks coming from all around the world to experience the "Wheels of Steel Night" at The Roxy, but in 1982 Blue decided to take an ensemble of her regular artists on tour to England and France as the first international Hip Hop tour. Known as the Roxy Tour, it brought a twenty-five-member entourage, including Afrika Bambaataa and the Soul Sonic Force, Rock Steady Crew, the World Champion Fantastic Four Double Dutch Girls, FUTURA, DONDI, Grandmaster D.ST & the Infinity Rappers, RAMMELLZEE, and FAB 5 FREDDY, to numerous locations to perform in school gymnasiums, clubs, and various venues to an often curious and attentive audience (Chang 2005, 182–184). For two weeks, French and British audiences who had previously experienced the sights and sounds of Hip Hop only secondhand were able to see it firsthand from the great innovators themselves. Organized by Blue with the assistance of French journalist and indie record-label owner Bernard Zekri, the tour left such an impression that international journalists and documentary filmmakers sent crews to the United States, and specifically to The Roxy, to capture every beat, every piece, every move, and every rhyme of the great cultural commodity from the United States. People around the world wanted to check out Hip Hop's authentic and unique appeal for themselves.

Wild Style and Style Wars

The most effective tools for the dissemination of the thriving culture were two monumental documentaries that captured the performances, conversations, creations, and innovations of the Hip Hop pioneers on film. Viewers unable to visit New York City in person studied them and appropriated, adopted, and imitated the various elements of the Hip Hop scene. *Wild Style* (Wild Style Productions, 1982) and *Style Wars* (New Day Films, 1983) were passed around various global communities as cult flicks, offering viewers insight into the secrets of this unparalleled way of life that had never before been experienced outside of New York City.

When filmmaker Charlie Ahearn and legendary graffiti artists FAB 5 FREDDY and LEE (Lee Quiñones) sat down to talk in 1981 about the possibility of capturing the graffiti movement and its connection to Hip Hop Culture on film, the three had no idea of the influence their low-budget project would have on the world-wide audience. Hoping to capture footage of the rawest expression possible, Ahearn and his crew entered the Bronx, Harlem, and Brooklyn to contact pioneering Hip Hop artists on their own turf. They succeeded. The film featured Grandmaster Flash, Grand Wizard Theodore, Grandmixer D.ST, Rock Steady Crew, Chief Rocker Busy Bee, Double Trouble, the Cold Crush Brothers, the Fantastic Five Freaks, RAMMELLZEE, LEE, FAB 5, LADY PINK (Sandra Fabara), DONDI, and ZEPHYR. It captured their conversations and battles, including the historic battle between the Cold Crush Brothers and the Fantastic Five Freaks. The climax of the film takes place at a huge park jam underneath a large "Wild Style," a complex yet personalized style of graffiti, by LEE. It was actually a real party for the entire neighborhood, not just a staged event, and the essence of Hip Hop Culture came through.

Ahearn sought to screen the film in Times Square so that both the Hip Hop community and the non–Hip Hop community would have an opportunity to watch it together; however, this screening never took place (Chang 2005, 186). The film nevertheless was released in selected theaters nationwide. The effect of the film on the domestic audience was mild. U.S. citizens, primarily youth, took Hip Hop for granted because it was accessible and readily available. Yet the global audience had a different reaction. The reception of the movie was so huge in places such as Germany, Italy, and Japan that Hip Hop communities in each of these nations point to the 1983 release of the movie as a starting point for Hip Hop Culture in their countries (Mitchell 2001, 18, 209; Condry 2001, 241). The wide reception sparked a request for promotional tours, which were accomplished by numerous artists and b-boy/b-girl crews, most notably Rock Steady Crew. In Japan, Rock Steady Crew and other artists made appearances at department stores and discos, and Yoyogi Park in Tokyo ended up becoming a b-boy/b-girl and DJ haven (Condri 2001, 228). Local youth gathered weekly to show their moves and express their best imitations of what they saw on film and experienced during the promotional tour.

Similarly, *Style Wars,* a documentary on the graffiti and b-boy/ b-girl elements of Hip Hop by photographer Henry Chalfant and filmmaker Tony Silver, allowed for an intimate look at the street-driven culture. Featuring interviews and other footage of an extensive list of artists, including DONDI, SHY 147, KASE 2, CRASH, DEZ, Crazy Legs, Ken Swift, Frosty Freeze, SKEME, MIN ONE, IZ THE WIZ, and DOZE, *Style Wars* offered a different perspective on the movement because it also took a candid look at the views of the New York Metropolitan Transit Authority, Mayor Edward Koch, and the police. The film allowed the graffiti artists and b-boys/b-girls to be the spokespeople for their communities, emphasizing their role as activists for equal opportunity and access to the city's resources. *Style Wars,* which was broadcast by PBS, had more of an influence domestically than *Wild Style,* and it reached the global market through bootlegged and illegally duplicated copies.

"Rockit"

One of the most important recordings of Hip Hop because of the way it ushered the movement into remote places, such as Australia, parts of Africa, and beyond, was Herbie Hancock's "Rockit." This futuristic experiment in the mixture of funk, jazz, and electronica was one of the lead tracks on his *Future Shock* album (Columbia, 1983), and it showcased an array of talent, including Bill Laswell as producer and Grandmixer D.ST as featured DJ. The album offered two takes of the track, presenting early signs of the turntablism movement, as D.ST dialogued and blended into the ensemble as any good musician would. His characteristic scratching offered a fusion never before attempted with such a renowned and established musician as Herbie Hancock. Although the track won a 1983 Grammy Award for best R&B instrumental performance, it rose only to #71 on the U.S. pop charts. The accompanying video appeared frequently on the newly created Music Television (MTV), introducing Hip Hop to numerous domestic youth and hundreds of global youth who tuned in to see the cultural and musical innovations and trends (George 1998, 61). The video featured D.ST center stage behind the turntables, interfacing with robotic legs and other images of futuristic creativity. To many, D.ST became a household name and instant celebrity as an authentic representative of Bronx-based Hip Hop. He would tour in Hancock's band, traveling around the world performing the piece to audiences of thousands, particularly in Europe, where Hancock already had an established following, especially in the United Kingdom, where the track hit #8 (Brewster and Broughton 2000, 260).

The Saturation Period

The mid-1980s increased Hip Hop's circle of influence as numerous films, books, and media presentations offered access to the artistic phenomenon, which was no longer exclusive and no longer local. The 1983 multimillion-dollar film *Flashdance* (Poly-Gram Filmed Entertainment), which featured two scenes of Rock Steady Crew members displaying their skills to an international audience, ignited a tremendous outpouring of Hip Hop films in the following year. *Beat Street* (MGM/UA Home Entertainment), *Body Rock* (New World Pictures), *Breakin'* (Cannon Group), and *Breakin' 2: Electric Boogaloo* (Cannon Film Distributors) all debuted in 1984, with *Krush Groove* (Film Development Fund and Visual Eyes Productions) and *Rappin'* (Cannon Pictures) following in 1985. These films showcased the elements of Hip Hop up close and personal, offering an international audience more access to the extremely popular culture. Books such as *Rap Attack: African Jive to New York Hip Hop* (South End Press), *Hip-Hop: The Illustrated History of Breakdancing* (St. Martin's Press), and *Rap Music, and Graffiti* (St. Martin's Press) were published in 1984 to a receptive audience of global DJs, b-boys/b-girls, graffiti artists, and MCs thirsty for more information on their newly discovered passions.

The closing ceremonies of the 1984 Summer Olympics in Los Angeles, California, featured over 200 b-boys/b-girls on stage dancing while Lionel Richie sang the hit song "All Night Long" to a global audience. For many this was the first exposure to the impressive culture. Many, however, tuned in regularly for samplings of the cultural expression on sitcoms such as *What's Happening* or on variety shows such as *That's Incredible* or *Saturday Night 'Live,'* broadcast around the world via U.S.-based American Forces Network (AFN). In the case of Cuba, Miami radio and television stations offered an entry point. Hip Hop spread in the worldwide bloodstream, unified by passion, practice, and presence, but not necessarily by context or content. Afrika Bambaataa and the Universal Zulu Nation played a huge role during this and subsequent periods, encouraging nations to use the art form and culture to speak to their own unique needs and desires. Zulu Nation chapters were set up around the globe, as were Rock Steady Crew chapters, in an attempt to connect and share the beauty of the culture

Scene still from the movie Beat Street. *(Orion/The Kobal Collection)*

and its power to unite people through a global commitment to peace. By the 1990s, driven by the media, MC Hammer, Vanilla Ice, and gangsta rap had also spread around the globe. Local and regional global cultures appropriated, adopted, adapted, and in many cases imitated what they saw, heard, or experienced, whether in person, on film or video, in a book, or on a musical recording.

The process of incorporating Hip Hop Culture into various global communities occurred in different ways and over various spans of time. The remainder of this chapter will describe the form this process took in three different nations in an attempt to explore the draw, the reception, and the retention of Hip Hop Culture by international youth. Brief case studies offering the method of reception and then inclusion of Hip Hop in France, Japan, and Cuba provide three very different examples of what has occurred in hundreds of communities, regions, and countries worldwide.

French Hip Hop

Although the United States has admired France for its refined culture in fashion design and other areas for many years, France has also greatly admired the popular music and popular culture of the

United States. The jazz of the 1920s and 1930s found a warm reception within the French nation, particularly in Paris. During the 1940s and 1950s, Broadway show tunes were similarly well received, and in the 1950s and 1960s rock 'n' roll from both the United States and England received an overwhelming reception in France. Although the American folk revival landed in France during the 1960s and 1970s, it was the UK-influenced punk and the U.S.-influenced disco and hard rock that gave France's own *nouvelle chanson* (French rock) a run for its money. The rising global economy, and France's position as a major international power, provided the backdrop for international trade, and specifically for the import of music.

A new chapter in French youth culture began in 1982 as the sounds, movements, and images of New York–based Hip Hop made their way to the northern suburbs of Paris and other locations within the nation. Following the arrival of Afrika Bambaataa and the Soul Sonic Force, Rock Steady Crew, the World Champion Fantastic Four Double Dutch Girls, FUTURA, DONDI, Grandmaster D.ST and the Infinity Rappers, RAMMELLZEE, and FAB 5 FREDDY, slated as the Roxy Tour and led by manager and organizer Kool Lady Blue, France entered the world of Hip Hop quickly. French newspapers and periodicals began running feature stories on the New York Hip Hop artists, offering unique commentaries on Hip Hop fashions, the Hip Hop lifestyle, and any other unique and different aspect of Hip Hop that they could discern and highlight. Although the group Chagrin d'Amor quickly recorded a full-length album, it was the "smurfs" (French b-boys/b-girls) who first popularized and spread the new expression throughout the country. Inspired by the captivating performances of Rock Steady Crew (who were also featured in the film *Wild Style,* which was distributed in France around this time), the smurfs created their own underground movement with DJs and MCs to provide a sonic backdrop for the dancers.

As the Hip Hop movement spread, the shift from imitation to adoption and adaptation occurred subtly. French youth began to understand the movement as a tool for expression and particularly as an instrument for demanding social justice, social change, and cultural and ethnic recognition. Many of the new French Hip Hop artists were African, Arab, or from the lower class. Although French Hip Hoppers did not understand or recognize all of the social, political, economic, cultural, or religious references included in the U.S.-based Hip Hop that was imported into France, what they did understand was the common reality of oppression

Hip Hop Culture is prominent in France's Nord Region, 1998. (Said Belloumi/Corbis Sygma)

and the urgent sounds of oppressed people. It was these urgent expressions that captivated French youth, many of whom lived in neighborhoods of high-rise, government-subsidized apartments that were plagued, like the neighborhoods of their American mentors, with the sights and sounds of violence, drugs, and other crimes (Prevos 1996, 714). These suburbs (or ghettos) of Paris, Strasbourg, Toulouse, and Marseilles, to name a few, gave rise to smurfs and smurf groups such as Frank II Louise, Gabin Nuissier, Fred Bendongué, Traction Avant, and Black Blanc Beur.

A unique style of Hip Hop emerged in France as French Hip Hop artists adapted the genre and made it their own. The lyrics of French Hip Hop were most often in French, of course, but as French popular music since the late nineteenth century had featured the use of lyrical techniques such as alliteration, onomatopoeia, and the creative use of puns, many of the verbal techniques of Hip Hop translated easily into French usage. French Hip Hop did not, however, retain the Afrocentric ideology that had been prominent in the Hip Hop of the United States during the 1980s. Many of the French Hip Hop innovators were Algerian or other North African exiles, and thus their families had departed their home countries and the continent of Africa for reasons quite different from those compelling Black Americans to look toward Africa. Nevertheless, the majority of early French Hip Hoppers opposed French social, political, and economic systems in the form of antiestablishment raps aimed at the nation, the national army, French public servants, and French politicians. Inherent in these raps was the constant reference to the government's oppression of racial and ethnic minorities.

Early French Hip Hop was highly influenced by Afrika Bambaataa's visit. His Universal Zulu Nation and its primary beliefs united Hip Hop communities around the world as peaceful, unified entities with a passion for life, a respect for difference, and a belief in the positive effects of peaceful coexistence. The Zulu Nation philosophy focuses on "knowledge, wisdom, understanding, freedom, justice, equality, peace, unity, love, respect, work, fun, overcoming the negative with the positive, economics, mathematics, science, life and truth" (www.zulunation.org, "The Beliefs of the Universal Zulu Nation"). The French chapter of the Zulu Nation was quickly chartered following the Roxy Tour visit.

Yet by 1987, with a few exceptions, such as Les Little and Sens Unik, most French Hip Hop groups and artists no longer boasted affiliation with the Zulu Nation. Bambaataa and his positivist utopian considerations had already begun to give way to the rising mainstream hard-core French rap that was so popular in the late 1980s through the 1990s. Popularized by groups such as Suprême NTM, Ministère Amer, and Assassin, this style of rap was loud, crude, and "in your face," borrowing from the look and feel of the U.S. mainstream, which had turned to hard-core gangsta rap around the same time. The French version, while not as violent, used localized jargon, metaphors, and socially, politically, and economically relevant commentary. During this period France rose to become the second-largest Hip Hop market in the world (after the United States) and the fifth-largest global music market (Negus 1994, 159–160). During the rise of hard-core French rap, Hip Hop programming on national network television debuted as well as numerous Hip Hop–oriented magazines. As Hip Hop icons Vanilla Ice and MC Hammer rose to prominence in the United States and abroad, French artist MC Solaar rose in France and abroad, including in the United States. Hip Hop has remained a vibrant expression in France, not as an American import, but as a French expression based on early American influence.

Japanese Hip Hop

Hip Hop in Japan began shortly after the release of *Wild Style* and the subsequent promotional tour of Hip Hop artists to Japan in 1983. The cadre of featured artists from the film exhibited the various elements of Hip Hop to captivated audiences at department stores and area discos in Tokyo. Enthralled by the b-boys/b-girls from the United States, and specifically by the performances of Rock Steady Crew, numerous Japanese youth imitated the moves, routines, and postures, bringing Hip Hop to Japan via the dance. Expression through dance circumvents language barriers, and in this case it provided an entrée for Japanese youth into the new expression. Japanese Hip Hop fans began by producing tracks that dancers might dance to. Japanese b-boys/b-girls, such as pioneer Crazy A and pioneering crews Tokyo B-Boy Crew, Be-Pop Crew, and Funky Jams, took to the streets of the Shibuya and Roppongi sections of Tokyo, battling one another as they had witnessed Americans do on *Wild Style* and subsequent films, such as *Beat Street, Breakin', Flash Dance,* and *Breakin' 2*. Return visits to Japan by Rock Steady Crew, Boogaloo Shrimp (a.k.a. Turbo from *Breakin'* and *Breakin' 2*), the Electric Boogaloos, and other U.S.-based b-boy/b-girl crews added to the popularity of the dance expression in Tokyo and Osaka. By 1986, Crazy A and Crazy Legs (Rock Steady Crew) initiated plans to launch Japan's own Rock Steady Crew chapter in Japan, a feat publicized in the early 1990s.

As Hip Hop began to take hold in Japan, Yoyogi Park, famous for its thriving street musicians, became such a haven for Japanese b-boys/b-girls that it was informally renamed B-boy Park, a name still in use twenty years later. The park is most noted for its weekly Sunday Hip Hop gatherings of b-boys/b-girls and DJs, who perform exhibitions, battle, and showcase the latest Hip Hop gear, much of which is imported from the United States. B-boy Park is also noted for the annual Hip Hop festival, held each year in August since 1999, which features more than 10,000 spectators paying homage to the elements of Hip Hop via exhibitions and battles.

From the scene at B-boy Park, DJs Krush, Yutaka, and Honda rose as pioneering DJs capable of scratching, mixing, and creating clever music tracks from which Japanese MCs would rhyme or rap over. DJing in Japan became so popular by the late 1980s that it has been said that turntable sales outranked guitar sales. Japanese youth had been formerly immersed in U.S.- and UK-based rock, but the expressions of Hip Hop offered an opportunity to revise the Japanese youth culture for a new generation of global citizens.

By 1986, Hip Hop clubs were opening in the Shibuya section of Tokyo, offering new venues for the exploration, performance, and appreciation of the culture. In 1987, the Harlem Club opened as a full-fledged Hip Hop nightclub and began to hold its widely popular "Daddy's House" on Friday nights (Neate 2004, 69). The premier club's name paid homage to the prominent section of New York City and insinuated a connection to P. Diddy. For global Hip Hop performers, many from the United States, it offered a place to perform and hang out with Japanese Hip Hop headz.

Following the lead of U.S. Hip Hop, which distinguishes between underground and mainstream forms of the genre, Japanese Hip Hop headz draw a distinction between J rap (Japanese rap) and J Hip Hop (Japanese Hip Hop). J rap is the commercial or mainstream version, and J Hip Hop is the underground. Over 90 percent of Hip Hop participants and artists (both J rap and J Hip Hop) are male. The audience for J rap, however, is 90 percent female. Groups such as Scha Dara Parr, East Eno X Yuri, and Dassen Trio, which offer catchy songs often referred to as "party music," are promoted as J rap groups. The audience for J Hip Hop groups such as King Giddra, Microphone Pager, and Rhymester, which deliver socially relevant and conscious material, is 80 percent male (Condry 2000, 177).

The biggest difference between U.S. Hip Hop and J rap or J Hip Hop is the absence of any ultra-political or radical racial commentary within the lyrics of the latter. This is because Japan is a highly regulated, homogeneous country with limited racial- and class-oriented diversity. Much of the oppression articulated in the lyrics by Japanese MCs deals more with generational challenges and the need for individual empowerment rather than echoing the anti-establishment cries prevalent in the United States and other interpretations of global Hip Hop. In fact, the Japanese MC did not fully rise to prominence until the mid-1990s. This was partly because the linguistic nuances of Japanese, and in particular the tonal nature of the language, made it difficult to adapt MC techniques. Yet by 1996 this was no longer an issue as Japanese MCs developed their own unique style of rhyming that catered to a growing number of Japanese Hip Hop patrons eager to purchase Japanese Hip Hop instead of U.S. Hip Hop produced in English.

The expression of rap, as well as of graffiti, which was also co-opted by Japanese Hip Hoppers, offered Japanese youth street credibility in a society not burdened by the same problems present in the United States—violence, crime, narcotics, alcohol abuse, and popular media stereotypes of all these difficulties. The expressions of Hip Hop in general allowed Japanese youth to identify with the underdog (Black Americans) and simultaneously offered a new definition of machismo for the men and of "sexy" for the women. Both appropriated U.S.-based Hip Hop fashion, hairstyles, and mannerisms. In fact, numerous Japanese Hip Hop headz and non–Hip Hop affiliates wear dreads (or dread wigs) and afros (or afro wigs) in addition to using skin tanners (both tanning beds and skin creams) in an effort to identify with Black American Hip Hop pioneers, physically showing appreciation and admiration for Black Americans as well as for the authenticity, empowerment, and creative genius of what they perceive as Black Americans' expression (Condry 2000, 173).

By the late 1980s, Japanese Hip Hop made its entrance into Japanese popular media in print and on television. The 1989 Japanese version of the U.S. *Soul Train, Dada LMD,* featured a section introducing trendy new dances and a closing line dance reflective of its model, yet the show was limited to the local Tokyo audience. *Dance Dance Dance,* another local show, also offered the best in trendy U.S.-based dances. *Dance Koshien,* a Sunday night show that also debuted in 1989, offered the first national network exposure of Hip Hop, featuring street dance competitions for high school–aged students. Although numerous Japanese-based fashion lines, record labels, and other producers of mass culture are in operation, Japanese Hip Hop continues to look to the United States for inspiration and guidance while maintaining its own identity and unique application of the global culture.

Cuban Hip Hop

Cuba has had an extremely complicated relationship with the United States dating back to the wars for independence against Spain during the last years of the nineteenth century. Yet culturally, Cuba and the United States have a deep admiration for one another, especially relative to artistic expression. During the late 1970s and early 1980s as rap music and Hip Hop Culture were spreading across the United States, Cubans, particularly in Havana, were tuning in to Miami-based radio stations WEDR 99 Jams and WHQT Hot 105 to hear the new sounds of U.S.-based popular music. Many also tuned in to U.S. television stations to watch shows such as *Soul Train.* This was extremely prevalent in Alamar, a large housing project on the east side of Havana.

Cubans would erect large antennas on the rooftops of the tall apartment buildings to boost the reception of Miami radio and television broadcasts. Through this medium, Hip Hop extended to Cuba.

Shortly after "Rapper's Delight" debuted across the United States in 1979, the instant hit was also heard by and was well received by Cuban youth. Cuban *raperos* (rappers) soon began imitating the lyrics of the pioneering MCs, and as time progressed, Run-DMC, Public Enemy, Queen Latifah, and NWA became local favorites. By the late 1980s, the imitation had led to a huge dilemma, as neither the members of Cuba's older generations nor government officials liked the influx of lyrics glorifying thug activity, gangsta lifestyles, crime, and violence and promoting misogyny and materialism. These topics did not gel well with the realities of an extremely economically deprived Cuba suffering from the fall of the Soviet Union. Indirect charges of cultural invasion were launched at the United States; however, many in Cuba realized that the expressions of Hip Hop could be good and beneficial to the youth. These commentators suggested that instead of simply imitating their U.S. neighbors, raperos should integrate Hip Hop into Cuban traditional culture as a fusion. By doing so, they said, Cuban Hip Hoppers could avoid aiding in the proliferation of America's problems and pay more attention to the Cuban challenges of poverty, prostitution, police harassment, limited free speech, and economic hardships. Aided by Pablo Herrera, who would rise as Cuba's top hip hop producer, and Nehanda Abiodun, known as the "Godmother of Hip Hop in Cuba," Cubans, and particularly Habaneros (residents of Havana), developed their own style of Hip Hop.

Herrera, a former English professor at the University of Havana, helped Cuban groups to develop their own sound, providing background tracks for them with limited equipment. Due to the trade embargo, Cuba had no turntables, vinyl records, or record shops. In fact, Cuba had no CD plant to press and distribute CDs. Cubans used cassette tapes to mix and produce tracks by manipulating a dual cassette deck, recording from one side to another, and adding sounds, samples, and the like via a plugged-in microphone. The standard DJ setup consisted of a portable CD player or two plugged into a PA system. In fact, this remains the primary setup for Cuban Hip Hop producers.

Nehanda Abiodun, a U.S. Black Liberation Army activist and a political exile in Cuba since 1990, also played a dominant role in the transformation and creation of Cuban Hip Hop. Her intimate knowledge and understanding of Black culture, the Black power movement, the civil rights movement, and the legacy of Malcolm X (an icon in Cuba among many raperos) aided in contextualizing the lyrics as well as the verbal and physical symbolism that raperos were imitating. She helped them to analyze the significance of specific references, discouraged the adoption of gangsta rap, and recommended the incorporation of traditional Cuban musical (and dance) styles such as *danzón, son, mambo,* and *rumba* as well as the use of traditional Cuban instruments such as the bata, guagua, and congas.

Although the raperos wore clothing similar to that of U.S. Hip Hop artists, including hoodies, skullies, big boots, bulky jackets, and gold chains, there are many differences between the two expressions. Cuban Hip Hop, unlike U.S. Hip Hop, is based largely on live instrumental accompaniment as opposed to DJs and break beats, although the latter are present. Most Cuban Hip Hop does not celebrate violence, and the lyrics do not typically contain misogynistic commentary. Cuban Hip Hop also does not promote anti–music industry lyrics, largely because the Cuban government is a fan of Hip Hop and supports limited industry avenues for its expression. During the fall of 2002, in an effort to demonstrate support and validation for the authentic expression of Cuban culture via Hip Hop, the Cuban Rap Agency (Agencia Cubana de Rap) was created, providing a state-run record label (EGREM), a Hip Hop–oriented magazine (*Movimiento*), a Hip Hop–oriented radio show (Esquina de Rap), and a Saturday afternoon Hip Hop–oriented television show. The agency also helps to support the Festival de Rap Cubano that had been held annually in Alamar, the noted birthplace of Cuban Hip Hop, every August since 1995. Founded through the collaboration of East Havana collective Groupo Uno, rock promoter Rodolfo Renzoli, and Asociación Hermanos Saíz (AHS), an offshoot of the Communist Youth Organization promoting youth artists, the festival offers performances by international artists, workshops, clinics, film screenings, and battles. The four-day event draws thousands from all over the world to take part.

Graffiti and graffiti artists are present in Cuba, but not prominent. Cuban b-boys/b-girls are also present, but because of Cuba's rich heritage in dance in its own right, the U.S. style of Hip Hop dance has been less influential than in other countries where Hip Hop has been adopted. The raperos, instead, are center stage within Cuban Hip Hop. Most are not known throughout the world, however, owing to Cuba's lack of positioning in the global

Cuban rap band Macumba Hop performs at the Alamar neighborhood amphitheatre during the first concert of the 9th Havana Hip Hop Rap Festival, celebrated in Havana, Cuba, 2003. (Cristobal Herrera/AP Photo)

entertainment market. In 2003, more than 500 Hip Hop groups were estimated to be practicing some form of Hip Hop on the island (West-Duran 2004, 9). The most popular Cuban group, Amenazas, left Cuba in the late 1990s to pursue a record deal in Europe. After encountering internal challenges, the group dissolved; two of the members reunited to form a group called the Orishas and signed a deal with EMI France. Other prominent groups include Obsecion, RCA, and the all-female group Instinto.

Attempts to foster relationships between U.S. Hip Hop artists and Cuban raperos have been championed by Monifa Bandele and the Black August Hip-Hop Collective, a Brooklyn-based advocacy group serving as a liaison to schedule exchanges from the United States to Cuba and vice versa. To date, Black Star, Common, dead prez (subsequently fined $2,000 by the United States for violating a travel ban to Cuba), Roots, FAB 5 FREDDY, and others have traveled and performed in Cuba, either through the efforts of Black August or on their own. In October 2001, Cuban raperos Obsecion, RCA, and Anónimo Consejo performed in New York as a part of the exchange.

Summary

The October 1979 release of Sugar Hill Gang's "Rapper's Delight" not only spread the once-local musical and cultural phenomenon based in Bronx nationally, it also allowed for the recorded rap music to be disseminated around the world. During the 1980s, Hip Hop Culture spread internationally via various forms of media, such as television and radio; through live performances and other visits and tours to overseas locations from U.S. Hip Hop artists; and through recorded music, video, and film.

Three early internationally released recordings offered the world a first audio example and glimpse of rap music and Hip Hop Culture. Blondie's rap-influenced track "Rapture," featuring a rap by lead singer Deborah Harry and including a name check of FAB 5 FREDDY and Grandmaster Flash; Afrika Bambaattaa's widely influential and broadly sampled masterpiece "Planet Rock"; and Malcolm McLaren's creative yet gimmicky "Buffalo Gals" offered informative perspectives on the new expressions hailing from New York's inner city.

The rise of various major hot spots, such as The Mudd Club and Disco Fever, offered a unique opportunity for various enclaves of creative and often eccentric people to mingle, bringing together the punk rock scene and the increasingly popular Hip Hop scene. Kool Lady Blue's "Wheels of Steel Night," piloted at the Negril club but known as an internationally acclaimed hot spot at The Roxy, enabled folks of all walks of life to experience and enjoy the various elements under one cover. International journalists and media representatives could then come to one location to gain a perspective on the rising culture. The popularity of Blue's achievement and her London-based network led to the first international Hip Hop tour of artists. Known as the Roxy Tour, a twenty-five-member ensemble traveled to England and France to offer curious audiences a firsthand look at Hip Hop as performed by the very pioneers of the culture.

The films *Wild Style* and *Style Wars* captured the landscape and soundscape of the birthplace of Hip Hop, giving viewers an insightful look at the evolution and early development of the culture. These two documentaries became hot commodities for a young global audience that desired to view the authentic and personalized expressions of the pioneers without having to travel to New York City. They served as international training tapes, and subsequent promotional tours by U.S. Hip Hop groups provided further instruction in the elements of Hip Hop. Overseas youth began to appropriate, adopt, and imitate the sound, look, and feel of the culture, proving that it did not matter whether someone spoke English or understood the political, economic, social, cultural, or religious references within the culture of origination. Elements of Hip Hop were thus transformed as they became grafted into other cultures around the world.

The dissemination of "Rockit" in 1983, featuring Grandmixer D.ST, via MTV further advanced Hip Hop, bringing it more into the mainstream of U.S. culture. Herbie Hancock's worldwide appeal lent a unique nod of validation to Hip Hop and marked its acceptance by a new pool of prospective Hip Hop fans.

During the mid-1980s, numerous motion pictures included various aspects of the culture as major components of their plots, ushering in a new wave of participants who were intrigued by the depictions on film. Informative books on Hip Hop Culture were released, a sign that Hip Hop music and culture were more than a passing fad. These helped to formalize the culture both on the street and in intellectual circles. Important internationally broadcast examples of Hip Hop, such as the closing ceremonies of the 1984 Summer Olympics, provided further validation of this inner-city-based expression as something to be proud of in U.S. culture. By the 1990s, Hip Hop had spread worldwide, not only as a U.S. cultural commodity, but also as an art form that international youth could transform on their own terms in order to redefine themselves and critique their own social, political, economic, cultural, and religious settings.

French Hip Hop was ignited by the Roxy Tour and was popularized by the smurfs. Initially focused on dance, French MCs eventually took to the microphone to address their demands for social justice, social change, and cultural and ethnic recognition for the oppressed population, largely made up of people of African and Arab descent. Although early French Hip Hop was strongly influenced by Afrika Bambaataa and the Universal Zulu Nation, the rise of mainstream hard-core Hip Hop and the opportunity for fame and international prominence soon overshadowed Bambaataa's positivist, utopian beliefs. France remains the second-largest Hip Hop market and the fifth-largest global music market.

Japanese Hip Hop was initially a response to the film *Wild Style* and the subsequent Wild Style promotional tour. As in France, in Japan the b-boys/b-girls first popularized Hip Hop, and they became so popular that one of Tokyo's major parks was renamed from Yoyogi Park to B-boy Park. Nightclubs in the Shibuya section of Tokyo provided the main venues for both J rap (commercial/mainstream) and J Hip Hop (underground). Japanese fascination with Black American culture became clear, and Hip Hop remains a prominent expression and lifestyle in Japan.

Cuban Hip Hop was fueled by its close proximity to Miami, Florida, and the accessibility of Miami-based radio and television broadcasts. Cuban raperos, though challenged by members of the older generations, by government authority, and by the lack of Hip Hop–oriented equipment, appropriated Hip Hop, transforming it into a uniquely Cuban style incorporating traditional music and dance styles and traditional instruments. Based on live performance and addressing the social, political, and economic challenges facing Cuba in the wake of the fall of the Soviet Union, Cuban Hip Hop now thrives as a vibrant, nationally accepted art form with full support of the government. Although travel between the United States and Cuba is made difficult by travel restrictions imposed by the United States, the annual Festival de Rap Cubano, organizations such as the Black August Hip-Hop Collective, and other forums have aided in keeping the Hip Hop communities connected.

References

Banes, Sally. 2004. "Breaking." In *That's the Joint!: The Hip-Hop Studies Reader,* ed. Murray Forman and Mark Anthony Neal, 13–20. New York: Rutledge.

"The Beliefs of the Universal Zulu Nation," http://www.zulunation.org.

Bennett, Andy. 2004. "Hip-Hop am Main, Rappin' on the Tyne: Hip-Hop Culture as a Local Construct in Two European Cities." In *That's the Joint!: The Hip-Hop Studies Reader,* ed. Murray Foreman and Mark Anthony Neal, 177–200. New York: Rutledge.

Brewster, Bill, and Frank Broughton. 2000. *Last Night A DJ Saved My Life: The History of the Disc Jockey.* New York: Grove.

Castleman, Craig. 2004. "The Politics of Graffiti." In *That's the Joint!: The Hip-Hop Studies Reader,* ed. Murray Foreman and Mark Anthony Neal, 21–29. New York: Rutledge.

Chang, Jeff. 2005. *Can't Stop Won't Stop: A History of the Hip-Hop Generation.* New York: St. Martin's.

Condry, Ian. 2001. "A History of Japanese Hip-Hop: Street Dance, Club Scene, Pop Market." In *Global Noise: Rap and Hip-Hop Outside the USA,* ed. Tony Mitchell, 222–247. Middletown, CT: Wesleyan University Press.

———. 2000. "The Social Production of Difference: Imitation and Authenticity in Japanese Rap Music." In *Transactions, Transgressions, and Transformations,* ed. Heide Fehrenbach and Uta G. Poiger, 166–184. New York: Berghan.

Forman, Murray. 2002. *The Hood Comes First: Race, Space and Place in Rap and Hip-Hop.* Middletown, CT: Wesleyan University Press.

George, Nelson. 1998. *Hip Hop America.* New York: Viking.

Hager, Steven. 2002. *Adventures in the Counterculture: From Hip Hop to High Times.* New York: High Times Books.

Haskins, James. 2000. *One Nation under a Groove: Rap Music and Its Roots.* New York: Hyperion.

Heibutzki, Ralph. 1997. "What's the Deal?: Rappin' & Rockin' the House that Sugar Hill Built." In *Accompanying Booklet to the Sugar Hill Records Story,* 12–21. Rhino Records R2 72449.

Hernandez, Deborah Pacini, and Reebee Garfalo. 1999/2000. "Hip Hop in Havana: Rap, Race, and National Identity in Contemporary Cuba." *Journal of Popular Music Studies* 11–12: 18–47.

Holman, Michael. 2004. "Breaking: The History." In *That's the Joint!: The Hip-Hop Studies Reader,* ed. Murray Foreman and Mark Anthony Neal, 31–39. New York: Rutledge.

Light, Alan, ed. 1999. *The VIBE History of Hip Hop.* New York: Three Rivers.

Mitchell, Tony, ed. 2001. *Global Noise: Rap and Hip Hop Outside the USA.* Middletown, CT: Wesleyan University Press.

Neate, Patrick. 2004. *Where You're At: Notes from the Frontline of a Hip-Hop Planet.* New York: Riverhead.

Negus, Keith. 1994. *Producing Pop: Culture and Conflict in the Popular Music Industry.* London: Edward Arnold.

Ogg, Alex, and David Upshal. 2001. *The Hip Hop Years: A History of Rap.* New York: Fromm International.

Perkins, William Eric, ed. 1996. *Droppin' Science: Critical Essays on Rap Music and Hip Hop Culture.* Philadelphia: Temple University Press.

Prévos, André J.M. 2001. "Postcolonial Popular Music in France." In *Global Noise: Rap and Hip-Hop Outside the USA,* ed. Tony Mitchell, 39–56. Middletown, CT: Wesleyan University Press.

———. 1996. "The Evolution of French Rap Music and Hip Hop Culture in the 1980s and 1990s." *French Review* 69 (April): 713–725.

Ro, Ronin. 1997. "Sugar Hill: Birth of an Industry." In *Accompanying Booklet to the Sugar Hill Records Story,* 4–11. Rhino Records R2 72449.

Strauss, Neil. 1999. "Rap and Rock." In *The VIBE History of Hip Hop,* ed. Alan Light, 239–249. New York: Three Rivers.

Toop, David. 2000. *Rap Attack 3: African Rap to Global Hip Hop,* 3d ed. London: Serpent's Tail.

West-Duran, Alan. 2004. "Rap's Diasporic Dialogues: Cuba's Redefinition of Blackness." *Journal of Popular Music Studies* 16 (1): 4–39.

Hip Hop Culture Chronology

1965

The graffiti movement begins in Philadelphia, popularized by a young Black teenager using the name CORNBREAD.

1967

In November, the father of Hip Hop Culture, Clive Campbell (later known as DJ Kool Herc), moves from Kingston, Jamaica, with his mother to the Bronx at age twelve.

1968

The Savage Seven organize in East Bronx. The group later changes its name to the Black Spades.

1969

Don Campbell, a street dancer in Los Angeles, California, invents the "Campbellock," the nickname for the funk-oriented street-dance style developed by Don Campbell during the 1970s and made popular by many b-boys/b-girls.

1970

The godfather of Hip Hop Culture, father of electro-funk, and founder of the Universal Zulu Nation, Afrika Bambaataa (Kahyan Aasim, b. 1957), begins DJing.

1970 (continued)

Two groups based in Oakland, California, the Black Messengers and the Black Resurgence, begin developing a dance style based around ROTC cadence drills. They create the "Catch On" style, which leads the way to other funk dance forms such as "Stickin'" and "Stepin.'"

The Last Poets record their album *The Last Poets* (Metrotone), reciting spoken word over jazz beats and instrumentation.

1971

TAKI 183 (Demetrius, a Greek teenager from Washington Heights, New York) becomes the first graffiti artist to gain recognition for his tags in the news media with an article in the *New York Times.* This influences many others to start writing.

The Experienced Vandals (a.k.a. Ex-Vandals), one of the earliest crews in graffiti art history, includes PHASE 2, SUPER KOOL, LIONEL 163, STAY HIGH 149, EL MARKO, SWEET DUDE, and KOOL HERC.

Top-to-bottom graffiti artwork is popularized by FLINT 707.

A historic gang truce meeting at the Bronx Boys Club is called forth by the Ghetto Brothers upon the murder of member Black Benjie (Cornell Benjamin), who was killed while attempting to pacify a gang battle on December 2. At the December 8 meeting, which is supported by funding from the youth services agency, the gym is filled with gang members and leaders as well as reporters and photographers covering the meeting.

The New York Police Department (NYPD) Bronx Youth Gang Task Force is created under the command of Deputy Inspector William Lakeman.

1972

The "Soul Artists" graffiti crew is formed by TRACY 158, ALI, and FUTURA 2000.

Graffiti on a wall in New York. (iStockphoto.com)

United Graffiti Artists (UGA) is created by Hugo Martinez in order to bring recognition to graffiti artists and to serve as an artistic activist group.

SUPER KOOL 223 sets the criteria for creating "pieces." He also replaces the cap on his spray-paint can with one from an oven-cleaner can, influencing a new style of writing.

Soul Train begins airing on television.

TRACY 168, who created the phrase "Wild Style," forms a writing crew called Wanted.

1973

In August, Father of Hip Hop DJ Kool Herc begins to DJ block parties on the west side of the Bronx at 1520 Sedgwick Avenue in the

1973 (continued)

recreation room of his apartment building, after DJing house parties for a few years. During these jams, he lengthens the instrumental breakdown segments of records and invents break beats.

Afrika Bambaataa organizes the Universal Zulu Nation on November 12. This marks the formal beginning of Hip Hop Culture.

The "Taki Awards" are given for the best graffiti pieces by *New York Magazine.* SPIN is the first artist to win this award (for best grand design).

A drawing done by SNAKE 1 and EL MARKO is featured in an article in *New York Magazine.* This marks the beginning of the use of black books (artists' sketch pads).

The Razor Gallery in the SoHo district of New York City becomes the first place to hold a show of graffiti pieces.

The legendary battle between b-boys Sau Sau and Tricksie takes place, with Sau Sau emerging victorious.

1974

After quickly making a name for himself on Sedgwick Avenue and during a quick stint at the Twilight Zone on Jerome Avenue, Kool Herc begins playing the Hevalo (at Burnside and Jerome) and the Sparkle (1590 Jerome Avenue).

Love Bug Starski, a noted MC and DJ, begins using the term "Hip-Hop." He is one of the people responsible for coining the slang term as a name for the culture.

DJs begin to speak over the records they are spinning (similar to the Caribbean style of "toasting"). Lines such as "And ya don't stop" are used, marking the beginning of MCing.

1975

MCing evolves from party shouts. Coke La Rock and Clark Kent are the first MC team. They, along with DJ Timmy Tim, hook up with Kool Herc to form Kool Herc and the Herculoids.

DJ Grand Wizard Theodore invents the scratch.

1976

On July 4, graffiti artists CAINE, MAD 103, and FLAME ONE become the first to paint an entire train (called "the freedom train"). Painting trains is the greatest form of graffiti art at the time.

Afrika Bambaataa's first official DJ battle against Disco King Mario takes place at Junior High School 123.

Grandmaster Flash invents quick mixing (the process by which short sounds are combined to create longer, more intricate sounds). Flash and Ray Chandler open the "Black Door" to have their parties in the Bronx (on Boston Road and 169th Street), naming the club after the black door at the entrance.

The first boombox, the Superscope by Marantz, is sold.

LEE (Lee Quiñones) begins painting murals with advanced techniques that are full of political commentary.

1977

The Crash Crew forms in Harlem. It eventually becomes one of the first MC crews to be recorded.

Street and block parties primarily in Bronx, Harlem, and Queens are regular occurrences.

DJ Disco Wiz is known for being the first Latino DJ.

DJ Kool Herc gets stabbed at one of his parties and temporarily disappears from the scene.

Grandmaster Flash develops the techniques of cutting, back-spinning, and phasing on turntables.

"Trans-Europe Express" is released by the German band Kraftwerk. The song inspires electro-funk artists such as Afrika Bambaataa.

1977 (continued)

The FABULOUS FIVE (graffiti artists) paint an entire train (the second entire train to be painted), calling it "The Christmas Train."

Jimmy D and JoJo form Rock Steady Crew in the Bronx. Early members also include Jimmy Lee and Mongo Rock.

"Popping," started by Boogaloo Sam, is considered the first hip hop dance. "Locking" is also popularized.

Boogaloo Sam and Slide found the Electric Boogaloo Lockers and recruit dancers Robot Joe, Toyman Skeet, Tickin Will, Twist-O-Flex Don, and Ant Man.

Jack the Rapper (Jack Gibson) puts together his first annual music convention (the Jack the Rapper Music Convention). This is the first music convention ever to include rap music.

1978

The music industry begins to use the term "rap music."

Disco Fever opens in the Bronx and becomes the first club that plays only rap music.

The Roland 808 is created and becomes the most used electronic drum machine.

Grandmaster Flash becomes Kurtis Blow's DJ for several months.

The Robot (dance) is introduced to the mainstream by Charlie Robot.

The Electric Boogaloos perform on *Soul Train* and become popular worldwide.

1979

The first record label dedicated to rap music (Sugar Hill Records) is founded by Sylvia Robinson. The first release, Sugar Hill Gang's

"Rapper's Delight," becomes the first rap hit record, selling 2 million copies, and the first rap single to hit the Top 40. Sugar Hill Records uses a live band to cover Chic's "Good Times." Chic sues for copyright infringement and wins.

An MC group, the Cold Crush Brothers, is formed with members Charlie Chase, Tony Tone, Grand Master Caz, Easy Ad, JDL, and Almighty KG. They perform live shows around the Bronx and become well known before the Sugar Hill Gang release of "Rapper's Delight." Their shows set the standard for future live hip hop shows.

Grandmaster Flash (Joseph Saddler) forms the group Grandmaster Flash and the Furious Five. In addition to Flash, members include Melle Mel (Melvin Glover), Kidd Creole (Nathaniel Glover), Cowboy (Keith Wiggins), Rahiem (Guy Williams), and Mr. Ness a.k.a. Scorpio (Eddie Morris).

The single "Superrappin" is released by Grandmaster Flash and the Furious Five.

The first known female rapper, Sweet Tee (Tanya Winley), records the single "Vicious Rap."

The Universal Zulu Nation celebrates its fifth anniversary.

Kurtis Blow records the single "Christmas Rapping," which helps him to become the first rapper to sign a major record deal with a major record label (Mercury Records).

Sony introduces the first walkman (TPS-L2).

Rock Steady Crew further develops breakdancing by adding more acrobatics. Crazy Legs and Lenny Len also join Rock Steady Crew.

LEE (Lee Quiñones) has an exhibition in Italy.

The movie *Warriors,* which tells the stories of New York City's street gangs and subway graffiti artists, is released.

1980

Kurtis Blow (Harlem) has the first rap single to be certified gold ("The Breaks"); it eventually goes platinum. He also has the first rap album on a major label (*Kurtis Blow,* Mercury Records) and performs "The Breaks" on *Soul Train* (October), becoming the first rapper to appear on national TV.

Blondie gives graffiti artist FAB 5 FREDDY props on her song "Rapture," introducing rap to mainstream. Lead singer Deborah Harry is credited as the first white rapper. This song appears on their album *Autoamerican.*

BET (Black Entertainment Television) goes on the air.

Members of High Times Crew are arrested for breakdancing at Washington Heights subway and photos appear in the *New York Post.* These are some of the first photos of breakdancing to be published.

The Sequence Girls (the first all-female group on wax) appear on charts with their single "Funk You Up" (Sugar Hill Records) and inspire more females to pursue rap.

1981

Funky 4 Plus One More perform "That's the Joint" live on NBC's *Saturday Night Live* on February 14, becoming the first rap group to appear on national television.

The Music Television channel (MTV), a twenty-four-hour music video channel, begins broadcasting on August 1.

Grandmaster Flash and the Furious Five's "Adventures of Grandmaster Flash on the Wheels of Steel" becomes the first rap record to bring the sound of live scratching and DJing to wax. This song appears on their album *The Message.* The group also releases the single "The Message."

Disco Daddy and Captain Rapp's "Gigolo Rap" is the first West Coast rap single on vinyl.

ABC's *20/20* offers the first national television coverage of the "Rap Phenomenon."

Ed Koch, the mayor of New York City, spends millions to prevent further graffiti in subway areas.

Tommy Boy Records is founded.

Afrika Islam, a member of the Universal Zulu Nation, starts the first Hip Hop radio show, *Zulu Beats,* on New York's WHBI 105.9 FM.

The first white rap group, the Beastie Boys, is formed by Kate Schellenbach. Members include John Berry, Mike Diamond, and Adam Yauch.

One of the first major articles on breakdancing appears in the *Village Voice* by Sally Banes.

Beat boxing is invented by Doug E. Fresh.

NOC paints a whole train car from top to bottom; the resulting work is called "Style Wars."

1982

"The Message," by Grandmaster Flash and the Furious Five, which introduced social commentary into rap lyrics, is chosen as one of the most influential songs of the decade by *Billboard* magazine.

The first international hip hop tour, the Roxy Tour, takes place in Europe, with Afrika Bambaataa, FAB 5 FREDDY, RAMMELLZEE, Grandmixer DXT (formerly D.ST) & the Infinity Rappers, Rock Steady Crew, the Double Dutch Girls, and graffiti artists PHASE 2, FUTURA, and DONDI.

Afrika Bambaataa and the Soul Sonic Force release "Planet Rock." The record eventually goes gold. The video for the song is one of the first music videos to use special effects. Through "Planet Rock," Bambaataa introduces electro-funk and establishes the Roland 808 drum machine and synthesizers as Hip Hop instruments.

1982 (continued)

The Hip Hop feature film *Wild Style* is released. It is the first full-length account of all four elements of Hip Hop. After its release, the Wild Style tour, featuring DJs, MCs, dancers, and graffiti artists, travels around the world promoting both the film and Hip Hop Culture to a global audience.

The Roxy on 18th Street in New York becomes one of the most popular clubs in the city. The infamous battle between Rock Steady Crew and the New York City Breakers takes place here. Footage from the battle appears in *Wild Style*.

Rock Steady Crew appears on *ABC News* for its Lincoln Center battle against the Dynamic Rockers. This battle, and all of its publicity, help to bring b-boying/b-girling to the mainstream. The battle appears in the 1983 film *Style Wars*.

The Beastie Boys release their first EP, *Pollywog Stew*, on Ratcage Records.

Chuck D, Flavor Flav, Terminator X, Professor Griff, Hank Shocklee, and Bill Stepheny form Public Enemy, based in Long Island, and are signed to Def Jam Records. Chuck D invites Flava Flav to be a part of his radio show as a regular guest co-host.

1983

Run-DMC is formed by Run (Joseph Simmons), DMC (Darryl Mc-Daniels), and Jam Master Jay (Jason Mizell). They release "It's Like That" and "Sucker MC's." "Sucker MC's" is one of the first crossover records to cater to both hip hop and rock fans. Run-DMC's "Rock Box" becomes the first rap video to be played on MTV.

Herbie Hancock and Grandmixer D.ST release "Rockit," the first fusion of hip hop and jazz.

After learning the "moonwalk" from a Los Angeles crew, Michael Jackson performs the move on "Motown's 25th Anniversary Television Special."

Grandmaster Flash and Melle Mel's "White Lines (Don't Do It)," an anticocaine single, becomes a rap classic and an international hit.

Afrika Bambaataa's *Looking for the Perfect Beat* (Tommy Boy Records) features the first recorded use of digital sampling, introducing the Emulator synthesizer. The success of the album turns Tommy Boy Records into a major hip hop/dance label.

Ice-T releases "Cold Winter Madness" and "Body Rock/Killers" the first West Coast gangsta raps.

The documentary *Breakin' and Enterin'* about West Coast "popping" and "locking" airs on cable. It was recorded in Los Angeles, California.

The graffiti film *Style Wars* airs on PBS.

Michael Stewart, a twenty-five-year-old Black artist, dies in the hospital in September after being beaten by police for writing graffiti in a Manhattan subway station.

DJ Red Alert begins his radio show on WRKS New York 98.7 FM. This station plays hip hop and dancehall.

Elektra signs the group Fearless Four, who become the first rap group to be signed to a major record label.

The SL-1200MKII turntable is introduced, setting a new standard for DJ equipment.

The movie *Flashdance* is released with an appearance by Rock Steady Crew. Crazy Legs performs a backspin as a substitute for actress Jennifer Beals.

Malcolm McLaren's video for the song "Buffalo Gals" is the first that features breakdancing (by Rock Steady Crew), live graffiti, and scratching.

Malcolm McLaren releases the album *Duck Rock*.

1983 (continued)

Dr. Dre, at age eighteen, begins to DJ at clubs that he is too young to go to. He also provides mixes for the rap station 1580 KDAY AM (Los Angeles, California) on Saturday nights.

Grandmaster Flash and the Furious Five split up.

Michael Holman forms the New York City Breakers. Among other prestigious places, they perform for President Ronald Reagan and become the first Hip Hop group to perform at the White House.

1984

UTFO records "Roxanne, Roxanne," a diss on a fictional woman that sparks more than 100 "response records." One of the most notable responses, "Roxanne's Revenge" by fourteen-year-old Roxanne Shante, sells more than 250,000 copies in the New York area alone.

1580 KDAY AM (Los Angeles) becomes the first rap-only radio station in the United States.

The Hip Hop documentary *Beat Street* by Harry Belefonte is released.

The closing ceremonies for the Summer Olympics feature more than 200 breakdancers performing with Lionel Richie.

Rick Rubin and Russell Simmons form Def Jam Records and release LL Cool J's "I Need a Beat," which eventually sells more than 100,000 copies.

A major Hip Hop concert tour (the Fresh Fest) makes about $3.5 million performing on twenty-seven dates. The concerts feature Run-DMC, Kurtis Blow, Whodini, Fat Boys, and Nucleus.

Video Music Box, started by Ralph McDaniels and Vid Kid (Lionel Martin), becomes the first Hip Hop television show of music videos.

The Hip Hop documentary *Breakin'* is released.

DJ Kool Herc plays his last old-school party.

Michael Holman creates the dance show *Graffiti Rock* for television, but it is not picked up by any of the major networks and canceled after one show.

Run-DMC's first album, *Run-DMC,* becomes the first rap album to go gold in December.

1985

Run-DMC's *King of Rock* is the first rap album to go platinum.

Doug E. Fresh, inventor of the human beat box, releases "The Show/La Di Da Di," featuring Dana Dane and Slick Rick. The song rises as the best-selling rap 12-inch record of the year.

The Hip Hop documentary *Krush Groove* is released.

Sugar Hill Records goes bankrupt and is no longer active in the record industry.

On May 21, the Washington Wives, formerly known as the PMRC (Parents Music Resource Center), lobbies for legislation to create a rating system for explicit lyrics and sexual content (known as "the sticker").

1986

Eric B. (Eric Barrier) and Rakim (William Griffin, Jr.) release "Eric B. Is President," once again changing the style of MCs by drawing focus to the lyrics and away from the music.

Schoolly D (Jesse B. Weaver, Jr.) invents gangsta rap on the East Coast with "P.S.K. What Does It Mean?" (Park Side Killers).

Run-DMC's *Raising Hell* becomes the first multiplatinum rap album and the first rap album to be on the U.S. Top 10. The group's members take hip hop to the pop charts with their rap version of Aerosmith's "Walk This Way," and they become the first rap artists to appear on the cover of *Rolling Stone*. While performing "My Adidas" in Philadelphia, they tell the audience to hold

1986 (continued)

their Adidas in the air. They thus become the first Hip Hop artists to earn an endorsement—from Adidas shoes. A film of this is sent to a firm in Germany that, after witnessing the rapid rise in Adidas sales, attempts to advocate for the manufacture of Run DMC-endorsed models of the Cadillac.

Kurtis Blow is featured in a Sprite commercial.

The Geto Boys form in Houston. The original members include Sir Rap-A-Lot, MC Raheim, MC Jukebox, DJ Ready Red, and Little Billy (Bushwick Bill).

The Beastie Boys release their first full-length album, *Licensed to Ill,* on Def Jam Records. The group quickly rises as rap's most popular artists, with over 4 million record sales.

"Sampling" becomes popular in rap music. Recording over other artists' music becomes easier and more common because of advances in sampling and digital technology. Ultramagnetic MCs becomes the first group to use a sampler as an instrument.

One of the longest battles in Hip Hop history begins between MC Shan of the Juice Crew, with his song "The Bridge," and Boogie Down Productions' KRS-One with his response, "The Bridge Is Over."

Hip Hop Slam, a media company with a record label, radio show, videotape series, and Web site, is founded.

1987

The Beastie Boys' debut *Licensed to Ill* becomes the first rap album to go to #1 on the pop chart.

Salt-n-Pepa release the single "Push It." It becomes one of the first rap songs to be nominated for a Grammy Award.

LL Cool J is the first rap artist on *Billboard*'s Black Singles chart to hit #1 with his song "I Need Love."

Eric B. and Rakim release the song "Paid in Full," and it appears on their album *Paid in Full.*

Criminal Minded is released by Boogie Down Productions.

DJ Scott LaRock of Boogie Down Productions is killed in the South Bronx while trying to intervene in an altercation.

The Soul Train Music Awards introduce the first rap category to the list of awards offered.

1988

Public Enemy releases *It Takes a Nation to Hold Us Back,* which includes the song "Black Steel in the Hour of Chaos."

Jazzy Jeff & the Fresh Prince release the song "Parents Just Don't Understand," which is on their album *He's the DJ, I'm the Rapper* released in 1989.

The Jungle Brothers release the album *Straight Out of the Jungle.*

Ultramagnetic MCs release the album *Critical Breakdown.*

Stetsasonic releases the album *In Full Gear.*

Slick Rick releases the song "Children's Story," on his album *The Great Adventures of Slick Rick.*

NWA releases the song "Straight Outta Compton," which is on *Straight Outta Compton.* The album goes gold and popularizes West Coast gangsta rap.

EPMD releases the song "You Gots to Chill," which appears on the album *Strictly Business.*

Kid 'n Play release the song "Rollin' with Kid 'N Play," on the album *2 Hype.*

Yo! MTV Raps debuts with FAB 5 FREDDY on MTV.

The Source magazine is founded by David Mays and Jon Shecter.

Russell Simmons and Rick Rubin (founders of Def Jam) split up. Simmons keeps control of Def Jam while Rubin starts Def American Records.

1989

KRS-One begins the Stop the Violence Movement and releases the single "Self-Destruction," featuring Public Enemy, Kool Moe Dee, Stetsasonic, MC Lyte, and others, to combat violence and the association of violence with Hip Hop. This movement raises about half a million dollars for the National Urban League.

Tone Loc's *Loc'd After Dark* becomes the first rap album to go #1 on the pop charts. The feature song, "Wild Thing," becomes the highest-ranking and best-selling rap single to date in the United States when it hits #2 on the *Billboard* Hot 100 on February 18.

De La Soul releases *3 Feet High and Rising,* the first of the group's albums featuring numerous musical interludes and segues in the form of skits. The group is also a part of the Native Tongues Posse (which at this time also includes Queen Latifah and Jungle Brothers, given the name by Afrika Bambaataa).

Salt-n-Pepa's single "Push It" goes platinum. The group becomes the first female rap group to go platinum.

The Hip Hop genre is acknowledged by the Grammy Awards, American Music Awards, and MTV Awards and gets its own category in each.

DJ Jazzy Jeff & the Fresh Prince release the first rap double album, *He's the DJ I'm the Rapper.* Over 2.5 million copies of the album are sold. Their 1998 song "Parents Just Don't Understand" wins them the first rap Grammy for best performance.

Karl Kani (Carl Williams) develops his clothing line in Los Angeles. His styles set the standard for the urban fashions that follow.

Public Enemy releases the song "Fight the Power," which appears one year later on the album *Fear of a Black Planet.*

A Tribe Called Quest forms in Manhattan, originally as a part of the Native Tongues Posse.

Mellow Man Ace releases his debut album *Escape from Havana* and becomes the first Latin rapper to go platinum.

Queen Latifah releases the song "Ladies First," which appears on her album *All Hail the Queen.*

NWA releases the song "F*** Tha Police," and it appears on the album *Straight Outta Compton.*

Young MC releases the song "Busta Move," which is on his album *Stone Cold Rhymin'.*

Tone Loc releases the song "Wild Thing," on his album *Loc-ed After Dark.*

The Beastie Boys release the album *Paul's Boutique.*

3rd Bass releases *The Cactus Album.*

De La Soul releases the album *3 Feet High and Rising.*

1990

The Deejay Stretch Armstrong & Bobbito show launches on New York's WKCR 89.9 FM on January 16. It lasts until 1998.

Will Smith's Hip Hop–influenced sitcom *The Fresh Prince of Bel-Air* debuts on September 10. It runs until 1996.

The 2 Live Crew ends up in a number of court cases for allegedly breaking obscenity laws with its *As Nasty as They Wanna Be* album. They eventually battle the charges successfully.

Tupac joins Digital Underground.

Schoolly D appears on *The Phil Donahue Show* to talk about the topics of "Money & Rap Music."

MC Hammer's *Please Hammer Don't Hurt 'Em* is nominated for best album. His song "U Can't Touch This" wins for best rap performance. This song, as well as Vanilla Ice's "Ice Ice Baby," become worldwide hits.

Cross Colors clothing is introduced and becomes popular among members of the Hip Hop population.

1990 (continued)

Public Enemy accuses the Grammy Awards of racism and boycotts the show.

Mr. Wiggles forms a new group called the Rhythm Technicians. He also dances at the American Music Awards.

Salt-n-Pepa release the song "Let's Talk about Sex," which appears on the album *Blacks' Magic.*

Whodini releases the song "Magic's Wand," which is included on his *Greatest Hits* album.

Kid 'n Play members star in the movie *House Party,* which earns $20 million, and it is followed by several sequels.

Rap Pages is founded by Larry Flint Publications.

1991

LL Cool J debuts as an actor in *The Hard Way,* playing an undercover cop.

NWA's *Efil4zaggin* sells 954,000 copies in its first week of release, becoming the first hard-core rap album to hit #1.

Tung Twista (later known as Twista) is listed in the *Guinness Book of Records* as the world's fastest rapper after the release of his debut album *Runnin' off at da Mouth.*

A Tribe Called Quest releases *The Low End Theory,* fusing jazz and poetry (an alternative to gangsta rap).

Cypress Hill releases *Cypress Hill.* The members of the group become supporters of the legalization of hemp and musical spokesmen for the National Organization to Reform Marijuana Laws.

Los Angeles, California, radio station 1580 KDAY AM is sold and its all-rap programming ends.

Ice Cube is featured in a St. Ides Malt Liquor commercial.

Public Enemy and Anthrax's rap/metal remake of "Bring the Noise" gets a wider audience to listen to rap.

Fox TV debuts Hip Hop video show *Pump It Up* with Dee Barnes.

LL Cool J is the first rapper to perform on MTV's *Unplugged*.

2 Live Crew releases the first live rap album, *Live in Concert*.

Boogie Down Productions releases *Live Hardcore Worldwide*.

SoundScan monitoring starts being used in more locations, proving that rap artists such as Ice Cube are outselling many rock groups.

Sway and Tech begin hosting *The Wake Up Show* on San Francisco's radio station KMEL.

Naughty by Nature releases the song "O.P.P.," which appears on the album *Naughty by Nature*.

A Tribe Called Quest releases the song "Scenario," which is on the album *The Low End Theory*.

DJ Jazzy Jeff & the Fresh Prince release the song "Summertime," which appears on their album *Homebase*.

The Geto Boys release the song "My Mind's Playing Tricks on Me," and it appears on their album *We Can't Be Stopped*.

Ice-T releases the album *O.G. Original Gangster*.

Main Source releases the album *Breaking Atoms*.

Dr. Dre and Ed Lover give out the first Source Award on *Yo! MTV Raps*.

1992
Dr. Dre starts Death Row Records with Suge Knight.

1992 (continued)

Ice-T's "Cop Killer" gets a response from President George H. W. Bush. The song appears on his heavy metal group's album *Body Count*.

Rap duo Eric B. & Rakim break up.

Puff Daddy founds Bad Boy Entertainment after leaving Uptown and becomes known as the "King of the Remix." He cofounds the marketing and research firm Blue Flame and starts Bad Boy Films. He also produces several of his own rap albums.

The Disposable Heroes of Hip-Hoprisy record the first anti-gay-bashing single "Language of Violence," and it appears on their album *Hypocrisy Is the Greatest Luxury*.

FUBU (For Us By Us) Clothing is established by Daymond John, Carl Brown, Keith Perrin, and J. Alexander Martin.

Russell Simmons forms Phat Fashions (Phat Farm's parent company).

Pete Rock and C. L. Smooth release the song "They Reminisce over You (T.R.O.Y.)," on their album *Mecca & the Soul Brother*.

Tupac releases the song "Brenda's Got a Baby," which is on his album *2Pacalypse Now*.

Arrested Development releases the songs "Tennessee" and "People Everyday," which are on the album *3 Years, 5 Months, and 2 Days in the Life Of*.

Kriss Kross releases the song "Jump," which appears on the album *Totally Krossed Out*.

Ice Cube releases the song "It Was a Good Day," on his album *The Predator*.

Pharcyde releases the song "Passing Me By," on the album *Bizarre Ride II the Pharcyde*.

Das EFX releases the album *Dead Serious*.

Gang Starr releases the album *Daily Operation.*

Dr. Dre releases the song "Nuthin' but a 'G' Thang," which appears on his highly successful solo debut *The Chronic.* The album introduces Snoop Dogg and eventually sells more than 4 million copies. It was the first debut album that entered at #1 on the *Billboard* charts.

James Thompson founds the Hip Hop Hall of Fame Awards.

1993

Wu-Tang Clan releases the song "C.R.E.A.M.," and it appears on the album *Enter the Wu-Tang (36 Chambers).*

HOT 97 in New York switches from a dance format to become "Where Hip Hop Lives," and Funk Master Flex arrives at the station.

Quincy Jones launches *VIBE* magazine.

Arrested Development wins a Grammy Award for best new artist, becoming the first rap artists to do so. Their song "Tennessee" wins them a Grammy Award for best rap performance by a duo or group.

Lugz becomes the first company to feature a signature shoe by Funkmaster Flex.

Guru releases his influential jazz-rap album *Jazzamatazz.*

Naughty by Nature releases the song "Hip Hop Hooray," and it appears on the album *19 Naughty III.*

Nas releases the album *Illmatic.*

The Ecko Unlimited clothing line is launched by Mark Ecko.

Snoop Dogg releases his hit songs "What's My Name" and "Gin & Juice," and they appear on his album *Doggystyle.*

The Invisibl Skratch Piklz win the World DJ Championship.

1993 (continued)

Cypress Hill's second album, *Black Sunday,* reaches #1 on the *Billboard* chart.

Digable Planets release the song "Rebirth of Slick (Cool Like Dat)," and it appears on their album *Reachin' (A New Refutation of Time and Space).*

A Tribe Called Quest releases the song "Award Tour," on the album *Midnight Marauders.*

MC Lyte releases the song "Ruff Neck," on her album *Ain't No Other.*

1994

First annual Source Awards take place on April 25. It is here where the East Coast–West Coast rivalry surfaces.

Da Brat is the first female rap artist to go platinum with her debut album *Funkdafied.*

Notorious B.I.G. (Christopher Wallace) releases a debut album, *Ready to Die,* with the backing of Sean "Puffy" Combs. It includes the song "Juicy."

Nas releases his debut album *Illmatic* and it goes gold.

Source magazine gives Crazy Legs the Hip Hop Pioneer Award.

VIBE magazine holds its first anniversary. The Sugar Hill Gang, LL Cool J, and Heavy D perform live.

Tupac is shot five times and robbed in a studio in New York. He holds Puff Daddy and Notorious B.I.G. of Bad Boy Entertainment responsible.

The first televised Source Awards show takes place.

Common releases the song "I Used to Love H.E.R.," and it appears on his album *Resurrection.*

Warren G releases the song "Regulate," on his album *Regulate . . . G Funk Era.*

1995

Eazy-E dies of AIDS on March 26.

The second annual Source Awards show takes place on August 3.

Queen Latifah wins a Grammy Award for best rap solo performance for "Unity."

The final episode of *Yo! MTV Raps* is aired.

LL Cool J begins starring in the NBC sitcom *In the House.*

Bone Thugs-n-Harmony release the song "Crossroad," which appears on their album *E. 1999 Eternal.*

Mobb Deep releases the song "Shook Ones Pt. 2," on the album *The Infamous.*

Coolio releases the song "Gangsta's Paradise," which is on his album *Gangsta's Paradise.*

Marley Marl releases the song "Symphony Vol. 1," on his album *Marley Marl's House of Hits.*

Marvel Comics does comic books of Public Enemy, Snoop Doggy Dogg, Dr. Dre, and Onyx.

The first documented b-boy summit takes place in San Diego, California.

Tupac signs to Death Row Records after Suge Knight gets him out of jail on $1.4 million bail. Tupac was found guilty on sexual assult charges in 1994 and was sentenced to four and a half years on February 7, 1995. He served eight months before Knight bailed him out.

Buff the Human Beat Box of the Fat Boys dies from a heart attack on December 10.

1996

The Fugees release *The Score,* an album blending hip hop, soul, blues, jazz, and reggae.

Nike and Sprite feature KRS-One in commercials.

Reebok and St. Ides Special Brew feature Method Man in commercials.

Nas releases the song "If I Ruled the World," which appears on his album *It Was Written.*

Jay-Z and Notorious B.I.G. release the song "Brooklyn's Finest," and it appears on Jay-Z's album *Reasonable Doubt.*

Xzibit releases the song "Paparazzi," on his album *At the Speed of Life.*

Bone Thugs-n-Harmony's song "Crossroad" breaks the record for fastest-rising single.

Tupac releases the song "Hit Em Up," and it appears on his album *Death Row Greatest Hits.* His album *All Eyez on Me* is also released. In September, Tupac is murdered in Las Vegas.

1997

Notorious B.I.G. releases the song "Hypnotize," and it appears on his album *Life after Death.* Later in the year Notorious B.I.G. is murdered in Los Angeles.

Missy "Misdemeanor" Elliott wins Billboard Video Music Awards for best clip (rap) and best new artist clip (rap) for her song "The Rain" on the album *Supa Dupa Fly.*

Queen Latifah wins the Aretha Franklin Award for "Entertainer of the Year" at the Soul Train Lady of Soul Awards.

Busta Rhymes' hit songs "Put Your Hands Where My Eyes Can See" and "Dangerous" are released and appear on his album *When Disaster Strikes.*

Company Flow releases the song "The Fire in Which You Burn," on the album *Funcrusher Plus.*

The Hip Hop documentary *Rhyme & Reason* is released.

The *Guinness Book of World Records* lists P. Diddy as the "Most Successful Rap Producer."

1998

The Guinness Book of World Records lists Rebel XD (Seandale Price) as the fastest rapper.

Lauryn Hill is listed as one of the "25 Most Intriguing People of 1998" in *People* magazine.

Missy Elliot is nominated for three Grammy Awards.

P. Diddy's Sean Jean clothing line is formed. P. Diddy also opens his first Justin's restaurant in Manhattan.

Tupac's song "Changes" is released posthumously, and it appears on his *Greatest Hits* album.

Mos Def and Talib Kweli release the album *Black Star.*

The Johnny Blaze Collection clothing line is launched by Patrick Ying and Larry Zimmer.

DMX releases "Ruff Ryders Anthem," which appears on his album *It's Dark and Hell Is Hot.*

Lauryn Hill releases the song "Doo Wop (That Thing)," on her album *The Miseducation of Lauryn Hill.*

DMX and Nas star in the movie *Belly* directed by Hype Williams.

1999

The first collaborative East/West meeting for aerosol art is held at Martinez Gallery in January.

1999 (continued)

Big L is shot and killed on February 15 in Harlem.

Freaky Tah of the Lost Boyz is shot and killed on March 28 in Queens.

The Rock and Roll Hall of Fame and Museum in Cleveland, Ohio, presents the "Roots, Rhymes, and Rage: The Hip Hop Story," its first major exhibition on Hip Hop Culture, in November. The exhibit runs until August 2000.

Lauryn Hill (formerly of the Fugees) wins five Grammy Awards, "legitimizing" rap (hip hop), after being nominated for ten, setting a new record for most awards won by a female artist. She also becomes the first rap artist to win the best album award.

Eve releases the album *Let There Be Eve . . . Ruff Ryders First Lady,* and it becomes the first album by a female rapper to enter the American charts at #1.

Jay-Z wins a Grammy for best album for his *Vol. 2 . . . Hard Knock Life,* but he claims that the Grammys do not respect rap and does not attend the show.

Eminem releases *The Slim Shady LP.*

Missy Elliott receives a nomination for an NAACP Image Award. She is also nominated for a Brit Award for best British video.

A Kung Fu Playstation game based on members of the Wu-Tang Clan is made. It is called "Taste the Pain."

OutKast is sued by Rosa Parks for using her name for the song entitled "Rosa Parks" on their album *Aquemini.* The initial charges were dismissed and later partly reinstated, and in 2003 the U.S. Supreme Court refused to intervene, essentially allowing her to continue her lawsuit against the group. See listing for 2005 for outcome.

Jay-Z and Damon Dash begin the Rocawear Clothing line.

The Hustle: A Gangsta Rap Documentary is released.

The Guinness Book of World Records lists Master P as the "Highest Paid Entertainer in Hip Hop."

The third Source Awards show takes place after a four-year hiatus.

2000

Puerto Rican rapper Big Pun dies of a heart attack on February 7.

The Ruff Ryders launch the Ruff Ryders Collection clothing line on August 30.

The "Hip Hop Nation: Roots, Rhymes, and Rage" exhibition runs from September through December at the Brooklyn Museum of Art in Brooklyn. It contains hundreds of items related to Hip Hop from the 1970s on.

Nelly puts St. Louis on the charts with the multiplatinum *Country Grammar.* The hit song "Country Grammar" appears on this album.

Eminem's *The Marshall Mathers LP* sells about 2 million copies in the first week. He also becomes the first white rapper to win a Grammy under the rap category (best rap album, for *The Slim Shady LP*). He wins another Grammy Award for best rap solo performance.

Missy Elliott's song "Hot Boyz" becomes the longest-running #1 song (eighteen weeks), breaking *Billboard*'s Rap Charts record.

The group dead prez releases one of the most influential albums in rap, entitled *Let's Get Free.*

Jurassic 5 releases the album *Quality Control.*

Wu-Wear is relaunched along with the "Wu-Deville" shoe.

Ice-T begins starring in the television series *Law and Order: Special Victims Unit (SVU).*

OutKast releases the song "Ms. Jackson," which appears on the album *Stankonia.*

2000 (continued)

Rapper Mos Def stars in the movies *Monster's Ball* and *Bamboozled.*

Three Hip Hop documentaries are released: *Backstage, East Coast Mix 1,* and *The Jump Off.*

The Invisibl Skratch Piklz break up.

For the third time in a row, DJ Craze wins the Technics DMC World DJ Championship.

The fourth Source Awards show takes place.

2001

Missy Elliott's song "Get Ur Freak On" is voted "Best Single of the Year" by *Rolling Stone* critics.

Eminem's *The Marshall Mathers LP* is nominated for album of the year at the Grammy Awards, but it is heavily protested due to its lyrical content. He wins the remaining rap categories.

Jay-Z releases the album *The Blueprint.*

Method Man and Redman begin commercials for Right Guard Xtreme Power Stripe deodorant.

Method Man and Redman star in the movie *How High.*

OutKast's OutKast Wear clothing line is formed.

Snoop Dogg launches his Snoop Dogg clothing line.

Nelly launches his Vokal clothing line.

The Hip Hop documentaries *Breath Control: The History of the Human Beatbox* and *Battle Sounds* are released.

DJ Q-bert releases *Wave Twisters,* the first feature-length graffiti-animated movie in history.

The fifth Source Awards show takes place.

2002

Russell Simmons's Hip Hop Summit extends to the West Coast in February.

On February 25, Run-DMC becomes the first Hip Hop group to have its members' handprints cast in cement along Hollywood Boulevard's Walk of Fame.

The Hip Hop Super Conference and Expo takes place in March at the Puck Building in New York. It is called "the world's largest all business hip-hop conference."

Lisa "Left-Eye" Lopes (the rapper of the female R&B trio TLC) is killed in a tragic automobile accident while vacationing in Honduras on April 25.

Wild Style is released on DVD in September.

Jam Master Jay of Run-DMC is murdered in his Queens studio on October 30.

November becomes the official month for celebrating the history of Hip Hop. The Hip Hop History Month resolution, passed by the New York State Senate, sponsored by state senator Pedro Espada, Jr., and championed by Afrika Bambaataa, says, "Due to the contributions of the . . . many hip hop legends, youth throughout the world have found means of supporting themselves. . . . The hip hop art forms have become a means of making a positive difference in this world."

The movie *8 Mile,* starring rapper Eminem, is released. The soundtrack features Eminem's song "Lose Yourself."

Nelly releases the song "Air Force Ones," which appears on his album *Nellyville*.

The song "In Da Club" is released by 50 Cent, on his album *Get Rich or Die Tryin'*.

Hip Hop Story: Tha Movie is released.

2002 (continued)

The Hip Hop documentary *The Freshest Kids* is released by QD3 Entertainment and Brotherhood Films.

Several Hip Hop documentaries are released: *Scratch; Hip Hop 4 Life; Heroes of Latin Hip Hop; Graffiti Rock (and Other Hip Hop Delights); Word: A Film of the Underground Hip Hop;* and *Hip-Hop Uncensored, Vol. 3: Hustlemania (The Road Trip Project)*.

Lil' Bow Wow stars in the basketball movie *Like Mike*.

Coca-Cola officials choose the Roots to appear in the company's "Nu Classic Soul" ad campaign.

Tupac and Notorious B.I.G. are inducted into the Hip Hop Hall of Fame.

Will Smith is nominated for an Oscar for his role as Muhammad Ali in the movie *Ali*.

At the 2002 Urban Fashion Awards, Russell Simmons wins the Urban Fashion Humanitarian Award, Karl Kani wins the Urban Fashion Pioneer Award, and Sean John wins the Best Menswear Design.

2003

Jay-Z appears in a Heineken USA commercial called "The Takeover."

Adidas releases a new sneaker (Jam Master Jay Ultra Star). Designed in part by Jay's three sons, it sells for $100 a pair. Five thousand pairs are made and all proceeds are donated to Jay's Scratch DJ Academy.

The DJ group X-ecutioners releases *Scratchology*, dedicated to Jam Master Jay.

Grandmaster Flash and the Furious Five's "The Message" is one of the first fifty songs to be put into the National Recording Registry. The registry is set up to preserve historical recordings of all genres.

Snoop Dogg pays a family's travel and lodging expenses to see him record an episode of his comedy show *Doggy Fizzle Televizzle*. He also begins doing commercials for America Online.

Missy Elliott is featured in commercials for the Gap.

Lil' Romeo and Master P star in a television series on Nickelodeon called *Romeo!*

Nelly starts marketing Vokal (his brand of vodka), his Vokal clothing line, and an energy drink (Pimp Juice).

Reebok and 50 Cent successfully launch the "G-Unit Collection by RBK," a collection of footwear, and 50 Cent launches the G-Unit clothing line.

Ruff Ryders launch the Dirty Denim clothing line. Their pet food, "Game Dog," is also introduced, along with pet apparel (collars, harnesses).

Eminem launches the Shady Gear clothing line.

Missy Elliott becomes a spokesperson for Vanilla Coke.

The Source holds a press conference to address current issues in Hip Hop.

Ride with Funkmaster Flex airs on Spike TV.

Brian "Baby" Williams (CEO of Cash Money Records) and his brother Ronald (Slim) launch a charitable organization, the Cash Money for Kids program. They also establish the Johnny and Gladys Williams Foundation to provide scholarships and food for needy families. In addition, Williams and Karl Kani launch the Life clothing line in March.

Eve begins starring in her UPN television sitcom, entitled *Eve*.

Mos Def is featured in the remake of the film *The Italian Job*.

Ice-T launches his IceWear clothing line.

2003 (continued)

Master P launches his P. Miller clothing line.

The Tony Silver and Henry Chalfant Hip Hop documentary *Style Wars,* which originally aired on PBS in 1983, is released on DVD with additional material. In addition, several new documentaries on Hip Hop are released, including *Soundz of Spirit; Street Legendz; Freestyle: The Art of Rhyme; Bomb the System; Beef; and Chuck D's Hip Hop Hall of Fame.*

Eminem's "Lose Yourself" becomes the first rap song to win an Oscar.

The sixth Source Awards show takes place.

2004

Karl Kani is awarded the Living Legend Award at the second annual Urban Fashion Awards Show on February 25.

The *Dirty States of America* documentary is released in June.

P. Diddy's Sean Jean clothing line wins the prestigious Menswear Designer of the Year Award from the Council of Fashion Designers of America—a first for an African American as well as the first for a Hip Hopper—in June.

Method & Red debuts on Fox in June with thirteen episodes, and continues through September.

The first National Hip-Hop Political Convention takes place in Newark, New Jersey, at Essex County College, New Jersey Institute of Technology, and Rutgers University from June 16 (Tupac Shakur's birthday) to June 19 (Juneteenth). Activists, executives, workers, artists, professionals, and educators discuss and attempt to develop a national political agenda for the Hip Hop community.

Ol' Dirty Bastard dies from a drug overdose on November 13.

InStyle magazine names Jay-Z "Man of Style" for the month of December.

OutKast's double CD, *Speakerboxxx/The Love Below,* wins Grammy Awards for album of the year and best rap album.

Esquire magazine acknowledges Andre 3000 as "Best Dressed Male."

P. Diddy stars in the Broadway return of Lorraine Hansberry's 1959 play, "A Raisin in the Sun," as Walter Lee Younger. The show plays at the Royale Theater and also stars Phylicia Rashad, Audra McDonald, and Sanaa Lathan.

Lugz announces its release of "The Birdman" shoe in May. The shoe is launched by Brian "Baby" Williams.

Xzibit begins hosting the MTV series *Pimp My Ride.*

The Hip Hop documentaries *Hip Hop Immortals* and *B Boy Masters* are released.

Lil' John releases an energy drink called "Crunk."

The Makaveli Branded clothing line is introduced by Tupac Shakur's mother, Afeni Shakur.

Nelly's Pimp Juice creates the P.I.M.P. Scholars Program. The acronym stands for Positive Intellectual Motivated Person.

Snoop Dogg hosts Spike TV's Video Game Awards show. He also is featured in a T-Mobile commercial, launches his Doggy Biscuitz sneaker line, releases his Snoop WRFF bike, and hosts MTV2's show *Sucker Free Sunday.*

P. Diddy designs new team uniforms for the NBA's Dallas Mavericks.

The seventh Source Awards show takes place.

2005

The Makaveli Branded clothing line holds its first fashion show on January 1.

The "Feminism and Hip Hop" conference, held in Chicago, addresses topics such as black women in Hip Hop and sexual politics on April 7–9.

"Hip Hop Conference 2005: Political Action and Social Responsibility in Hip-Hop" takes place at Oberlin College in April.

The 1999 lawsuit over the use of Rosa Parks's name as the title of OutKast's 1998 hit without her permission is settled in April. Parks, known to many as the mother of the civil rights movement, dies on October 24 at the age of 92.

Biz Markie is featured on the VH1 reality show *Celebrity Fit Club*.

Da Brat is featured on the fourth season of VH1's reality show *The Surreal Life*.

Wyclef Jean wins a Golden Globe Award for his song "Million Voices" from the soundtrack to *Hotel Rwanda*.

Rap moguls Irv Gotti and Chris Gotti surrender to the FBI in New York for laundering illegal drug money through their record label The Inc. They were eventually cleared of charges by a federal jury in December.

Snoop Dogg hosts his first Snooper Bowl (with his youth football team playing against a youth all-star team from Jacksonville, Florida).

Nelly is featured with Tim McGraw in a Budweiser commercial.

The RZA and Ray Acosta, former Vice President of Musica Latina, launch Wu-Tang Latino, a new record label featuring Hip Hop and reggaeton.

The Tupac Amaru Shakur Center For The Arts and Peace Garden opens in Stone Mountain, Georgia.

AJ Calloway and Free, longtime hosts of the popular BET Hip Hop show *"106 & Park"* abruptly resign. The reason was not disclosed.

Jay-Z launches Roc La Familia, a new record label focused on reggae, calypso, West Indian music, and reggaeton.

Nelly enters long-term partnership with Reebok to produce a signature collection of athletic foot wear, apparel, and accessories.

Lil' Kim (Kimberly Denise Jones) is sentenced to a year and a day in prison for lying to a grand jury regarding a 2001 shooting outside of Manhattan, New York's Hot 97 radio station.

Kurtis Blow is inducted into the Bronx Walk of Fame.

Hurricanes Katrina and Rita rip through the Gulf Coast killing many and displacing many more. Local, regional, and national Hip Hop artists respond, including an unscripted statement by Kanye West during a benefit concert broadcast live on NBC who shocks viewers by saying' "George Bush doesn't care about Black people."

Kanye West appears on the cover of *Time* magazine heralded as one of the smartest people in Hip Hop.

Books on Hip Hop that are released include *The Psychology of Hip Hop* and *Can't Stop Won't Stop: A History of the Hip-Hop Generation.* The latter, by Jeff Chang, is the recipient of the 2005 American Book Award offered by the Before Columbus Foundation in recognition of "Outstanding Literary Achievement."

Documentaries, *Rize, Hip Hop Task Force,* and *Hip Hop 411* are released.

The Millions More Movement, on the tenth anniversary of the Million Man March, has great support by local, regional, and national Hip Hop artists.

Russell Simmons and the Simmons/Lathan Media Group team up with Comcast to launch Def on Demand (DOD), an on-demand cable channel dedicated to Hip Hop and urban music.

2005 (continued)

Movies prominently featuring Hip Hop are released, including *Hustle and Flow* and *Get Rich or Die Tryin'*.

Many in the Hip Hop community rally to support the call for clemency for cofounder of the Crip gang, Stanley "Tookie" Williams who was convicted in 1979 of the murder of four individuals and sentenced to the death penalty. Governor Arnold Schwarzenegger denies the request and Williams is executed on December 13.

Biographical Sketches

his chapter offers forty-seven biographical sketches of some of the most influential pioneers, innovators, and practitioners within Hip Hop Culture. The list includes DJs, graffiti artists, b-boys/b-girls, producers, music video and film directors, journalists, historians, activists, designers, and moguls in an attempt to offer in-depth and insightful background information on the who's who of Hip Hop Culture.

To guide the final selection of the individuals and groups included, I first created a set of criteria. In accordance with these guidelines, each of the individuals and groups selected has made a lasting contribution to the development, presentation, and/or dissemination of Hip Hop Culture both nationally and worldwide. In addition, each has attained a high level of public admiration and has been prominent in the genre over a substantial period of time. Finally, each has influenced subsequent artists and practitioners within the culture and has been regarded as an innovator by these artists and practitioners. Although numerous other individuals and groups could have been added to this list, they certainly could not have replaced any of the selections presented. For ease of use as a resource and reference, the list is presented in alphabetical order by first name or group name.

Afrika Bambaataa

http://www.zulunation.com/
Known as the "Master of Records" for his remarkable ability to recall and select certain choice breaks and sections on records, whether obsolete or prominent, Afrika Bambaataa reigns internationally as one of the superior DJs of numerous genres and the undisputed Godfather of Hip Hop Culture. Born Kevin Donovan

"Master of Records" and "Godfather of Hip Hop Culture," Afrika Bambaataa rocks the party. (S.I.N./Corbis)

in the Bronx on April 10, 1960, he would rise as one of the most unrecognized and underappreciated world leaders of the late twentieth and early twenty-first centuries. A young gang warlord affiliated with the Black Spades, Bambaataa aided an entire generation, helping his peers turn away from gang violence and warfare to music, dance, and art.

The former Adlai E. Stevenson High School student with an amazing prowess as a DJ began throwing block parties in 1973. Influenced by Kool DJ Dee and DJ Kool Herc, Bambaataa used the new sounds of Hip Hop to inspire peace and unity. With the inception of his Bronx River Organization in 1973, a name he later shortened to simply "Organization" and which by 1974 had become the Universal Zulu Nation (influenced by the legacy of the South African Zulus and their king, Shaka Zulu), he led inner-city youth away from a life of violence through a particular philosophy and approach. In 1982, Bambaataa and his Soul Sonic Force gave birth to electro-funk with the single "Planet Rock," one of the most sampled records in the history of Hip Hop. Bambaataa's stage presence is most influenced by Sly & the Family Stone and "Uncle" George Clinton, although he often credits many artists for their legacy and influence. Besides the generally accepted four elements of Hip Hop, Bambaataa has suggested a fifth element, captured in the slogan "Knowledge, Culture and Overstanding" (see Chapter 2).

Through the Universal Zulu Nation, Hip Hop has spread to numerous nations around the world. Bambaataa also encouraged the adoption of November as Hip Hop History Month, as it was in this month in 1973 when he launched his organization, which united DJs, graffiti artists, b-boys and b-girls, and MCs.

Beastie Boys

http://www.beastieboys.com/
The first major all-white Hip Hop crew, the Beastie Boys rose to become one of the most successful groups of the golden age of Hip Hop even though critics and other artists marked them as cultural pirates infringing on other people's territory and cultural practices. First formed as an underground punk band in 1981, upper-middle-class Jewish childhood friends Mike D (Michael Diamond, drummer, born November 20, 1966) and MCA (Adam Nathaniel Yauch, bassist, born August 5, 1965) invited drummer Kate Schellenbach and guitarist John Berry to play the underground scene in New York City. In 1983, after one EP release, Schellenbach and

MCA (L), Mike D (C), and Ad-Rock (R) of the Beastie Boys pose for reporters at a news conference on April 21, 2003, after headlining the first Tibetan Freedom Concert before an ethnic Chinese audience in Taipei. The Tibetan Freedom Concert, which began in 1996, raises money to support the human rights movement in Tibet. (Lynn Goldsmith/Corbis)

Berry left for other ventures, and Diamond and Yauch added guitarist ad-Rock (Adam Horovitz, born October 31, 1967) to complete the trio. In 1984, the group abandoned punk for the new sounds of rap, signing with Def Jam Records.

The crew landed wide national exposure as the opening band for Madonna's 1985 Virgin Tour, which was followed by an opening spot on Run-DMC's Raising Hell Tour. In 1986, the Beastie Boys released *Licensed to Ill* on the Def Jam label. Even though critics attacked the sarcastic and comedic stage presence of the trio, the album sold more than 750,000 copies in the first six weeks, largely because of the popularity of "Fight for Your Right (to Party)," a song recognized in 1995 by the Rock 'n' Roll Hall of Fame as one of the "500 Songs That Shaped Rock and Roll." The album was the first Hip Hop album to break 5 million in sales and was one of the biggest sellers of the 1980s.

In 1988, due to a contractual conflict, the Beastie Boys left Def Jam en route to Capitol Records in California. With the assistance of the Dust Brothers, their second album, *Paul's Boutique* (Capitol, 1989), capitalized on their cult-like following of collegiate and alternative rock communities. The success of the second album spurred the creation of the Grand Royal record label in 1993, and shortly after, the *Grand Royal* magazine, which began as a newsletter to update their fan base on the events and initiatives of the record label. In 1994, Yauch converted to Buddhism and initiated his long-standing humanitarian campaign against the injustices of China toward Tibet. The group's members would become huge supporters of the Milarepa Fund as well as regulars at the Tibetan Freedom Concert.

Beastie Boys recordings continued to sell throughout the 1990s and into the 2000s, and by 2003 they were ranked second in all-time sales of Hip Hop albums, with an estimated 21 million records sold (behind Tupac Shakur, with 35 million sold, and slightly ahead of Eminem, with 20 million). The group, which now includes DJ Mix Master Mike on occasion, was also ranked as #11 in a list of the "50 Greatest Hip Hop Artists" by the cable television music station VH1 in 2003.

Beat Junkies

http://www.beatjunkies.com/

One of the seminal groups to lead the revival of the Hip Hop DJ, and most specifically the rise of turntablism in the 1990s, the Beat Junkies formed under the leadership of DJ J-Rocc (Jason Jackson) of Orange County, California, in 1992. This crew of battle DJs exemplifies the multicultural reality of Hip Hop in the 1990s as the artists are from different racial and ethnic backgrounds. Armed with the signature Green Lantern rings, the crew of over ten members, the most notably, DJ Rhettmatic (Nazareth Nizra), DJ Melo-D (David Mendoza), and DJ Babu (Chris Oroc), who joined the crew in 1995, created one of the most famous DJ collectives to date. DJ Shortkut (Jonathan Cruz), a cofounder of the Invisibl Skratch Piklz, also joined later and now enjoys simultaneous membership in two of the leading groups showcasing turntablism.

As a team, the Beat Junkies accomplished world champion titles at the International Turntable Federation (ITF) competitions in 1997 and 1998, the last years that they entered competition. Their monumental recording, *The World Famous Beat Junkies, Vol. I*, in 1997 on the PR record label furthered the turntablist movement, emphasizing a DJ's ability to record album-length works that would cater to an audience. In 2001, following the creation of Beat Junkies, Inc., an umbrella organization that manages and supports the various business ventures of the Beat Junkies, J-Rocc launched the Beat Junkie Sound record label. The crew of radio personalities, individual award winners, and notable DJs and producers of other well-known groups have aided in expanding the vocabulary and techniques of Hip Hop DJs, dedicating themselves to perfecting cuts, beat juggling, mixes, and scratches with extreme precision and unparalleled showmanship.

Davey D

http://www.daveyd.com/

Born in the Bronx, Davey D began his long and influential career in Hip Hop as an MC in 1977 with the Total Def Krew (TDK) in the Co-op City area of the Bronx as well as with the Avengers, who hailed from the Marble Hill section of the Bronx. Upon graduation from high school, Davey D traveled to California's Bay Area, where he attended the University of California, Berkeley, and began DJing on the radio. The veteran of KALX, KPFA, and KMEL served as director of the PROs Record Pool during the late 1980s and into the early 1990s. The former journalism major is also a member of the Bay Area Black Journalist Association (BABJA).

Among his greatest contributions to Hip Hop Culture are his monumental Web site, Davey D's Hip Hop Corner, which is the oldest, largest, and most notable Hip Hop–oriented Web site on the Net, as well as his popular newsletter, *FNV*, boasting a subscriber base of more than 100,000 people and growing. In 2002, Davey D launched a second newsletter, the *Hip Hop Political Newsletter (HHPN)*. As a Hip Hop historian, journalist, and community activist, he has appeared on CNN's *Talk Back Live,* ABC's *Nightline,* BBC Radio, Australia's *Lateline,* PBS's *The Tavis Smiley Show,* and numerous other programs and/or documentaries on BET, VH1, MTV, and more. He has been featured as an author or as the focus of articles in *Source* magazine, *VIBE* magazine, *Rolling Stone* magazine, the *Washington Post,* the *New York Times,* the *New York Post,* the *Oakland Tribune, USA Today,* and numerous other publications. As a featured speaker or panelist, he participated in the 2000 Democratic National Convention, the Rainbow Push Coalition, the Congressional Black Caucus, and dozens of smaller events at high schools, community service centers, and universities.

Don Campbell & the Lockers

Don Campbell was born in St. Louis, Missouri, during the 1950s and raised in Los Angeles, California. A talented artist specializing in facial profiles and pictures of nature, Campbell attended Los Angeles Trade Technical College as a student of commercial art. He was also a track athlete. By 1970, Campbell had befriended both Sam Williams and Sweet T (Michael Moore), fellow students at Trade Tech and street dancers influenced by the funk music and funk culture of the Los Angeles scene. Williams encouraged Campbell to enter a dance contest, where Campbell debuted his version of the "funky chicken." He did not win, but the lack of early success did not deter Campbell from developing his unique dance into what Williams later referred to as the "Campbell-lock." Soon, Campbell was a lead competitor in the Los Angeles urban dance scene and a rising urban legend among the urban dance community. While hanging out at Los Angeles's Maverick's Flat, a local club that Campbell frequented, he met and befriended local dancer Fred Berry.

In 1971, when former newscaster Don Cornelius relocated his dance program *Soul Train* from Chicago's WCIU-TV to Los Angeles's KTTV, the urban dance scene in Los Angeles exploded with opportunity. As a black alternative to Dick Clark's renowned *American Bandstand, Soul Train* offered an opportunity that became for many youths the urban equivalent to dancing on Broadway. Cornelius's signature closing line, "Peace, love and soul," appealed to them. Campbell and Berry quickly seized the opportunity and became regular and somewhat featured dancers on the show. Their presence on the show not only earned them featured coverage in the urban magazines *Soul* and *Right On!,* but also paved the way for other urban dancers, who displayed the poppin' and lockin' style to gain entry onto the show. Yet the opportunity was short lived. When Campbell and Berry and a host of other poppers and lockers requested $50 pay per show, Cornelius quickly refused and removed the dancers from the show.

Though angry about this response, they were encouraged by their immediate rise to fame and the numerous opportunities that their presence on *Soul Train* created. Campbell formed the Campbellock Dancers in 1973, considered by some the first professional urban dance group to feature the locking style. The nucleus of the group was made up of Campbell, whose style became (and remains) one of the most imitated and appropriated urban dance styles to ever appear on the scene; the Penguin (Fred Berry), Slim the Robot (Bill Washington), Fluky Luke (Leo Williamson), Campbellock Jr. (Greg Pope), and Toni Basil. Other members at various times included Deney Terrio, Shabadoo (Adolfo Quinones), Alpha Omega Anderson, and Go-Go (Tony Lewis).

Wearing large apple hats, knickers, striped socks, and suspenders and adorned in many bright colors, the Campbellock Dancers (who later changed their name to "the Lockers") appeared on stage with numerous artists, including Frank Sinatra, Bob Hope, Sammy Davis, Jr., Dean Martin, Bill Cosby, Stevie Wonder, Aretha Franklin, Roberta Flack, Richard Pryor, and Bette Midler. They also appeared on numerous television shows, such as *The Dick Van Dyke Show, The Carol Burnett Show, The Tonight Show, Starring Johnny Carson* (first as the Campbellock Dancers and again as the Lockers), *What's Happening* (as the Rockers), *ABC In Concert* (as the Lockers), and *Saturday Night Live* (the first non-musical performance on the show), and on numerous Grammy and Oscar award shows. With over eighty credits, the group was also featured in a commercial for Schlitz Malt Liquor Beer in 1973.

When the group dispersed in the late 1970s and 1980s, numerous members went on to achieve great success. Berry played a lead role in the syndicated sitcom *What's Happening,* starring as "Rerun." Basil went on to record a #1 pop tune, "Mickey (You're So Fine)," in 1982. Terrio earned the host slot on the popular show *Dance Fever.* Quinones went on to star as "Ozone" in *Breakin'* (Canon Group, 1984) and *Breakin' 2: Electric Boogaloo* (Cannon Film Distributors, 1984). Campbell, who continues to have a presence on the Los Angeles urban dance scene, still teaches his style to many. Some of his original outfits are housed and often displayed at the Rock 'n' Roll Hall of Fame Hip Hop exhibit.

Doug E. Fresh

http://www.dougefresh.com/

The legendary entertainer and first noted human beat box of Hip Hop, Doug E. Fresh was born Doug E. Davis in Barbados on September 17, 1966. Known for his ability to replicate and reproduce perfect note-for-note imitations of drums, effects, samples, scratching, and a host of other sounds, Fresh first appeared with Spoonie Gee and DJ Spivey on a 1983 recording, "Pass the Budda," on the Spotlight label. Yet it was his appearance in the 1984 film *Beat Street* (MGM Home Entertainment, 1984), where he beat boxed behind the Treacherous Three, that gave him his first national exposure.

Fresh's big break came in 1985, when he and his Get Fresh Crew (including Barry Bee, Chill Will, and MC Ricky D [a.k.a. Slick Rick]) landed a hit and set a Hip Hop standard with "The Show/La Di Da Di." Although his later works, including a 1992 album on MC Hammer's Bust It label, did not match his early success, his partner Slick Rick (Richard Walters) achieved great success with his unique ability to deliver humorous, captivating stories in his heavy British accent.

Dynamic Rockers/ Dynamic Breakers

The Dynamic Rockers hail from Queens and were one of Rock Steady Crew's most notable rivals. They are best known for their legendary battle against Rock Steady Crew in front of New York's Lincoln Center in 1982 as well as for their United Skates of America (USA) battle, which is depicted in *Style Wars* and other documentaries. Known for their use of gymnastics and acrobatics, the crew added a new dimension to street dancing.

During the late 1980s, Dynamic Rockers members Airborne, Spinner, Kano, and Flip formed a new group, the Dynamic Breakers, taking advantage of an opportunity to sign a management deal with Breakdance International Management. The four former high-school gymnastic team members added a New Jersey breaker, Deuce, to the crew and began a string of performances. The Dynamic Breakers appeared in movies such as *Delivery Boys* (Pegasus Pictures, 1984) and *The Last Dragon* (Delphi III, 1985) as well as on television shows such as *That's Incredible* and NBC's *The New Show,* where they helped actress/comedian Penny Marshall accomplish a head spin on camera. In addition to recording two singles on Sunnyview Records, the Dynamic Breakers have performed with Run-DMC, Whodini, Kurtis Blow, the Fat Boys, Grandmaster Flash, Magnificent Force, and Uptown Express. They were also a part of the historic Fresh Fest and Fresh Fest 2 tours that aided in spreading Hip Hop nationwide.

The Electric Boogaloos

http://www.electricboogaloos.com/

After viewing a television show featuring a performance of Don Campbell and the Lockers in 1975, Sam Solomon was compelled to create his own style of dance showcasing his unique sense of rhythm and style. The Fresno, California, resident spent the next few years developing the "Boog style" (later called Boogaloo, inspired by James Brown's hit, "Do the Boogaloo"), the poppin' style, and the "Electric Boogaloo," which combines the two. In 1977, Solomon, as "Boogaloo Sam," formed the group the Electric Boogaloo Lockers along with cofounder Slide (Nate Johnson). They soon added Slim (Joe Thomas, a.k.a. Robot Joe), Tickin' (Will Green), and Twist-o-Flex (Darnell McDowel) as well as Toyman Skeet and Ant Man.

In 1978, the Solomon family relocated to Long Beach, California, where Boogaloo Sam initiated a new group, the Electric Boogaloos, that would quickly rise to the top and remain as one of the leading groups promoting and performing the funk-based street dancing that would eventually be adopted into Hip Hop. The original Electric Boogaloos included Boogaloo Sam, Popin' Pete (Timothy Solomon), Robot Dane, Puppet Boozer, Creepin Sid, and Scarecrow Sculley as well as Tickin' Deck, King Cobra, and King Python. Over the past thirty years, the Electric Boogaloos have collectively and individually starred in numerous television shows, movies, and videos, and they continue to maintain an active schedule of performances and international clinics.

Eminem

http://www.eminem.com/

Born Marshall Bruce Mathers III on October 17, 1972, in St. Joseph, Missouri (outside of Kansas City), Eminem (a.k.a. Slim Shady) is known as the first critically accepted white MC. Raised on the east side of Detroit, the skilled wordsmith and quick-witted freestyler rapped with the New Jacks and Soul Intent prior to traveling to Los Angeles to participate in the 1997 Rap Olympics, an opportunity he had landed with the assistance of Rap Coalition's Wendy Day. While in Los Angeles, Eminem was invited to the world-famous Wake Up Radio Show with Sway and Tech, where he freestyled on air. He was quickly signed to Dr. Dre's Aftermath record label. Eminem's rise to prominence was so quick that the

Rapper Eminem performs "Without Me" during the 2002 MTV Movie Awards. (Scott Gries/ImageDirect/Getty Images)

Hip Hop media had him on the front page of numerous trade magazines even before the release of his 1999 debut *The Slim Shady LP*, which sold 4 million copies in five weeks. His next album, *The Marshall Mathers LP*, sold close to 2 million copies in one week, making it the fastest-selling Hip Hop album ever (at the time).

Known for his charged and graphically animated lyrics, Eminem has been accused of presenting homophobic, sexist, and misogynistic lyrics. He is most noted, though, for his lyrical jabs at

Christina Aguilera, 'NSYNC, Ricky Martin, Britney Spears, Ray Benzino & David Mays, and a host of others. The multi-award-winning artist added acting to his list of successes with his feature role in *8 Mile* (Imagine Entertainment, 2002), a film loosely based on his life and rise from Detroit to worldwide success. Eminem has since launched Shady Records, releasing a project by his Detroit crew, D12.

FAB 5 FREDDY

Frederick Braithwaite was born in 1959 in the Bedford-Stuyvesant (Bed-Stuy) section of Brooklyn. A student of art, with an emphasis on painting in college, Braithwaite entered the realm of graffiti during the 1970s. Under the name of BULL, Braithwaite's tag 99-BULL 99 became well known (he also tagged Showdown 177). Interested in the work of the FAB (FABULOUS) 5 graffiti crew, Braithwaite, an adult, walked into the high-school classroom of FAB 5 crew member Lee Quinones, a student, to express his interest. He was quickly thrown out of the classroom, but as a result of this meeting Braithwaite and Quinones became friends. Braithwaite joined the crew of LEE, MONO, DOC, SLUG, and SLAVE as FAB 5 FREDDY.

During 1978, a mass shift from painting trains to painting walls occurred as New York City tightened up the security on subway train lay-ups. Known for his passion and knowledge of pop art and his skills as an extraordinary networker, FAB 5 FREDDY was able to bridge numerous artistic communities, in effect helping to spread Hip Hop. During the late 1970s, he frequently partied with Deborah Harry and Blondie, Jean-Michel Basquiat, Keith Haring, and Andy Warhol at the Mudd Club in downtown New York City. These relationships led to an April 1981 endeavor in which he served as curator for an art show entitled "Beyond Words: Graffiti-Based, -Rooted and -Inspired Works" at the Mudd Club. Featuring the works of LEE, PHASE 2, LADY PINK, ZEPHYR DONDI, Basquiat, Haring, John Sex, Alan Vega, RAMMELLZEE, and numerous others, he bridged the punk, subway graffiti, and street art scenes with the blossoming Hip Hop movement. The Cold Crush Brothers, the Fantastic Freaks, and Afrika Bambaataa's Jazzy Five MCs all performed at the opening.

The famous shout-out that both FAB 5 FREDDY and Grandmaster Flash received on Blondie's 1980 #1 pop hit "Rapture" raised both to a level that FAB 5 FREDDY would greatly utilize.

Through an affiliation with the artist collective Co-LAB, FAB 5 FREDDY met Charlie Ahearn, with whom he partnered to produce the film *Wild Style* (Wild Style Productions, 1982). FAB 5 FREDDY not only coproduced the documentary but also starred in the film and composed original music for the film. After the film project was completed, FAB 5 FREDDY moved to directing music videos and commercials. He collaborated in these projects with Queen Latifah, KRS-One, Nas, Snoop Doggy Dogg, Pepsi, and others. He also served as associate producer for the film *New Jack City* (Warner Brothers, 1991). He made his most visible contribution, however, as the first host of MTV's *Yo! MTV Raps.* Following the success of the August 6, 1988, pilot, Ed Lover and Dr. Dre were added as cohosts, and the show earned the much-coveted Saturday night slot as the first nationally broadcast TV show dealing exclusively with Hip Hop. The show quickly rose to become the network's most watched show and the only MTV program broadcast on MTV affiliates throughout the world. FAB 5 FREDDY remains one of Hip Hop Culture's earliest and most recognizable international icons.

FUBU

http://www.fubu.com

Founded by five childhood friends, FUBU stands as one of the most successful clothing manufacturers associated with Hip Hop Culture. The five owners grew up in the Hollis section of Queens, listening to the sounds of rap music and witnessing the growing Hip Hop Culture. They also witnessed non-Black-owned businesses such as Nike, Adidas, Gucci, and others capitalize on the predominantly Black consumer base in Queens. Aiming to capture a portion of the same market, lead founder and CEO Daymond John used a $100,000 loan against his home to initiate the company.

The company set out to create baseball caps and T-shirts that were "For Us, By Us." By 1993, the company had secured Hollis native LL Cool J as its biggest advertiser. With the new endorsement deal, LL Cool J would wear and highlight the FUBU line on tour, in concert, and in public appearances. This national and international advertising not only boosted sales but also added legitimacy and validation to the fledgling company from within Hip Hop. FUBU quickly moved away from attempting to capture only a Black audience in order to capture a broader range of youth who identified with Hip Hop Culture. Expanding their merchandise to

LL Cool J wears FUBU Hip Hop clothing. (Richard Chung/Reuters/Corbis)

include jerseys, jeans, swimwear, and intimate and formal wear, the founders created lines for women, men, and children.

As Hip Hop continued to travel worldwide during the mid-1990s, so did FUBU. A partnership with Samsung America helped FUBU to expand its manufacturing and global distribution. The addition of Platinum FUBU, which features both the Fat Albert and the Harlem Globetrotters lines along with a line of fragrances, is partly responsible for the company's continued success, and the company further benefited from the additions of FB Entertainment and FUBU Films. However, the vision of the founders and their ability to stay "current" is the real secret. By 1999, the company was turning a $200 million a year profit and in the same year grossed over $380 million. The company greatly profited from a deal with the National Basketball Association (NBA), which licensed FUBU to make official jerseys and sweat suits. Over the years, FUBU has won many awards, including accolades from Congress, the NAACP, the Queens Borough President, the Pratt Institute, and *Essence* magazine, among many others.

The Fugees

http://www.sonymusic.com/artists/Fugees/

Formed in South Orange, New Jersey, in 1987 by Columbia High School schoolmates Pras (Samuel Prakazrel Michel) and Lauryn Hill as the Tranzlator Crew, the duo performed the local circuit before adding Pras's cousin, Wyclef Jean. In addition to doing performances with the crew, Hill was an actress on the soap opera *As the World Turns,* earning money that helped to subsidize the group's early equipment purchases. The former "Amateur Night at the Apollo" contestant would later star in the film *Sister Act 2: Back in Habit* (Touchstone Pictures, 1993). Before changing their name to the Fugees (short for "Haitian refugees"), the group signed to Ruffhouse/Columbia and released the chart-topping album *The Score* (1996). The multiplatinum and multi-award-winning album earned the group worldwide recognition.

Recognized as one of the first major Hip Hop albums to utilize reggae, this album further expanded the reach of Hip Hop. In 1997, the group split, and each member of the trio began to accomplished solo work. Pras's hit "Ghetto Superstar (That Is What You Are)" earned him producer credits. Lauryn Hill's debut solo project, *The Miseducation of Lauryn Hill* (Ruffhouse) in 1998 boosted her worldwide fame, earning her a #1 spot on *Billboard*'s Top 200 chart, selling more than 400,000 units in the first week, and earning five Grammys, then unprecedented for a female artist. Wyclef Jean is lauded as a leading producer/remixer, having worked with Destiny's Child, the Neville Brothers, Celia Cruz, Canibus, Whitney Houston, Michael Jackson, Mick Jagger, Santana, Simply Red, Bond, and a host of others. His work on the 2005 *Hotel Rwanda* (Commotion Records) soundtrack earned a Golden Globe award.

Grandmaster Flash

http://www.grandmasterflash.com/

The creator of the cue system that allowed him to pre-hear records in his headphones before playing them over the loudspeaker, Grandmaster Flash also developed cutting, backspinning, and phasing. Born Joseph Saddler in Barbados, West Indies, on January 1, 1958, he was raised in the Bronx and attended Samuel Gompers Technical School, receiving a degree in electronics. Influenced by DJ Kool Herc and Pete DJ Jones, Saddler spent a year in his 167th Street apartment experimenting with turntables and his extensive record collection. His speed and precision, as well as his development of the Quick Mix (quickly mixing from one break to another in seamless fashion), earned him the name Flash.

Eager to put a group together, Flash invited Cowboy (Keith Wiggins) to join him as his first MC. Shortly thereafter, he added Kidd Creole (Danny Glover), who brought his brother Melle Mel (Melvin Glover). The crew was known first as Grandmaster Flash and the 3 MCs. Flash would soon add Duke Bootree (Ed Fletcher) and Kurtis Blow (Kurtis Walker) to form the Furious Five. These two were soon replaced with Mr. Ness (Eddie Morris, a.k.a. Scorpio) and Rahiem (Guy Williams). This later group launched their debut recording "Super Rappin'" (Enjoy Records, 1979) shortly after the release of Sugar Hill Gang's "Rapper's Delight." Enticed by the quick success of the Sugar Hill Gang, Grandmaster Flash and the Furious Five signed with Sugar Hill Records prior to Flash's historic "Adventures of Grandmaster Flash on the Wheels of Steel," the first hip hop single to use samples, scratching, and a DJ.

The group's greatest success and demise came with the release of the Hip Hop classic "The Message" in 1982. Due to contractual disagreements, all five of the Furious Five were not allowed to rap on one of the first socially, politically, and economically conscious tracks within the history of Hip Hop. Flash, Kid Creole, and Rahiem left Sugar Hill for Elektra, while Melle Mel led the remaining members, Cowboy and Scorpio. The group would eventually reunite in 1987 to settle their differences, but the death of Cowboy in 1989 put an end to any plans for future work as a group. Flash attempted a career as a solo artist but found no success. During the 1990s, he worked for New York's Hot 97 WQHT and WBLS while continuing to DJ parties and jams. Flash continues to be featured in numerous documentaries on Hip Hop, and DJing in particular.

Grandmixer DXT

Born Derek Showard, Grandmixer D.ST is one of the most notable and revered of the second-generation Hip Hop DJs. Influenced by the innovations of DJ Kool Herc, he began DJing in around 1975–1976, taking on the name D.ST because it is short for "Delancy Street," one of his main Manhattan hangouts. One of the accomplished drummer's first crews was called the Baby Herculords, signifying his admiration for Kool Herc. A self-described b-boy who not only DJs but also rhymes and dances on occasion, D.ST was of special interest to legendary DJ Afrika Bambaataa, who invited D.ST to join the Universal Zulu Nation and enter a select cadre of Zulu DJs. During the 1980s, D.ST performed with numerous crews, including Infinity Four MCs, Bill Laswell's Material, and Praxis. In addition, he recorded and performed with Herbie Hancock, producing the influential song "Rockit" from the *Future Shock* album (Columbia, 1983). D.ST was also a part of the first Hip Hop tour to Europe in 1982 along with Bambaataa, RAMMEL-LZEE, PHASE 2, FUTURA, and DONDI.

Known as an expert and advocate of the use of digital recording, effects processors, laptop computers, and software, D.ST also remained well versed and well equipped to accomplish DJing tasks with analog equipment. In fact, D.ST, who during 1989–1990 changed his name to DXT, remains one of the most precise record scratchers and one of the most entertaining showpersons in Hip Hop. DXT's greatest contribution to Hip Hop may be his conceptual approach to DJing, an approach he called playing the "turn fiddle." Raising the turntable above his shoulder and holding it as a fiddle, he approaches performing on the turntable the same way other musicians approach performing on musical instruments, subtly controlling melody, pitch, rhythm,

Grand Mixer DXT speaks at the Hip-Hop Appreciation Week press conference in New York City, 2001. (Reuters/Corbis)

texture, pulse, and other musical nuances. For many of his contemporaries, his televised performance of "Rockit" with Herbie Hancock served as their introduction into the world of DJing and, more specifically, into the realm of turntablism. Many within this same fold consider Grandmixer DXT as a father of turntablism.

Hammer

During the 1990s, MC Hammer was one of the most popular MCs of Hip Hop. He would rise as one of the richest rappers in the world prior to his 1996 declaration of bankruptcy. Born Stanley Kirk Burrell in Oakland, California, on March 30, 1962, he was given the nickname Hammer because of his alleged likeness to Oakland A's legend Henry "Hammerin' Hank" Aaron. Like his hero Aaron, Burrell attempted professional baseball, yet, unsigned, he ventured off into the navy for three years. Upon his return, the former member of the rap group the Holy Ghost Boys entered an agreement with baseball players Mike Davis and Dwayne Murphy, who financed Bustin' Records under the helm of Burrell. Under the name MC Hammer, he released the 1987 album *Feel My Power,* which caught the attention of Capitol Records and landed him an unprecedented $750,000 advance. Capitol re-released *Feel My Power* as *Let's Get It Started* (1988).

The extremely popular album led to endorsement deals with British Knights footwear and Pepsi. His follow-up, *Please Hammer Don't Hurt 'Em* (Capitol, 1990), went multiplatinum, selling more than 17 million units due to the prominence of its lead track, "U Can't Touch This." This single stands as one of the most recognized songs of the decade and introduced many people to rap music and Hip Hop Culture. In 1991, the noted entertainer, heralded for his creative choreography as well as for his unique dress, dropped the "MC" from his name and released *Too Legit to Quit* (Capitol), which sparked VH1 to create an original movie of the artist. The movie quickly rose as the second most popular movie in VH1's history.

At the height of his career, Hammer owned a $12 million estate in Fremont, California, seventeen luxury cars, and a private jet and had a staff of more than 250 employees. He also had his own cartoon, *Hammerman,* and a Mattel Hammerman action figure was made, armed with a ghetto blaster. In 1994, as sales and concerts began to slow, Hammer signed with Suge Knight's Death Row Records, joining a roster of West Coast–based gangsta rappers. His album *The Funky Headhunter* (Giant, 1994) went gold. However, after breaking his leg, and after the brutal murder of his friend and label-mate Tupac Shakur in 1996, Hammer left the label and filed for bankruptcy. The subject of a 1997 VH1 *Behind the Music* show, he resurfaced in the late 1990s as the night pastor of his own service, called "Hammertime," at the Jubilee Christian Center in San Jose, California, under senior pastor Reverend Dick Bernal. In 2003, Hammer served as a celebrity judge on ABC Family's *Dance Fever* and as a house-mate in VH1's reality show *The Surreal Life*.

Hype Williams

Born Harold Williams, "Hype" has single-handedly revolutionized the nature of Hip Hop music video. The former painter attended Andrew Jackson High School of Art and Music in New York. Upon matriculation in 1987, Williams attended Adelphi University in Long Island, where he majored in film production. During the mid-1990s, Williams directed some of the most notable and long-standing contributions to Hip Hop music video.

With his desire to offer artists control over plot and concept and his innovative use of various lenses, unorthodox costumes, make-up, color, and textual contrast, Williams has made great contributions to music video through his approach to directing. Examples include videos such as Busta Rhymes' "Dangerous," "Whoo-Hah Got You All in Check," and "Put Your Hands Where My Eyes Can See"; Missy Elliott's "The Rain"; Will Smith's "Getting' Jiggy Wit It"; and "California Love" featuring Suge Knight and Tupac Shakur. Williams has directed more than 100 music videos, including ones by P. Diddy (Puff Daddy), Nas, Poor Righteous Teachers, Jay-Z, and many other hip hop, R&B, and rock artists.

In 1999, Williams directed his first film, *Belly* (Big Dog Films, 1998), starring DMX, Nas, T-Boz, and Method Man. Williams has also entered the realm of video games, working with Electronic Arts (EA). His work is featured in games such as "NBA Street V3," "Fight Night 2," and "The Urbz: Sims in the City." His awards include Billboard Music Video Awards, MTV Video Music Awards, and the People's Choice Favorite International Artist Award from the Music Video Awards in Canada.

Invisibl Skratch Piklz

http://www.asphodel.com/bio/invisblskratchp_.html

The Invisibl Skratch Piklz, a seminal DJ crew known for promoting and exposing the world to turntablism, grew out of a group that formed earlier and went through several name changes. The name Invisibl Skratch Piklz came into use in 1995. The initial group, formed in 1990 and called Shadow of the Prophet, included Oakland/San Francisco Bay Area DJs Q-Bert (Richard Quitevis), Mix Master Mike (Michael Schwartz), and Apollo (Apollo Novicio). They later were deemed the "Rock Steady DJs" by Rock Steady Crew's member Crazy Legs. Under that name, they won both the U.S. and World Championships of the Technics Disco Mixing Club (DMC) Competitions in 1992. The group's other names prior to Invisibl Skratch Piklz were FM20, Dirt-Style Productions, and Tern Tabel Dragunz. In 1995, Mix Master Mike and DJ Disk (Lou Quintanilla) conceived the name Invisibl Skratch Piklz, although DJ Disk soon left to pursue other goals.

Mix Master Mike, DJ Q-Bert, and DJ Shortkut (Jonathan Cruz) set out on a mission to perform "turntable jahz." Acknowledging the turntable as a musical instrument, the crew of distinguished DJs elevated practices such as scratching, cutting, beat juggling, and other effects. As a turntable orchestra, the group won so many national and international competitions that they were banned from further participation.

The crew later included DJ D-Styles (Dave Cuasito) and DJ Yoga Frog (Ritchie Desuasido), who handled most of the business affairs for Invisibl Skratch Piklz, Inc. The company was established in 1997 to oversee the various initiatives of the group, such as lecture tours around the world, scratch music tutorials, the annual Skratchcon convention, and the recording of *The Invisibl Skratch Piklz Vs. the Clams of Death* on the Asphodel label. In 1998, both DJ Q-Bert and Mix Master Mike were inducted into the DMC DJ Hall of Fame. Among their innovative projects was the graffiti-oriented animation film, *Wave Twisters: The Movie* (Image Entertainment, 2003). The crew officially disbanded in 2000, promising to return under a different name.

Jay-Z

http://www.jayzonline.com/
Born Shawn Corey Carter in the Marcy Projects of Brooklyn on December 4, 1970, by the early 1990s the street hustler known formerly as "Jazzy" would soon be the highest officer of one of the record labels that spread Hip Hop worldwide. The esteemed Hip Hop mogul began as a quick-witted, skilled, freestylin' MC running with Jaz-O and later the group Original Flavor before launching his own label, Roc-A-Fella Records, along with Damon Dash and Kareem "Biggs" Burke. His 1996 debut *Reasonable Doubt,* launched after he negotiated a distribution deal with Priority Records, portrayed the talented artist as a gangsta rapper; however, his second album, *In My Lifetime, Vol. 1,* released in 1997, moved away from the gangsta image toward a more commercially appealing, nonthreatening sound that matched his hot tracks, memorable verses, and catchy hooks.

His shift away from the hard-core gangsta style certainly gained critiques by other artists with whom he engaged in battles, including Nas in a popular series. However, by 2001 Jay-Z was not only a top-ranked artist but had made his Roc-A-Fella Records a house of hits. The label was a Hip Hop empire boasting a slew of talented artists and producers, including Beanie Sigel, Cam'Ron, M.O.P., Memphis Bleek, Just Blaze, and Kanye West. With the assistance of a loyal MTV crowd, his street credibility, and his string of albums, Jay-Z rose as a popular-culture icon and an extremely influential businessman. Besides the record label, his Roc-A-Fella empire eventually included Roca Wear clothing line, Roc-A-Fella Films (which released big-budget Hollywood films, including *State Property*), Armandale Vodka, and the 40/40 Club (an exclusive sports bar in New York City). He also endorsed the S. Carter line of footwear through Reebok as the first nonathlete to have a signature shoe.

Jay-Z is also a humanitarian with a passion for underprivileged youth, particularly those in situations similar to the one he experienced as a youth. He gives an enormous amount of money annually through Team Roc, the Shawn Carter Scholarship Fund, and his annual Jay-Z Santa Claus Toy Drive. In 2004, Jay-Z became a part owner of the New Jersey Nets, and on January 3, 2005, he was announced as the president and CEO of Def Jam Records. His Roc-A-Fella label will remain as an imprint of Def Jam.

Sean "P. Diddy" Combs (L) and Jay-Z at the Roca-Wear fashion show, New York, 2002. (Steve Azzara/Corbis Sygma)

Karl Kani

http://www.karlkani.com/

Carl Williams was born in the Flatbush section of Brooklyn. His interest in fashion design from an early age led him to leave New York in 1988 for Los Angeles. Although he opened his own clothing shop soon after his arrival, it was his 1991 partnership with Carl Jones under the business name of Threads 4 Life (Cross Colours) that enabled him to make a name for himself. He was a lead designer for the Cross Colour brand, which became highly regarded within Hip Hop, particularly after the firm obtained commercial endorsements by groups such as Kriss Kross. The line became widely available in department stores. Yet mismanagement and internal conflict caused a decline in 1993.

In November of that year, Williams launched Karl Kani Infinity with $500,000. Focused on his trademark style of baggy jeans, oversized casual wear, and urban fashion for men and women, Kani earned $34 million in revenues in his first year and $60 million in his second, after expanding his merchandise to England, Germany, and Australia. Kani has since added Kani Footwear, a Big & Tall line, and a Men's Couture line. He has expanded distribution to Turkey, the Philippines, Belgium, France, Japan, Switzerland, China, and other countries. Although Kani's business suffered greatly in 1999 owing to the rising popularity of counterfeit Kani wear, his business savvy and ability to secure distribution in numerous department and retail stores moved the company further up the ladder of success. In 2001, Williams launched the Kani Life record label. He developed a new clothing line, Life Line, in March 2003, in partnership with Baby (a.k.a. Birdman) of Cash Money Millionaires.

Kool Herc

Born Clive Campbell in Kingston, Jamaica, Kool Herc would rise as the first Hip Hop DJ and father of Hip Hop, merging Jamaican DJ setups with the sounds of the U.S. inner city. He migrated to the United States in 1967 as a young adolescent and lived in the Bronx. While attending Alfred E. Smith High School, Campbell was nicknamed "Hercules" for his tall frame, broad stature, and superior athleticism. He learned to dance and write graffiti and eventually joined the famed Ex-Vandals crew using the tag "Kool

Herc." Avoiding the peer pressure of gangs, Herc turned to his passion for music and his love for records. He began DJing, and by 1971 he was a popular house-party DJ. With his understanding of the importance of dance, Herc developed a way to extend the breakdown section on popular records. Using two of the same record, he would create a manual loop by catching the end of one section with the beginning of the same section on a duplicate record. The result was known as the break beat. The technique was popular, and Kool Herc became one of the most heralded DJs around, particularly for dancers.

During 1973 the crowd at his parties grew too large for the confined space of an apartment, so Kool Herc began to throw large jams in other locations. The first was at 1520 Sedgwick Avenue in a recreation room. From there he played at the Twilight Zone, at Hevalo, and at Sparkle. By this time, Herc had added Coke La Rock (a.k.a. A-1 Coke and Nasty Coke), and later he added Timmy Tim and the original Clark Kent to form his crew the Herculords. Herc's parties brought together b-boys/b-girls, graffiti artists, and fans of the music. He rarely made a profit from the jams but used the money he did make to purchase more equipment to expand his enormous and unparalleled sound system, drawing direct influence from the Jamaican sound systems of his youth. Besides uniting the graffiti artist and the DJ to formulate the early stages of Hip Hop Culture, he is also responsible (according to many) for coining the term "b-boy," a dancer who uses the break beat as inspiration for uniquely creative moves.

While playing at the Executive Playhouse in 1977, Kool Herc was stabbed, and the injury removed him from the limelight for many years. In the 2000s, as numerous celebrations and acknowledgments of Hip Hop's thirty-plus years took place, Kool Herc resurfaced and received wide international recognition for his early developments. In 2005, along with pioneers Afrika Bambaataa, Grandmaster Caz, Melle Mel, Chief Rocker Busy Bee, Sha-Rock, and Ray Riccio, he launched the Sedgwick & Cedar clothing line, acknowledging the place where it all began.

KRS-One

http://www.krs-one.com/
Formerly known as "the Blastmaster" and "the teacher," KRS-One remains one of Hip Hop's most influential artists of all time. Born Lawrence Krisna Parker in the Bronx on August 20, 1965, he left

home at fourteen to travel the streets of New York as a homeless youth, frequenting local group homes and men's shelters. In 1984, under the guidance of ZORE from the Bronx-based Down to Bomb crew, Parker began writing graffiti, first tagging as KRS and then as KRS-One (Knowledge Reigns Supreme Over Nearly Everyone). In 1985, KRS met and befriended Scott Sterling, a social worker and local DJ/producer affiliated with the club Broadway International. The two formed the group Boogie Down Productions and released the classic Hip Hop album *Criminal Minded* (Sugar Hill, 1987).

KRS-One's MC style was very political and in-your-face, and it was often criticized as preachy. While the album rose on the charts, Sterling (DJ Scott LaRock) was murdered. KRS-One recruited his brother, Kenny Parker, to take over as DJ and released *By Any Means Necessary* (Jive, 1988), dramatically changing his style from the hard-core gangsta persona to a hard-core conscious persona frequently name-checking his slain partner. Constantly alluding to the political, social, and economic woes of the United States, KRS-One set a tone that has been followed by later generations of MCs. Following the death of a young fan in a fight after a BDP/Public Enemy concert, KRS-One was influenced by Tokyo Rose (Ann Carli) of Jive Records to launch the "Stop the Violence Movement."

With the help of journalist Nelson George, KRS-One gathered a slew of popular artists to record "Self-Destruction," a track that would raise more than $600,000 for the National Urban League. During the 1990s, KRS-One moved further away from the idea of gangsta rap music, instead advocating for the acceptance of Hip Hop as a legitimate Kulture. In 1991, KRS-One and Professor Z (Zizwe Mtafuta Ukweli) formed Human Education Against Lies (HEAL), again calling for Hip Hop stars to collaborate on a recording to raise money and bring awareness to social consciousness regarding inclusive history. A recording entitled "Civilization vs. Technology," was never released. In the following year, KRS-One became a tremendously popular lecturer on the university circuit, offering his advice on health, love, awareness, wealth, and "Hiphop Kulture."

KRS-One moved to Los Angeles in 1998 and accepted a position as vice president of A&R at Reprise/Warner Records, where he signed DJ Kool Herc, Kool Moe Dee, and numerous other pioneers and legends while also launching the Temple of Hiphop. However, in 2000 KRS-One left Los Angeles and Reprise/Warner to commit to the preservation, promulgation, and presentation of Hiphop Kulture through the Temple of Hiphop. During the fourth annual Hiphop Appreciation Week in May 2001, KRS-One introduced the Hiphop Declaration of Peace at the United Nations Headquarters in New York City (May 16). The author of two books, *The Science of Rap* (1996) and *Ruminations* (Welcome Rain Publishers, 2003), KRS-One has also received numerous humanitarian awards and remains a living legend of Hip Hop. The title of his 1990 album, *Edutainment,* has become a part of the vocabulary even in non–Hip Hop circles.

Kurtis Blow

The first superstar of Hip Hop, Kurtis Blow was born Kurtis Walker on August 9, 1959, in Harlem. The b-boy-turned-DJ (as Kool DJ Kurt) earned early recognition operating the turntables at outdoor block parties and as a club DJ at Smalls Paradise and Disco Fever, yet it was at City College of New York, where he met fellow student Russell Simmons and changed his name to Kurtis Blow, where he became an MC managed by Simmons. During the 1977–1978 year, Blow did local Harlem and Bronx shows. In 1979, he recorded the hit "Christmas Rappin'," cowritten by journalist Robert "Rocky" Ford and financier and cowriter J. B. Moore at Simmons's request. The record made the Top 10 R&B chart in 1980 but was overshadowed by the success of Sugar Hill Gang's "Rappers Delight." Kurtis Blow nevertheless became the first rapper to sign a major record contract (Mercury) and subsequently became the first prominent solo act.

Singles such as "The Breaks," "Hard Times" (the first recorded socially conscious Hip Hop anthem), and "If I Ruled the World" solidified Blow as a household name. His appearance in *Krush Groove* (Crystalite Productions, 1985) and his productions for the Fat Boys, Fearless Four, Dr. Jeckyll and Mr. Hyde, Sweet G., Luv Bug Starski, and others further solidified his contribution to rap music and Hip Hop Culture. The first rapper to have a certified gold record ("The Breaks," 1979), the first solo rapper to sign an endorsement deal (Sprite, 1985), the first MC to perform on *Soul Train,* and perhaps the first rap producer to compose music for a major network soap opera (*One Life To Live,* early 1990s), Kurtis Blow has done it all, leading to his recognition as one of the early innovators of Hip Hop.

LL Cool J

http://www.defjam.com/llcoolj/home.las

Known by the moniker "Ladies Love Cool James," LL Cool J has risen over the years as one of Hip Hop's most successful artists. Born James Todd Smith in the St. Albans section of Queens on January 14, 1968, he began rapping at age nine when his grandfather bought him some DJ equipment with which to begin making mix tapes. The young artist caught the attention of Russell Simmons and Rick Rubin, both college students and cofounders of the fledgling Def Jam Records. LL would soon drop out of school to be Simmons and Rubin's first act in 1984. His first single, "I Need a Beat," sold more than 100,000 copies with his debut album *I Can't Live Without My Radio* (Def Jam, 1985), achieving platinum status, as would his next five releases. He was the first rap artist to have six consecutive platinum albums and another six gold albums.

LL's b-boy style made him very popular with the ladies, and his machismo appeal and hard-core braggadocio lyrics made him popular with the men, enabling him to quickly achieve superstar status. His classic battles with Kool Moe Dee and Canibus, and his song "I Need Love," Hip Hop's first ballad, also contributed to his popularity. During the 1990s, the artist added actor to his list of accomplishments, starring in the UPN sitcom *In the House* (1996–1998, after one season on NBC). He has been featured in more than fifteen films, including: *Krush Groove* (Crystalite Productions, 1985), *Any Given Sunday* (Ixtlan Corporation, 1999), *Kingdom Come* (Fox Searchlight Pictures, 2001), and *S.W.A.T.* (Camelot Pictures, 2003). The multi-award-winning artist also served as the first MC to appear on *Saturday Night Live* as well as the first MC profiled in *Ebony* magazine (1988). He has served as a spokesperson for Major League Baseball, Coca-Cola, FUBU, and Gap. The author of *I Make My Own Rules* (St. Martin's Press/Ilion Books, 1997), he is also the founder of the Camp Cool J Foundation, a nonprofit organization providing educational, cultural, and recreational programs for youth as well as free camping events.

Marley Marl

Marley Marl was one of Hip Hop's first major producers and an early innovator of sampling, beats, and strong hooks. Born Marlon Williams on September 30, 1962, Marl was raised in the

Queensbridge housing project in Queens. After meeting Bronx-based DJ Breakout while in high school, Marl formed the Sureshot Crew and subsequently rose as a talented DJ and producer. With proceeds from "Sucka DJs," Marl's first recorded response to Run-DMC's "Sucker MCs," Marl bought a Roland 808 drum machine and some other equipment and set up his studio in his sister's apartment, naming it the "House of Hits."

Marl eventually moved away from the drum machine in exchange for his innovative technique of sampling drum sounds and creating patterns and loops. He soon assembled a collective of talented artists who would soon be leading figures in Hip Hop, the first collective of its kind. It included MC Shan (Marl's cousin), Big Daddy Kane (Antonio Hardy), Biz Markie (Marcell Hall), and Roxanne Shanté (Lolita Shante Gooden) as the Juice Crew. Later additions included Kool G. Rap and DJ Polo, Masta Ace (Duval Clear), Craig G., and Tragedy. A first big break for the crew was Roxanne Shanté's 1984 hit "Roxanne's Revenge," a response to U.T.F.O.'s "Roxanne Roxanne." The next big hit came with the unofficial Queens Anthem, "The Bridge," by MC Shan, which spurred an ongoing battle with Bronx-based KRS-One. During his rise Marl also worked with non–Juice Crew members such as radio personality Mr. Magic, Eric B. and Rakim, Heavy D and the Boyz, LL Cool J, TLC, King Tee, Capone-N-Noreaga, Fat Joe, MC Lyte, Monie Love, Tha Alkaholiks, and numerous others.

The Juice Crew is best known for one of the best collective recordings in Hip Hop, "The Symphony," a track released on the collective's 1988 album *In Control, Vol. 1*, on the Cold Chillin' label, where Marl would spend some years as the in-house producer. After years of success with Cold Chillin', he went through a host of court bouts with the label. The relationship was severed, and in 1998 Marl surfaced victorious. Throughout these legal troubles he maintained a vibrant presence on New York City local urban radio.

Master P

http://www.thenewnolimit.com/

Born Percy Romeo Miller on April 29, 1970, in the Calliope projects of the third ward of New Orleans, Louisiana, Master P epitomizes the Hip Hop rags-to-riches dream. After the divorce of his parents, Miller lived between New Orleans and Richmond, California. A star athlete, he went to the University of Houston on a basketball scholarship before injuring his knee and returning to California, where he completed an associate degree in business at Oakland's Merritt College. Equipped with this degree and $10,000 (sources dispute whether the sum of money was from a court settlement or an inheritance), Miller opened a record shop in the late 1980s in Richmond. Sparked by the heavy demand for rap music, Miller launched the No Limit record label, which shared the same name as his record store, in 1990. Becoming known primarily through word of mouth, Miller, now nicknamed Master P, sold over a million copies of his own releases prior to striking a distribution deal with Priority Records in 1995.

Master P understood how to record and distribute music with a limited budget, and he returned to New Orleans to create a Hip Hop empire, using the momentum of the rising genre of gangsta rap to make his mark. With his production team, which included Craig B. as well as KLC and Mo. B. Dick, known as Beats by the Pound, Master P recruited two of his brothers, Silkk the Shocker (Vyshonn Miller) and C-Murder (Corey Miller), to form the trio TRU. They released *Tru 2 Da Game* in 1997. In the same year, Master P made history by becoming the first artist to release a full-length, straight-to-DVD film along with an album. Known for promoting future endeavors with advertisements in the CD jackets of present releases, Master P continued to push the envelope as he moved into writing, directing, and producing his own films. By 1997, without the aid of radio or MTV, Master P had established a Hip Hop empire.

Never afraid to take a risk, Master P then returned to his passion for basketball, trying out with the Charlotte Hornets in 1997 and with the Toronto Raptors in 1998. Although he did not make either NBA roster, he did play for the Continental Basketball Association (CBA), the American Basketball Association (ABA), and the International Basketball League (IBL). Meanwhile, he was named to *Fortune* magazine's list of "America's 40 Richest Under 40," ranking number 28. He is the founder and CEO of No Limit Clothing, P. Miller Clothing and Footwear, No Limit Films, No Limit Toys, P. M. Properties, No Limit Sports Management, and Advantage Travel and also created Platinum Barbecue potato chips and the Master Piece line of watches. Always willing to redefine himself and expand, Miller moved distribution from Priority to Universal Music in 2001 and helped his son Percy Romeo Miller, Jr., known as Lil' Romeo, to establish himself as a talented, multiplatinum MC. Lil' Romeo also starred as an actor on his own Nickelodeon show, *Romeo!*, launched in September 2003. Master P, the mogul whose empire's worth exceeded $400 million in 2001, has been listed in the *Guinness Book of World Records* as the highest paid entertainer in the Hip Hop industry.

Missy Elliott

http://www.missy-elliott.com/

One of the most notable and influential MCs of the late 1990s and early 2000s, Missy "Misdemeanor" Elliott's writing, production, and MCing talents have led to changes in attitudes concerning the presence of women in Hip Hop. Challenging the hyper-sexual representations of women by Lil' Kim, Foxy Brown, and Trina, but not falling into the consciousness camp of Lauryn Hill and Erykah Badu either, Elliott established herself as a Hip Hop artist who could play as hard as the men and thrive. Born Melissa Arnette Elliott on July 1, 1971, in Portsmouth, Virginia, Elliott had an early passion for music. During high school she was part of a group called Sista that signed a contract with the DeVante Swing' label (of the R&B group Jodeci). Yet the label did not pan out and the group's work was never released. Elliott continued writing songs, singing back-up, and rapping, then signed with Elektra in 1996.

Her debut multi-award-winning, platinum album *Supa Dupa Fly* (Goldmind/Elektra, 1997) immediately made Missy a popular-culture icon. Her unique creativity and exceptional music videos, in particular "The Rain," have inspired new trends in hip hop music videos. Over the years, Elliott has written for, produced, and/or worked with stars in numerous genres, including Aaliyah, Whitney Houston, Janet Jackson, Destiny's Child, and Justin Timberlake. She also has humanitarian goals and in 2003 was named spokesperson for Break the Cycle, an organization aiming to help young people stop the chain of domestic abuse. In 2005, she launched her own talent variety show on UPN, *The Road to Stardom with Missy Elliott*.

Nation of Graffiti Artists (NOGA)

Influenced by the work of the United Graffiti Artists (UGA), Jack Pelsinger, a theater director, founded the Nation of Graffiti Artists (NOGA) in 1974. Aimed at achieving a more inclusive and less selective ensemble of artists than UGA, NOGA served as a strong platform for local graffiti artists inspired to see their artwork not only on trains, walls, and public edifices but also on canvas and in galleries. Taking over where UGA left off, NOGA helped to solidify graffiti as a commercial endeavor. In this endeavor, the organization offered to paint Metropolitan Transportation Authority (MTA) trains in New York City for $150 per car as a fund-raiser for the organization. The MTA refused, instead spending in excess of $1,500 per car to prevent them from being painted. NOGA, like UGA, diffused into the underground during the late 1970s.

Native Tongues

During the late 1980s and early 1990s, a group of like-minded, socially conscious artists combined to form a collective built on the promotion of Afrocentric, positive, thought-provoking music that would not sacrifice its realness or edge yet would not play into the negative media-based portrayal of young people of color. Called the Native Tongues, the collective members agreed to perform with and promote each other's work to allow for optimal exposure.

Originally composed of the Jungle Brothers (Mike Gee [Michael Small]), DJ Sammy B [Sammy Burwell], Baby Bam [Nathaniel Hall]), Queen Latifah (Dana Owens), and Universal Zulu Nation founder and leader Afrika Bambaataa, the collective was soon joined by De La Soul (Posdnous [Kevin Mercer], Trugoy the Dove [David Jude Jolicoeus], and Pasemaster Mase [Vincent Mason]), DJ/rapper/producer Prince Paul (Paul Huston), and Tribe Called Quest (Q-Tip [Jonathan Davis], Phife [Malik Taylor], and DJ Ali Shaheed Muhammed). The release of De La Soul's "Buddy" and the Jungle Brothers' "Doin' Our Own Dang" exemplified the spirit of the collective.

As the 1990s progressed, a new generation joined the collective. Black Sheep (Dres and Mista Lawnge), as well as Common (Lonnie Rashied Lynn, formerly known as Common Sense), Black Star (Mos Def [Dante Smith], Talib Kweli, and DJ Hi-Tek), Da Bush Babees (Babe-Face Kaos, Y-Tee, and Mister Man), and Leaders of the New School (MC Charlie Brown, MC Dinco D, MC Busta Rhymes, and Cut Monitor Milo), added to the enormously popular collective. Groups Gang Starr and Brand Nubian were collaborators but not officially affiliated with the collective. By the 1990s, the individual groups were so popular that the collective was no longer needed for exposure and it dissolved.

New York City Breakers

Many New York City Breakers members were already a part of the Floormasters crew when Hip Hop club promoter and artist Michael Holman assembled a group of top dancers under the new name. The group, a noted rival to Rock Steady Crew, performed in the televised pilot of Holman's show *Graffiti Rock,* the first Hip Hop dance show (along with Don Cornelius's popular dance show *Soul Train*). The same year, 1984, the NYC Breakers battled Rock Steady Crew in the classic Hip Hop movie *Beat Street* (MGM Home Entertainment, 1984), a movie that introduced many new fans around the country and around the world not only to Hip Hop but also to Hip Hop dance.

The crew originally consisted of Kid Nice (Noel Mangual), Mr. Wave (Tony Draughon), Action (Chino Lopez), Lil Lep (Ray Ramos), Glide Master (Matthew Caban), Icey Ice (Corey Montalvo), Powerful Pexster (Tony Lopez), and Flip Rock (Bobby Potts). The group has grown since its inception, but not before performing at the 1984 Summer Olympics opening ceremony in Los Angeles, at CBS's Kennedy Center Honors TV Extravaganza, and at President Ronald Reagan's second inaugural celebration—the latter two upon the request of fan Frank Sinatra. In addition to an appearance on Gladys Knight & the Pips' "Save the Overtime for Me" video (*Visions*, Columbia, 1983), the New York City Breakers have performed with KRS-One, Dr. Dre, Doug E. Fresh, DJ Hollywood, Cold Crush, Furious Five, MC Shan, and others.

Notorious B.I.G.

www.notoriousonline.com/

From the names Biggie Smalls, to Biggie, to Big Poppa, to Frank White, Notorious B.I.G. is often characterized as one of the most influential voices of Hip Hop. Born Christopher G. L. Wallace on May 21, 1972, in Brooklyn, the popular-culture icon turned to street hustling in his Bedford-Stuyvesant (Bed-Stuy) neighborhood. As an early member of the OGB (Odd Gold Brothers) crew and the Techniques, B.I.G.'s big chance came when a tape of him rapping landed in the hands of DJ Mister Cee, famed DJ for Big Daddy Kane. Mister Cee quickly sent the tape to *Source* magazine for review in the "Unsigned Hype" column, landing B.I.G. an invitation to rap on a compilation of top "Unsigned Hype" winners.

Legendary wordsmith, Notorious B.I.G. clutches Billboard Music Awards during the 1995 awards show held in New York City on December 6, 2005. (Lorenzo Ciniglio/Corbis Sygma)

His successful track led to a contract with Uptown Records and eventually Bad Boy Entertainment under the influence of P. Diddy.

B.I.G.'s debut album, *Ready to Die* (Bad Boy Records, 1994), earned multiplatinum status, but it was his next album, *Life after Death* (Bad Boy Records, 1997), that sold more than 700,000 units in the first week and eventually earned diamond status (over ten times the amount needed for platinum). It was largely because of this album that hard-core gangsta rap gained prominence in New York City following the influence of West Coast artists such as NWA, Ice Cube, and Dr. Dre.

The multi-award-winning MC was highly criticized for his lyrics, which were often challenged as sexist, misogynistic, and full of graphic, violent imagery depicting crime and sometimes death. Yet, in spite of these charges, B.I.G. was considered by many the Mayor of Bed-Stuy. He is most famous, however, for his widely publicized feud with Tupac, which drew media attention to an alleged East Coast versus West Coast war. B.I.G. was murdered on March 9, 1997, in Los Angeles eight months after the murder of Tupac. May 14 has been delegated Notorious B.I.G. Day and is widely celebrated on urban radio nationwide.

NWA

http://www.nwaworld.com/

Known for their explicit, violent, misogynistic, and often graphic lyrics, NWA (Niggaz With Attitude) stands as one of the most popular groups of the mid- to late 1980s, capturing a national audience encompassing both inner-city and suburban youth. Formed in Compton, California, in 1986 by Easy-E (Eric Wright), a former drug dealer, the group helped to pioneer gangsta rap, offering a hard-edged look at life in the inner city from the perspective of those who lived there. Wright solicited DJ/producer Dr. Dre (Andre Young) and DJ Yella (Antoine Carraby) to leave the group that they had founded, World Class Wrecking Crew, to join NWA. Wright also invited Ice Cube (O'Shea Jackson) and Arabian Prince (Mik Lezan). Simultaneously, he founded Ruthless Records as a mechanism for the dissemination of their records and gangsta rap records by others.

The group's 1987 debut, *N.W.A. and the Posse,* was largely ignored, but their next album, *Straight Outta Compton* (Priority, 1988), which included MC Ren (Lorenzo Patterson), would rise to legendary status in Hip Hop history. Boasting of the Southern California gang scene, violence, and drugs, the album and its headlining singles, "Gangsta Gangsta" and "Dopeman," received critical reviews by media and numerous adversarial groups. But it was the single "F—k the Police" that caused the Federal Bureau of Investigation (FBI) to investigate the group. The song nevertheless became an anthem drawing attention to police brutality, racial profiling, and disorderly conduct cases involving bad cops nationwide.

In 1989, Ice Cube left the group as a result of internal conflict. He launched a highly successful solo career as an MC, actor, and producer/director. His Cube Vision has conducted successful motion picture projects, such as the *Friday* series, *Barbershop I* and *II,* and the *Beauty Shop* offshoot. In 1992, Dr. Dre left, also because of internal conflict, and started Death Row Records along with Suge Knight. Dr. Dre has had a tremendously successful career as a solo artist and producer, launching the careers of Snoop Dogg, Eminem, 50 Cent, the Game, and others. NWA disbanded after his departure. Wright found success in a Cleveland group, Bone Thugs-n-Harmony, with whom he signed in 1995 following a rather unsuccessful outing as a solo artist. Wright died in March 1995 after complications from AIDS.

P. Diddy

http://badboyonline.com/

Born Sean Combs on November 4, 1969, in Harlem, P. Diddy, a talented artist and brilliant entrepreneur, has quickly risen as one of the most noted and prominent popular-culture icons of the late twentieth and early twenty-first century. The graduate of Mount St. Michael's Academy in the Bronx attended Howard University for two years as a business management major prior to accepting an internship in New York City at MCA affiliate Uptown Records. Within a year, Combs rose to vice president of talent and marketing, influencing the success of Mary J. Blige, Jodeci, Father MC, and Heavy D & the Boyz, and he signed Notorious B.I.G. to the label. After undertaking a number of risky experiments, Combs was fired. However, the entrepreneur went on to guide a $15 million distribution deal with Artista to found Bad Boy, where he quickly signed Notorious B.I.G. (who was also let go), Craig Mack, and a host of successful and prominent artists. The launch of Bad Boy Entertainment in 1993 gave rise to what by 2003 would be called Bad Boy Worldwide Entertainment Group, boasting almost $300 million in sales annually and 609 employees.

Under the umbrella is Notorious Entertainment, Sean John clothing, Justin Combs Music Publishing, Bad Boy Marketing, Bad Boy Productions, Daddy's House Studios, Daddy's House Social Programs, Bad Boy Technologies, Bad Boy Films, and Bad Boy Books. The famed CEO is also the owner of two Justin's Caribbean and Soul Food restaurants, which are located in Manhattan and Atlanta. Among numerous awards, he won the prestigious ASCAP (American Society of Composers, Authors, and Publishers) Songwriter of the Year prize in 1996. In 2002, P. Diddy, formerly known as Puff Daddy and Puffy, was nominated for an Oscar Award for his performance in the Broadway staging of *A Raisin in the Sun*. He also completed the New York City Marathon that year, earning $2 million for New York City public schools. Through all of his troubles with the law and numerous risky business decisions, P. Diddy has enjoyed unprecedented success in music, publishing, fashion, television, film, and numerous other ventures.

Public Enemy

www.publicenemy.com/

Perceived by some as a controversial and abrasive group, but admired by others as an empowering and needed voice in Hip Hop, Public Enemy stood as one of the most popular and prominent groups in Hip Hop during the 1980s. Led by Chuck D (Carlton Douglas Ridenhour, born August 1, 1960), a graphic arts student and campus radio station DJ at Adelphi University in Long Island, the group countered the rising gangsta rap groups by addressing race, injustice, inequality, and a slew of socially, politically, and economically oriented subjects.

While at Adelphi, Ridenhour met and befriended Hank Shocklee and Bill Stephany. They recorded a few demos and sent them to producer Rick Rubin, and Rubin signed Ridenhour as Chuck D to the Def Jam label. Rubin also brought on Shocklee as a producer, and Stephany as a publicist. Chuck D soon recruited DJ Terminator X (Norman Lee Rogers), Professor Griff (Richard Griff, a.k.a. Minister of Information), and Flavor Flav (William Drayton) to form Public Enemy. Chuck D also recruited four dancers/security persons under the name Security of the First World (S1Ws). Although the group's first album received critical praise, it flopped on the charts. Their second album, *It Takes Millions to Hold Us Back* (Def Jam, 1988), would prove revolutionary, however, due to Chuck D's political message, Flavor Flav's comical yet critical antics, and the phenomenal production of the Bomb Squad (Hank Shocklee, Keith Shocklee, and Vietnam [Eric Saddler]).

Public Enemy has long been the subject of controversial debate. Some have criticized the group's many positive endorsements of Nation of Islam minister Louis Farrakhan, and some have had concerns about the possibly anti-Semitic lyrics by Chuck D and the clearly anti-Semitic comments by Professor Griff. During the early 1980s, the group took a hiatus as Flavor Flav dealt with his troubles with the law.

In 1996, Chuck D accomplished a solo album, *Autobiography of Mistachuck* (Mercury). He was most active during this period as a widely-sought-after media pundit and lecturer, speaking to more than 500 colleges, high schools, and prisons, and as a community activist. In 1997, Chuck D authored the national bestseller *Fight the Power: Rap, Race and Reality* with Yusuf Jah (Delta). The group reunited in 1998 but left the Def Jam label, instead becoming the first mainstream group to sign with an Internet-based record label, Atomic Pop. Public Enemy's best-known single may be the Hip Hop anthem "Fight the Power" from Spike Lee's *Do the Right Thing* (40 Acres & a Mule Filmworks, 1989).

Queen Latifah

http://www.queenlatifah.com/

Known as the "First Lady" of Hip Hop, Queen Latifah has created a path unparalleled and perhaps unmatched by any other MC, whether female or male. Born Dana Elaine Owens on March 18, 1970, in Newark, New Jersey, she was given the nickname "Latifah" by a cousin at age eight. The Arabic word, meaning "sensitive" or "delicate," stuck. As a young girl, Owens clearly displayed a talent for singing and acting and participated in school productions. She also played basketball at Irvington High School. Yet it was her group Ladies Fresh in which she served as a human beat box that launched her career in entertainment.

While attending the Borough of Manhattan Community College, Latifah joined the Native Tongues Collective, the organization spearheaded by Afrika Bambaataa to bring a more Afrocentric consciousness to Hip Hop and help independent artists get their start. Latifah recorded a demo, it was released, and she was signed to Tommy Boy Records in 1988. The next year, her debut, *All Hail the Queen* (Tommy Boy, 1989), landed with the classic hit "Ladies First," a song that would later be selected by the Rock 'n' Roll Hall of Fame as one of the 500 songs that shaped rock 'n' roll. Her song "U.N.I.T.Y." would continue to communicate her unique social and moral stance by addressing sexism, misogyny, and other issues presented by gender-based discrimination. The Grammy Award–winning song, aided the album *Black Reign* (Motown, 1993), achieved recognition as the first gold record by a solo female rap artist.

Latifah, along with business partner Shakim Compere, founded Flavor Unit Entertainment and Management, the company responsible for discovering Naughty by Nature. Unlike many of her peers, her success in music is matched by her success on television and film. In addition to a five-year stint on the television sitcom *Living Single* (1992–1997), she hosted her own daytime talk show, *The Queen Latifah Show,* which ran in syndication from 1999–2001. She has been featured in more than twenty films, including *Jungle Fever* (40 Acres & a Mule Filmworks, 1992), *Set It Off* (New Line Cinema, 1996), *The Bone Collector* (Columbia

"First Lady" of hip hop and Academy Award nominee, Queen Latifah promotes her 2003 movie, Bringing Down the House. *(Steve Sands/New York Newswire/Corbis)*

Pictures Corporation, 1999), and *Beauty Shop* (Cube Vision, 2005). Her appearance in *Chicago* earned her recognition as the first MC to be nominated for an Oscar Award. The MC, actress, author, manager, and business owner has also appeared in commercials for Cover Girl, Courtyard Inn at Marriott, and the Freedom Card

Gold Master Card and serves as a spokesperson for Lane Bryant Clothing store. In addition to winning numerous other awards, Latifah was named one of the "Most Fascinating Women of 1990" by *Ladies Home Journal* and "Entertainer of the Year" for 2003 by *Essence* magazine.

Rakim

http://www.rakim.com/

Known as the "greatest MC to ever rock the mike," Rakim Allah, born William Griffin, Jr., on January 28, 1968, in the Wyandanch section of Long Island, changed the nature of the MC during the golden years of Hip Hop. The former high-school football star and prospective collegiate and professional football recruit turned to music at the suggestion of Eric B. (Eric Barrier), who worked at New York's WBLS radio station as a DJ prior to becoming Rakim's DJ. The two became the most recognized MC/DJ duo of the period and were the undisputed leaders in their specialty. Yet it was Rakim's move away from the prevalent party-calling and simple call-and-response patterns that brought them fame. *Paid in Full* (4th & Broadway, 1987) and *Follow the Leader* (UNI, 1988) quickly established the two as household names in hard-core Hip Hop.

Rakim's ability to rhyme not only at the ends of lines but also within the middle of his lines, while also conveying a message, influenced many of his contemporaries. As a convert to the Five Percent Nation, he developed lyrics that dealt with complex moral and spiritual issues. After he and partner Eric B. released four albums, the two separated over contractual and financial issues, leading to a five-year hiatus by the MC. Rakim returned in 1997 with *The 18th Letter* (Universal), which went platinum. His second solo album, *The Master* (Universal, 1999), had less success.

Rock Steady Crew

http://www.rocksteadycrew.com/

Founded in 1977 by JoJo (Joe Torres) and Jimmy D, this Bronx-based crew has revolutionized the art of street dance and spread the element of b-boying/b-girling across the globe. Rock Steady Crew is a household name among Hip Hop fans worldwide. With more than 100 members in chapters around the world, the crew is known for its process of recruiting and initiating new b-boys and b-girls through "battling." Rock Steady Crew has been featured in numerous movies, including *Flashdance* (PolyGram Filmed Enter-

Members of Rock Steady Crew arrive at the 2005 VH1 Hip Hop Honors held at Hammerstein Ballroom. (AP Photo/Mark Lennihan)

tainment, 1983), *Wild Style* (Wild Style, 1982), *Beat Street* (MGM Home Entertainment, 1984), *Style Wars* (Public Broadcasting Service, 1983), and *The Freshest Kids* (QD3 Entertainment, 2002). The members of literally every other crew judge themselves according to their battles with Rock Steady Crew or their ability to even reach the level of meeting this crew in battle.

The group's main rivals are the Dynamic Rockers and the New York City Breakers. Notable members include Crazy Legs (Richard Colón), who was added in 1979. The crew's longtime president, Crazy Legs is one of the world's most esteemed and recognized b-boys. Also notable are Prince Ken Swift (Kenny Gabbert), Mr. Wiggles (Steve Clemente), Orko (Roger Romero), Baby Love (Daisy Castro), and Frosty Freeze (Wayne Frost). During a 1982 gig with Afrika Bambaataa, the Godfather of Hip Hop invited the crew to join the Universal Zulu Nation, an invitation they accepted with honor. The crew was requested by the Queen of England to perform at a 1983 Artist Benevolent Fundraiser. They were the first b-boys to perform at Carnegie Hall (2001), and they have a park at the corner of 98th and Amsterdam named after them in New York City.

The Roots

http://www.theroots.com/

One of the most popular and highly regarded of all Hip Hop bands, the Roots, founded in 1987, have done more to present Hip Hop as a "live" interaction of versatile and talented artists than any other group in the recent history of the culture. Building on the legacy of Stetsasonic, schoolmates Black Thought (Tariq Trotter) and ?uestlove (Ahmir Khalib Thompson) formed a duo at Philadelphia High School for Creative Performing Arts. Since neither had money to purchase equipment, Thompson, a skilled drummer, played his drum kit, while Trotter rapped over the beats. Under the name Foreign Objects, the two would perform at school, on sidewalks, and in talent shows. As local clubs in Philadelphia and New York City offered openings, the duo expanded to add bassist Hub (Leon Hubbard) and MC Malik B. Upon a 1993 invitation to represent U.S. Hip Hop in Germany, the group changed its name to the Roots and recorded an album, *Organix* (Remedy Records, 1993), in order to have a product to sell.

Later that year, the group was signed to the DGC label, and in 1995 the group released the monumental album *Do You Want More?!!!??!* (DGC), boasting no samples or previously recorded materials, a rarity in the Hip Hop of that day. The album went unnoticed in the Hip Hop world but caught on among various alternative and college audiences. Two guests on the album, Rahzel the Godfather of Noyze (Rahzel M. Brown) and Kamal (Scott Storch), were added to the group. Still, the music was better received among non–Hip Hop audiences than among Hip Hop youth. It was not until their third album, *Things Fall Apart* (MCA, 1999), that their music met with applause in the Hip Hop world. In addition to their musical contributions, the group has a record label, Okay Player, and a Web site, and it hosts the Black Lilly forum, a renowned series of jam sessions based in Philadelphia.

Run-DMC

http://www.rundmcmusic.com/

Known as the most popular and perhaps the first hard-core group of the golden age of Hip Hop, Run-DMC has established an unmatched legacy. The childhood friends from the Hollis section of Queens first assembled under the name Orange Krush. Run (Joseph Simmons, born November 24, 1966), DMC (Darryl Mc-

Hip Hop icons Run-DMC from left to right: Run, DMC, and Jam Master Jay.
(Jonathan Alcorn/ZUMA/Corbis)

Daniels, born May 31, 1964), and Jam Master Jay (Jason Mizell,
born January 21, 1965, died October 30, 2002) would change the
name in 1982 to Run-DMC, and, under the management of Run's
brother, Russell Simmons, and his fledgling Rush Management,
the group would soon establish the new sound of hip hop and
lead the genre to national and international prominence during
the mid- to late 1980s.

Former drummer and guitarist Jam Master Jay reduced the hip
hop sound to a drum machine and his turntable, making the DJ
synonymous with the hip hop band. The group also set the early
look of Hip Hop with their black leather jackets, black jeans, Adidas sneakers, fedoras, and fat gold rope necklaces, giving rise not
only to a look not only for b-boys and b-girls but to urban sportswear in general. Among a long list of "firsts," the group bridged
the musical divide between rock and rap, collaborating with Aerosmith on the 1986 multi-award-winning remake of "Walk This
Way." The song took rap mainstream and introduced a new generation of suburban kids to the sounds of rap. The song was later
added to the Rock 'n' Roll Hall of Fame's "500 Songs that Shaped
Rock 'n' Roll."

The trio were the first nonathletes to endorse Adidas, fueling a multibillion-dollar relationship between Hip Hop and the athletic sportswear industry. Further, the group was the first in Hip Hop to have a music video played on MTV, the first rap group to appear on *American Bandstand* and *Saturday Night Live,* and the first to appear on the cover of *Rolling Stone* and *Spin* magazines. The group served as ambassadors of Hip Hop, becoming the first rap group to earn a gold album with *Run-DMC* (Profile, 1984), the first rap group to earn a platinum album with *King of Rock* (Profile, 1985), and the first rap group to go multiplatinum with *Raising Hell* (Profile, 1986). The group also turned to film and were featured in four movies: *Krush Groove* (Crystalite Productions, 1985), *Tougher Than Leather* (Def Pictures, 1988), *Who's the Man?* (New Line Cinema, 1993), and *The Show* (Rysher Entertainment, 1995). Yet, after the movies, recordings, and awards, and despite an immense amount of recognition as the most important group in the history of Hip Hop, the partnership of more than twenty years came to a halt when Jam Master Jay was murdered in his New York studio on October 30, 2002. His murder brought a close to one of the longest-standing units in Hip Hop and one of the last to prominently feature a DJ as part of the group.

Russell Simmons

http://www.phatfarmstore.com/
Russell Simmons has single-handedly changed the nature of the music business and built the Hip Hop business model. Born in the Hollis section of Queens on October 4, 1957, the former street hustler attended City College of New York (CCNY), Harlem campus, as a sociology major. In 1978, Simmons began promoting block parties and club shows in the Queens and Harlem areas. Around this time, he arranged to serve as manager to fellow CCNY student Kurtis Blow. Simmons successfully launched Blow's career, but it was his partnering with producer Rick Rubin in 1984 that would build Hip Hop's major empire, Def Jam.

The partnership launched the careers of LL Cool J, Run-DMC, Public Enemy, EPMD, Slick Rick, the Beastie Boys, and numerous other talents. In 1985, Simmons produced *Krush Groove,* a film loosely about his life and the rise and success of Def Jam. The movie was popular and launched Def Jam into the film business. In 1988, Rubin sold his portion of the company to Simmons, who was quickly building an empire that would eventually include Def Jam Records, Rush Artist Management, Phat Farm Clothing and

Footwear, Baby Phat, dRush Advertising, Rush Mobile, DefCon–3 energy drink, *One World* magazine, UniRush financial services, Def Comedy Jam (HBO), and Def Poetry Jam (HBO). Under the umbrella of Rush Communications, Simmons is worth hundreds of millions of dollars, up from an estimated $200 million in 2001. In 1999, Simmons sold his final shares of Def Jam to Universal Music for an unprecedented $100 million. Two years later, he established the Hip Hop Summit Action Network, catering to youth and young adults. He has given millions of dollars to various humanitarian and philanthropic funds, including scholarships. His own Rush Philanthropic Arts Foundation was established in 1995. For his profound success and influence, *Business Week* magazine in 2003 labeled Simmons a CEO of Hip Hop.

Salt-n-Pepa

The most notable female group in the history of Hip Hop, during the golden age of Hip Hop Salt-n-Pepa added to the male-dominated expression a pro-feminist touch as well as a renewed sense of fashion. Brooklyn native Salt (Cheryl James, born March 8, 1964) and Kingston, Jamaica, native Pepa (Sandra Denton, born November 9, 1969) met in Queens while working as telephone representatives for Sears. The two aspiring nurses also met Luv Bug (Hurby Azor), a coworker who was also a student of record production at the Center of Media Arts. Azor invited the two to record on one of his projects. His group, the Super Lovers, was recording a response to Doug E. Fresh's "The Show," entitled "Showstopper," at the time. The two remained under Azor's guidance and formally became Salt-n-Pepa, with Azor serving as manager and producer.

The rappers recruited Latoya Hanson to be their DJ. Under the name of DJ Spinderella, she added a female presence behind the turntables, something that was rarely seen at the time. Their debut album, *Hot, Cool & Vicious* (Next Plateau, 1986), with its commercially appealing sound and catchy pop hooks, went platinum, selling over a million copies in the United States and the United Kingdom. During their first year of success, Hanson was replaced by high-school student Deidre Roper (born August 3, 1971), who would continue under the name DJ Spinderella. Over the next ten years, the group maintained a dominant presence in Hip Hop. Along with offering party and love themes, they dealt with taboo topics in songs such as their 1991 single "Let's Talk about Sex" and their 1995 remake "Let's Talk about AIDS."

The only female group to continually present certified platinum albums over a ten-year period, Salt-n-Pepa traded in their microphones for business wear in 2002. Pepa operates a Hip Hop clothing store in Atlanta, Georgia, named "Hollyhood." DJ Spinderella is the proprietor of a salon and day spa in Queens named "She Things." Salt continues in the music industry as a song writer and producer.

Snoop Dogg

http://www.snoopdogg.com/

Snoop Dogg, a West Coast rapper, actor, and businessman, was born Calvin Broadus on October 20, 1972, in Long Beach, California. Nicknamed Snoop by his mother because of his alleged resemblance to Snoopy, the famed Peanuts character, he became a football player in high school but spent three years after graduation in and out of jail on drug charges. The known gangsta turned to music in pursuit of a better life and eventually became a multiplatinum-selling artist.

Snoop Dogg teamed up with Warren G (Warren Griffin III), the stepbrother of Dr. Dre (Andre Young), who helped him to become a popular-culture icon. After an appearance with Dr. Dre on the *Deep Cover* (Solar, 1992) soundtrack, Snoop went on to a feature role on Dr. Dre's 1992 *The Chronic* (Death Row). Under the name Snoop Doggy Dogg, Snoop released his debut album, *Doggystyle* (Death Row), in 1993. The album quickly went multiplatinum, adding to the popularity of the gangster rap subgenre. In the mid-1990s, however, Snoop was plagued by legal challenges as he was put on trial for the murder of a gang member. Snoop was acquitted in 1996 and used the momentum to launch a number of business ventures.

A new recording contract in 1998 moved Snoop from Suge Knight's Death Row Records to Hip Hop mogul Master P's New Orleans–based No Limit Records. In 2000, Snoop launched his own label, Dogg House Records, and his own clothing line, Snoop Dogg Clothing. In 2001, he made the *Snoop Dogg's Doggystyle* video series in conjunction with *Hustler* magazine. In 2003, he starred in *Doggy Fizzle Televizzle,* his own series on MTV, and in 2005 he helped introduce the Snoop De Ville luxury vehicle line from Cadillac, serving as spokesman. The author of *Tha Doggfather: The Times, Trials, and Hardcore Truths of Snoop Dogg* (William Morrow, 1999), Snoop has also been featured in a number of movies, including *Bones* (Heller Highwater Productions, 2001), *Training Day*

(Outlaw Productions, 2001), *The Wash* (Lithium Entertainment Group, 2001), and *Soul Plane* (Metro-Goldwyn-Mayer [MGM], 2004).

TAKI 183

TAKI 183 became the first widely known writer of graffiti art after a story about him was featured in a July 21, 1971, article in the *New York Times* entitled "Taki 183 Spawns Pen Pals." Born Demetrius, the Greek immigrant took the name TAKI 183 from his nickname "Taki," a diminutive of "Demetrius," and the number of the street on which he lived in Washington Heights, a working-class neighborhood at the north edge of Manhattan.

Introduced to the art of graffiti by a friend at the age of fifteen, TAKI recalled seeing the tags of JULIO 204 as early as 1967. Realizing that JULIO 204 was the same Julio who lived a few blocks down the street from him on 204th Street, Demetrius created his own moniker and followed along. During the summer of 1970, TAKI 183 wrote his first tag on an ice-cream truck. By fall, he had picked up a job as a messenger. One of his deliveries would take him to an art store, where he purchased an extra-wide marker and began to paint the town. Simultaneously, JULIO 204 had been arrested for vandalism and forced to retire from the practice of graffiti. TAKI, who primarily wrote on subways and East side walls, claims his extra-wide marker was what made his tags stand out above other tags of the day. His interview with the reporter and the article that resulted from it spawned the movement and popularized graffiti around the country and around the world.

Tupac Shakur

http://www.2paclegacy.com/

A widely acclaimed MC, poet, and actor, Tupac Amaru Shakur was born June 16, 1971, in Brooklyn. According to some reports, his birth name was Lesane Parish Crooks. The name that he is known by, however, is in honor of a famed Incan chief, Tupac Amaru. Tupac's father was a New York Black Panther Party member, Afeni Shakur.

During his childhood, Tupac lived between Bronx and Harlem until the family moved to Baltimore in 1986. While attending the Baltimore School of Arts, Tupac pursued his passion for theater and acting and began rapping under the name MC New York. In

1988, the family moved to Marin, California, where Tupac led a group named Strictly Dope and eventually auditioned for Shock G (Greg Jacobs). He was admitted into the group Digital Underground as a roadie, dancer, and MC. After taking a short break to take care of his mother, Tupac signed a solo deal with Interscope Records and formed the group Thug Life. Tupac's debut album, *2Pacalypse Now* (Interscope, 1991), earned him great appeal, but his entrance into the motion-picture industry in the 1992 film *Juice* (Island World, 1992) quickly multiplied his national and international appeal.

Tupac was plagued by legal problems and incarceration throughout 1993–1995 but nevertheless rose quickly as one of the most important voices in Hip Hop. After receiving a prison sentence of four years, Tupac was out of jail pending appeal in 1995 thanks to Death Row CEO Suge Knight, who had bailed him out for $1.4 million. Tupac quickly signed to Knight's label.

Tupac was accused of using misogynistic, violent lyrics glorifying crime and death. He was attacked by such luminaries as the late C. Delores Tucker, chair and founder of the National Political Congress of Black Women, and Vice President Dan Quayle. The influential MC and leader of the Outlawz is most noted, however, for his highly publicized feud with Notorious B.I.G., which was depicted by the media as an East Coast versus West Coast war. Tupac was murdered on September 13, 1996, in Las Vegas. Notorious B.I.G. was murdered eight months later.

The legacy of Tupac Shakur has been championed by such influential persons as award-winning poet and playwright, Sonia Sanchez, and widely regarded scholar, Michael Eric Dyson, and was celebrated by a symposium at Harvard University in 2003. Numerous posthumous, multiplatinum records by Tupac have been released through Amaru Records, owned by his estate.

United Graffiti Artists (UGA)

During the summer of 1972, City College sociology major Hugo Martinez worked on a federally funded program through Queens College dealing with street gangs. While in the field, Martinez learned of the graffiti world. He was introduced to the now historic "writer's corner 188," a wall at the corner of 188th Street and Audubon Avenue where legendary graffiti artists gathered, shared ideas, and traded views of their black books. Intrigued by the commendable and indisputable skills of these artists, Martinez invited twelve of them to come to City College to offer a demonstration on graffiti writing. In October 1972, he founded the United Graffiti Artists (UGA) to help provide exposure for the work of top graffiti innovators (primarily those working in the subway system) and to advocate for social acceptance of the genre as an art form.

Martinez further aimed to explore the option of graffiti as a viable commercial endeavor and articulated the desire to lead young artists away from dangerous street life into the safer and potentially profitable world of art galleries and work-for-hire. The UGA organized its first graffiti art exhibit in December 1972 at City College's Eisner Hall. From the exhibit, the group earned a $600 commission from the Twyla Tharp Dance Company for designing and painting a backdrop for the company's performance of "Deuce Coupe." Media coverage followed. The UGA moved into New York's Razor Gallery for an exhibit of twenty canvases of UGA art, drawing press from the *New York Times, Newsweek,* and others. Internal challenges, as well as strategic attacks on graffiti artists by the New York City Mayor's Office and the Metropolitan Transportation Authority (MTA), however, drove the UGA into the underground.

Will Smith

http://www.willsmith.net/

Born Willard Christopher Smith II in the Wynnefield section of Philadelphia on September 25, 1968, Will Smith would lead the Hip Hop movement to television and rise as a successful MC, actor, humanitarian, and business owner. While at a 1986 house party, Smith met and performed with DJ Jazzy Jeff (Jeffrey A. Townes, born January 22, 1965), one of Philadelphia's most renowned DJ/producers and innovative scratchers. Smith, whose nickname was "Prince," turned down a scholarship to the Massachusetts Institute of Technology (MIT) when the duo was signed to Jive Records.

Their first single, "Girls Ain't Nothing But Trouble," told in a comedic and commercially appealing manner, served as a preview of Smith's humorous stories. When their debut album, *Rock the House* (Jive), was released in 1987, it quickly went gold and received a huge reception on MTV. Yet it was the next album, *He's the DJ, I'm the Rapper* (Jive, 1988), that moved the Fresh Prince from behind the shadow of DJ Jazzy Jeff. The lead single of the double LP (one of the first in Hip Hop), "Parents Just Don't Understand," quickly rose as a youth anthem. It sold more than 2.5 million units after the single's video debuted on MTV, winning the first-ever Grammy in the rap category.

Smith's clean, positive, humorous, and nonthreatening image made him the perfect selection as the star of Quincy Jones's new show on NBC, *The Fresh Prince of Bel-Air*. The show ran for six seasons and enjoys syndication around the world. After a brief hiatus from music, the duo returned in 1991 with *Homebase* (Jive), which quickly went platinum, led by the hit "Summertime." In the 1990s, however, Smith again took a leave from music to focus on acting, this time on the big screen. He has been featured in more than fifteen films, including *Bad Boys* (Don Simpson/Jerry Bruckheimer Films, 1995), *Independence Day* (20th Century Fox, 1996), *Men in Black* (Amblin Entertainment, 1997), *Ali* (Columbia Pictures, 2001), and *Hitch* (Columbia Pictures, 2005). In 1997, Smith returned to music with his solo debut, *Big Willie Style* (Columbia), which sold 8 million copies, and his 1999 release, *Willenium* (Columbia), went double platinum.

Smith also started the Will and Jada Smith Charitable Foundation in partnership with his wife during the late 1990s. He co-owns Overbrook Entertainment with James Lassiter and is the cofounder of Treyball Development along with his brother Harry Smith.

Wu-Tang Clan

http://www.wutangclan.com/

One of the dominant forces in Hip Hop during the 1990s and early 2000s, the Wu-Tang Clan is composed of nine talented and extremely charismatic MCs, all of whom have multiple pseudonyms. The Staten Island crew was established by the Genius/GZA (Gary Grice, a.k.a. Justice and Maxi Million) and Ol' Dirty Bastard (Russell Jones, a.k.a. Unique Ason, Joe Bannanas, Dirt McGirt, Dirt Dog, and Osirus) in the early 1990s as a collective of skilled MCs and producers. It was RZA (Robert Diggs, a.k.a. Prince Rakeem, Rzarecta, Chief Abbot, and Bobby Steels), however, who would define the vision and the sound of the Clan.

As the producer or coproducer of all of their projects, RZA established the Clan as a major force in Hip Hop. Upon the release of their first single, "Protect Ya Neck," the Clan was offered numerous deals, but they agreed to accept only under terms that would allow each artist to do solo albums on any label of choice. This

Ghostface Killah, on left, and Raekwon of the Wu-Tang Clan perform during a party to celebrate the release of their new album Iron Flag *in New York City. (Chip East/Reuters/Corbis)*

type of offer was presented by Loud/MCA, which released the Clan's debut album, *Enter the Wu-Tang (36 Chambers),* in November 1993. The single "C.R.E.A.M." elevated the group to quick stardom, launching a string of solo projects from members prior to their second group release, a double CD entitled *Wu-Tang Forever,* which entered the charts at #1 and sold 600,000 copies in the first week.

Other group members include Method Man (Clifford Smith, a.k.a. Johnny Blaze, Ticallion Stallion, Shakwon, Methical, and MZA), Raekwon the Chef (Corey Woods, a.k.a. Shallah Raekwon and Lou Diamonds), Ghostface Killah (Dennis Coles, a.k.a. Tony Starks and Sun God), U-God (Lamont Hawkins, a.k.a. Golden Arms, Lucky Hands, Baby U, and 4-Bar Killer), Inspectah Deck (Jason Hunter, a.k.a. Rebel INS and Rollie Fingers), and Masta Killa (Elgin Turner, a.k.a. Jamel Irief, High Chief, and Noodles). The crew added Cappadonna (Darryl Hill) in 1995. The Clan, highly influenced by martial arts movies of the 1970s and 1980s, was highly affected, as was the entire Hip Hop community, at the sudden death of Ol' Dirty Bastard on November 13, 2004.

X-Ecutioners

http://www.x-ecutioners.net/

One of the seminal DJ crews, the X-ecutioners revitalized the role of the DJ in Hip Hop and helped to lead the way in the promulgation and performance of turntablism. The New York–based group was founded in 1989 by DJ Roc Raida along with DJ Steve D, DJ Johnny Cash, and DJ Sean Cee under the name X-MEN. With the goal of becoming the dominant battle DJ crew, and the specific agenda of defeating the prominent crew Clark Kent's Superman DJ Crew, the X-MEN perfected scratching, mixing, beat juggling, cutting, transforming, and other techniques of the most skilled DJs.

The crew became well known for its innovative drum patterns, which members achieved by manipulating and juggling individual kick, snare, cymbal, and tom sounds using a technique created by Steve D. Because of copyright issues, the X-MEN changed their name in 1997, and their personnel, while signing a recording contract with the Asphodel label. Under the new name X-ecutioners, but still led by DJ Roc Raida, the new crew featured DJ Total Eclipse (Keith Bailey), DJ Mista Sinista (Joel Wright), and DJ Rob Swift (Rob Aguilar). Their first non-mixtape release, *X-Pressions* (Asphodel, 1997), remains a well received and innovative album. Each member is now a renowned DJ in his own right. Roc Raida was given the title "Grandmaster" at a panel at the Cleveland, Ohio, Rock 'n' Roll Hall of Fame by DJ Kool Herc, Grandwizard Theodore, and Grandmixer DXT in 2000. In 2002, DJ Mista Sinista left the group to pursue individual interests, and DJ Rob Swift left in 2004 for the same reason. They were replaced by DJ Boogie Blind and DJ Precision.

Figures, Tables, and Documents

his chapter presents Hip Hop Culture through figures, tables, and documents. More than anything, though, this chapter reveals the need for more systematic study of the culture and its effects on national and global society. To date, most research on Hip Hop has been based on anecdotal evidence and used informal methods, and little formal statistic-gathering has been accomplished. In addition, the research has generally focused on very specific elements and entities within Hip Hop rather than taking a broad view of major themes. The goal of this chapter is both to offer Hip Hop–related data and to inspire others to document and chronicle Hip Hop, not only through narrative, but through all possible measures and means.

Figure 7.1   Percentage of U.S. Dollars Spent on Hip Hop 1989–2003

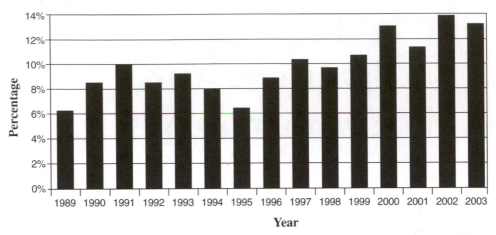

Note: Prior to 1991, data were collected by numerous agencies. Soundscan was created in 1991 and has since served as the industry-recognized authority on data collection.

Source: Recording Industry Association of America (RIAA) 1998–2003 Consumer Profile.

Figure 7.2   Percentage of U.S. Dollars Spent in the Five Major Music Categories

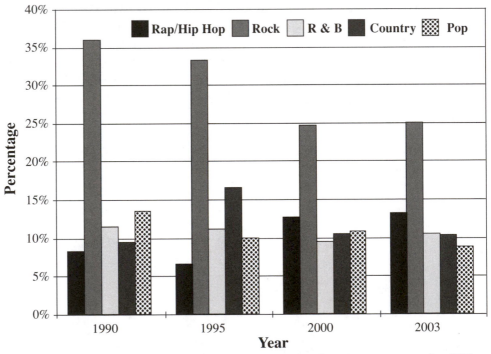

Note: Prior to 1991, data were collected by numerous agencies. Soundscan was created in 1991 and has since served as the industry-recognized authority on data collection.

Source: Recording Industry Association of America (RIAA) 1998–2003 Consumer Profile.

Figure 7.3   Percentage of U.S. Dollars Spent on Rap/Hip Hop and Rock 1989–2003

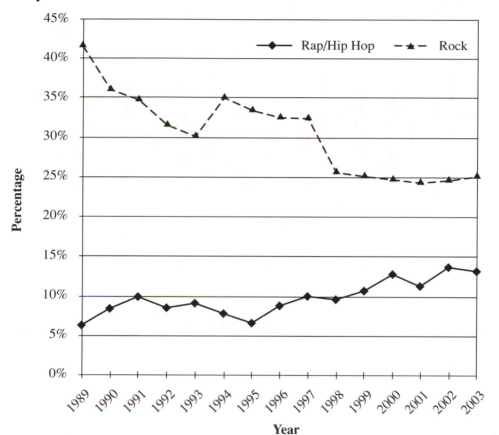

Note: Prior to 1991, data were collected by numerous agencies. Soundscan was created in 1991 and has since served as the industry recognized authority on data collection.

Source: Recording Industry Association of America (RIAA) 1998–2003 Consumer Profile.

Figure 7.4   Percentage of U.S. Dollars Spent on Rap/Hip Hop and Pop 1989–2003

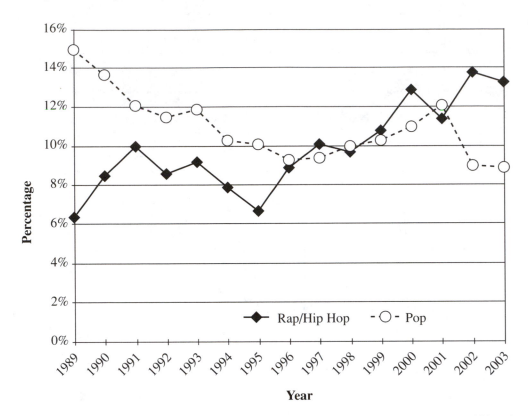

Note: Prior to 1991, data were collected by numerous agencies. Soundscan was created in 1991 and has since served as the industry-recognized authority on data collection.

Source: Recording Industry Association of America (RIAA) 1998–2003 Consumer Profile.

Figure 7.5   U.S. Dollars Spent on Rap/Hip Hop 1989–2003

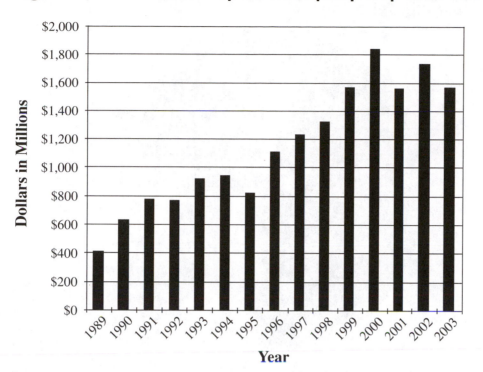

Note: Prior to 1991, data were collected by numerous agencies. Soundscan was created in 1991 and has since served as the industry-recognized authority on data collection.

Source: Recording Industry Association of America (RIAA) 1998–2003 Consumer Profile.

Figure 7.6 Radio Hip Hop Listeners by Age

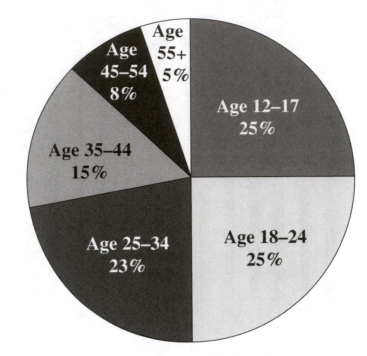

Source: "The Hip-Hop Lifestyle," Interep Research, 2003, Cume Composition

Figure 7.7   Radio Hip Hop Listeners by Ethnicity

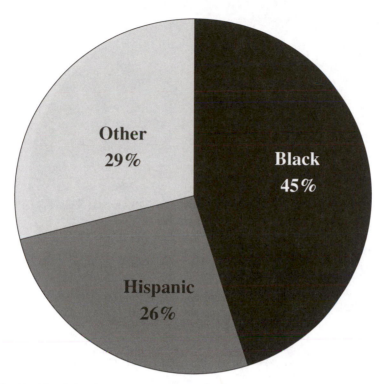

Source: "The Hip-Hop Lifestyle," Interep Research, 2003, Cume Composition

Figure 7.8   Radio Hip Hop Listeners by Gender

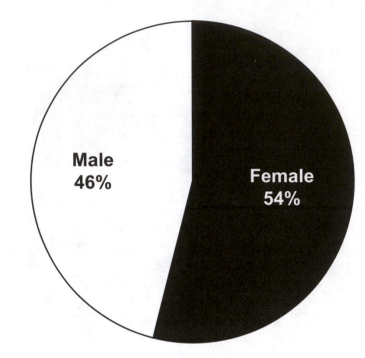

Source: "The Hip-Hop Lifestyle," Interep Research, 2003, Cume Composition

Figure 7.9   Trend of Adult (18–34) Hip Hop Radio Listeners 1999–2003

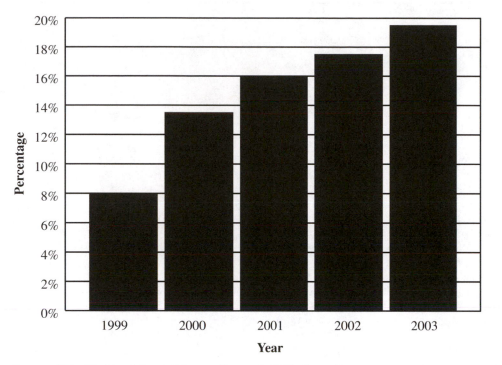

Source: "The Hip-Hop Lifestyle," Interep Research, 2003, Cume Composition

Table 7.1   Selected Hip Hop–Oriented Commercials and Advertisements, 1996–2005

Product/Company	Hip Hop Artist	Year
Major League Baseball	LL Cool J	1996
Gap	LL Cool J	1998
Sprite	Common, Fat Joe, Goodies Mob, Mack 10, Afrika Bambaataa, and Jazzy Jay	1998
Sci-Fi Channel	Busta Rhymes	1999
Mountain Dew	Busta Rhymes	2000
Lane Bryant	Queen Latifah	2000
Freedom Gold Mastercard	Queen Latifah	2000
Reebok Classic	Queen Latifah	2000
Pepsi	Wyclef Jean	2001
Cover Girl	Queen Latifah	2001
Ikea	LL Cool J	2001
XM Satellite Radio	Snoop Dogg	2002
Right Guard	Method Man and Redman	2002
Dr. Pepper	Black Eyed Peas	2002
Miller Lite	Busta Rhymes	2002
Virgin Mobile	Wyclef Jean	2002
Cover Girl Smoothers	Queen Latifah	2002
Dr. Pepper	Black Eyed Peas	2002
Dr. Pepper	LL Cool J and Run-DMC	2003
Coca-Cola	Common and Mya	2003
America Online	Snoop Dogg	2003
Coors[a]	Nelly	2003
"Got Milk" Campaign	Nelly	2003
Marriott Courtyard	Queen Latifah	2003
Pizza Hut	Queen Latifah	2003
Curvation Lingerie	Queen Latifah	2003
Reebok[b]	Jay Z and 50 Cent	2003
Gap	Missy Elliott	2003
Virgin Mobile	Busta Rhymes	2003
Heineken[c]	Jay Z	2004
Gatorade	LL Cool J	2004
Volvo	LL Cool J	2004
T Mobile	Snoop Dogg	2004
Right Guard	Xzibit	2004
Burger King	Snoop Dogg	2004
Burger King	P. Diddy	2004
NBA and ESPN[d]	Black Eyed Peas	2004
Caress Body Wash	LL Cool J	2005
Cover Girl Fantastic Lash and Wetslicks cosmetics	Queen Latifah	2005
Diet Pepsi	P. Diddy	2005
Diet Pepsi	Xzibit	2005
Lays Potato Chips	MC Hammer	2005

[a]Coors provided title sponsorship for Nelly's summer 2003 tour and created a special beer can commemorating twenty-five years of Hip Hop.

[b]Reebok sponsored the 2003 Summer Tour for Jay Z and 50 Cent.

[c]Jay Z was in a Heineken commercial featured during the 2004 Grammy Awards Show.

[d]The song "Let's Get It Started" was used to promote the 2004 NBA Playoffs.

Table 7.2   Selected Hip Hop–Oriented Programming on Network Television/Cable, 1988–2005

Television Show	Television Station	Year Launched
Yo! MTV Raps	MTV	1988
Rap City	BET	1989
Kid n' Play	NBC	1990
In Living Color	FOX	1990
Fresh Prince of Bel Air	NBC	1990
Living Single	FOX	1993
The Wayans Bros.	WB	1995
In the House	NBC	1995
Moesha	UPN	1996
The Steve Harvey Show	WB	1996
The PJs	WB	1999
Direct Effect	MTV	2000
106 & Park Top 10 Live	BET	2000
Making the Band	MTV	2002
Making the Band 2	MTV	2003
Ride with Funkmaster Flex	Spike TV	2003
Doggy Fizzle Televizzle	MTV	2003
Platinum	UPN	2003
Eve	UPN	2003
All of Us[a]	UPN	2003
Chappelle's Show	Comedy Central	2003
Romeo!	Nickelodeon	2003
Method & Red	FOX	2004
Pimp My Ride	MTV	2004
Dance 360	Syndicated	2004
Making the Band 3	MTV	2005
The Road to Stardom with Missy Elliott	UPN	2005

[a]Produced by Will and Jada Smith.

Figure 7.10   Gross Sales of Select Hip Hop–Oriented Motion Pictures

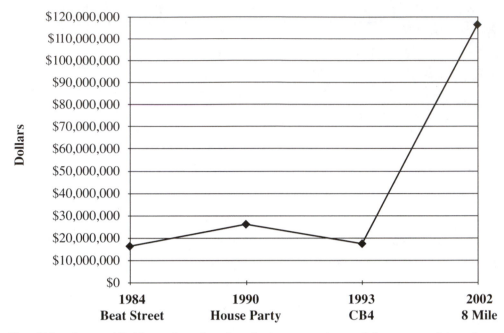

Note: Although most Hip Hop–oriented motion pictures cannot boast of the success of these four, the chart offers the growing trend in the potential for Hip Hop–oriented motion pictures to sell well into the millions.

Source: http://www.the-numbers.com.

Table 7.3   American Music Awardees in Rap/Hip Hop Category, 1989–2003

Year	Artist	Category	Album
1989	Young MC	Favorite Rap/Hip Hop Artist	
1989	MC Hammer	Favorite Rap/Hip Hop Artist	
1989	DJ Jazzy Jeff & the Fresh Prince	Favorite Rap/Hip Hop Artist	
1989	MC Hammer	Favorite Rap/Hip Hop Album	*Let's Get It Started*
1989	DJ Jazzy Jeff & the Fresh Prince	Favorite Rap/Hip Hop Album	*He's the DJ, I'm the Rapper*
1990	Vanilla Ice	Favorite Rap/Hip Hop New Artist	
1990	MC Hammer	Favorite Rap/Hip Hop Artist	
1990	MC Hammer	Favorite Rap/Hip Hop Album	*Please Hammer, Don't Hurt 'Em*
1991	Naughty by Nature	Favorite Rap/Hip Hop New Artist	
1991	MC Hammer	Favorite Rap/Hip Hop Artist	
1991	DJ Jazzy Jeff & the Fresh Prince	Favorite Rap/Hip Hop Album	*Home Base*
1992	Kris Kross	Favorite Rap/Hip Hop New Artist	
1992	Sir Mix-a-Lot	Favorite Rap/Hip Hop Artist	
1993	Dr. Dre	Favorite Rap/Hip Hop New Artist	
1993	Dr. Dre	Favorite Rap/Hip Hop Artist	
1994	Snoop Doggy Dogg	Favorite Rap/Hip Hop Artist	
1995	Coolio	Favorite Rap/Hip Hop Artist	
1996	2Pac	Favorite Rap/Hip Hop Artist	
1997	Bone Thugs-n-Harmony	Favorite Rap/Hip Hop Artist	
1998	Master P	Favorite Rap/Hip Hop Artist	
1999	DMX	Favorite Rap/Hip Hop Artist	
2000	Dr. Dre	Favorite Rap/Hip Hop Artist	
2001	Nelly	Favorite Rap/Hip Hop Artist	
2003	50 Cent	Favorite Rap/Hip Hop Male Artist	
2003	Missy Elliott	Favorite Rap/Hip Hop Female Artist	
2003	Lil Jon & the East Side Boyz	Favorite Rap/Hip Hop Band/Duo/Group	
2003	50 Cent	Favorite Rap/Hip Hop Album	*Get Rich or Die Tryin'*

Note: The first American Music Award given in the rap category was in 1989.

Source: http://www.rockonthenet.com.

Figure 7.11   Trend in Number of American Music Awardees in Rap-Hip Hop Category 1989–2003

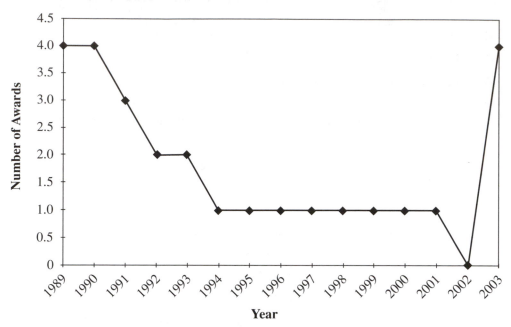

Note: The first American Music Award given in the rap category was in 1989.

Source: http://www.rockonthenet.com.

Table 7.4   Grammys Awarded in Rap Category, 1988–2003

Year	Artist	Category	Work
1988	DJ Jazzy Jeff & the Fresh Prince	Best Rap Performance	Parents Just Don't Understand
1989	Young MC	Best Rap Performance	Bust a Move
1990	Big Daddy Kane, Ice-T, Kool Moe Dee, Melle Mel, Quincy D. III & Quincy Jones	Best Rap Performance by a Duo or Group	Back on the Block
1990	MC Hammer	Best Rap Solo Performance	U Can't Touch This
1991	DJ Jazzy Jeff & the Fresh Prince	Best Rap Performance by a Duo or Group	Summertime
1991	LL Cool J	Best Rap Solo Performance	Mama Said Knock You Out
1992	Arrested Development	Best Rap Performance by a Duo or Group	Tennessee
1992	Sir Mix-a-Lot	Best Rap Solo Performance	Baby Got Back
1993	Digable Planets	Best Rap Performance by a Duo or Group	Rebirth of Slick (Cool Like Dat)
1993	Dr. Dre	Best Rap Solo Performance	Let Me Ride
1994	Salt-n-Pepa	Best Rap Performance by a Duo or Group	None of Your Business
1994	Queen Latifah	Best Rap Solo Performance	U.N.I.T.Y.
1995	Naughty by Nature	Best Rap Album	*Poverty's Paradise*

Year	Artist	Category	Work
1995	Mary J. Blige & Method Man	Best Rap Performance by a Duo or Group	I'll Be There for You/You're All I Need to Get By
1995	Coolio	Best Rap Solo Performance	Gangsta's Paradise
1996	Fugees	Best Rap Album	The Score
1996	Bone Thugs-n-Harmony	Best Rap Performance by a Duo or Group	Crossroad
1996	LL Cool J	Best Rap Solo Performance	Hey Lover
1997	Puff Daddy & the Family	Best Rap Album	No Way Out
1997	112	Best Rap Performance by a Duo or Group	I'll Be Missing You
1997	Will Smith	Best Rap Solo Performance	Men in Black
1998	Jay-Z	Best Rap Album	Vol. 2 … Hard Knock Life
1998	Beastie Boys	Best Rap Performance by a Duo or Group	Intergalactic
1998	Will Smith	Best Rap Solo Performance	Gettin' Jiggy Wit It
1999	Eminem	Best Rap Album	The Slim Shady LP
1999	Erykah Badu & the Roots	Best Rap Performance by a Duo or Group	You Got Me
1999	Eminem	Best Rap Solo Performance	My Name Is
2000	Eminem	Best Rap Album	The Marshall Mathers LP
2000	Dr. Dre & Eminem	Best Rap Performance by a Duo or Group	Forgot about Dre
2000	Eminem	Best Rap Solo Performance	The Real Slim Shady
2001	Outkast	Best Rap Album	Stankonia
2001	Eve & Gwen Stefani	Best Rap/Sung Collaboration	Let Me Blow Ya Mind
2001	Outkast	Best Rap Performance by a Duo or Group	Ms. Jackson
2001	Missy Elliot	Best Rap Solo Performance	Get Ur Freak On
2002	Eminem	Best Rap Album	The Eminem Show
2002	Kelendria Rowland & Nelly	Best Rap/Sung Collaboration	Dilemma
2002	Killer Mike & Outkast	Best Rap Performance by a Duo or Group	The Whole World
2002	Nelly	Best Male Rap Solo Performance	Hot in Herre
2002	Missy Elliott	Best Female Rap Solo Performance	Scream a.k.a. Itchin'
2003	Outkast	Best Rap Album	Speakerboxxx/The Love Below
2003	Eminem, Jeff Bass & L Resto	Best Rap Song	Lose Yourself
2003	Beyoncé Knowles & Jay-Z	Best Rap/Sung Collaboration	Crazy in Love
2003	Murphy Lee, Nelly & Sean Combs	Best Rap Performance by a Duo or Group	Shake Ya Tailfeather
2003	Eminem	Best Male Rap Solo Performance	Lose Yourself
2003	Missy Elliott	Best Female Rap Solo Performance	Work It

Note: The first Grammy awarded in the rap category was in 1988.

Source: http://www.grammy.com.

Figure 7.12   Trend in Number of Grammys Awarded in Rap Category 1988–2003

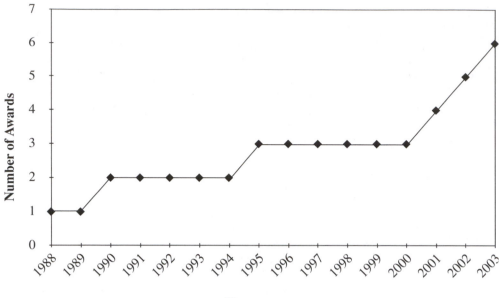

Note: The first Grammy awarded in the rap category was in 1988.

Source: http://www.grammy.com.

Document One: Temple of Hiphop Resolution for Hiphop Appreciation Week (May)

This Hiphop Declaration of Peace guides Hiphop Kulture toward freedom from violence, and establishes advice and protection for the existence and development of our Hiphop community. Through the overstandings of this Hiphop Declaration of Peace, we establish a foundation of health, love, awareness, wealth, peace and prosperity for ourselves, our children and their children's children, forever.

For the purpose of establishing a respectable international framework by which Hiphop Kulture may achieve and contribute to a lasting peace in the world we, the founders, pioneers, inventors, artists, photographers, authors, teachas, and other kultural contributors of Hiphop Kulture, ordain and decree, the manifestation of this Hiphop Declaration of Peace.

That Hiphop Kulture may come to know, and act upon, its true intention, meaning and purpose we, the B-Boys, B-Girls, Emcees, DeeJays, Writers, Beatboxers, and other legitimate contributors to Hiphop Kulture have united on this day May 16, 2002 at the United Nations headquarters in New York to document, establish, fulfill, and promote the vision of Hiphop as an International kulture for peace and prosperity.

For the clarification of Hiphop's meaning and purpose, or when the intention of Hiphop is questioned, or when disputes between parties arise, Hiphoppas shall have access to the advice of this document, the "Hiphop Declaration of Peace," as guidance, advice and protection.

First Overstanding

Hiphop is the name of our collective consciousness. It is commonly expressed through Breakin, Emceein, Graf, Deejayin, Beatboxin, Street Fashion, Street Language, Street Knowledge and Street Entrepreneurialism or Street Trade. Wherever and whenever the elements, and expressions of Hiphop Kulture manifest, this Hiphop Declaration of Peace shall advise its use and interpretation.

Second Overstanding

Hiphop Kulture respects the dignity and sanctity of life, without discrimination or prejudice. We shall consider our duty to protect the development of life, over and before our individual free choice to destroy it or seek to alter its natural development.

Third Overstanding

Hiphop Kulture respects the laws and agreements of its kulture, its country, its institutions, and those it does business with. Hiphop does not irresponsibly break laws.

Fourth Overstanding

Hiphop Kulture encourages womanhood, manhood, sisterhood, brotherhood and family. We are also conscious not to bring any disrespect to the dignity and reputation of our ancestors.

Fifth Overstanding

The right to define and educate ourselves shall be encouraged, developed, preserved, protected and promoted as a means toward peace and prosperity.

Sixth Overstanding

Hiphop honors no relationship, person, event, act, or otherwise, wherein the preservation and further development of Hiphop's Kulture, principles and elements are not considered nor respected. Hiphop Kulture does not participate in activities that clearly destroy its ability to productively exist.

Seventh Overstanding

The elements of Hiphop Kulture may be traded for money, honor, power, respect, food and other resources. However, Hiphop's Kulture is never for sale—nor can it be bought. It is priceless principle of our self-empowerment.

Eighth Overstanding

Companies, corporations, non and not-for profit organizations, as well as individuals and groups that are clearly benefiting from the use, interpretation and/or exploitation of Hiphop, and the expressions and terminologies of Hiphop; shall be encouraged to commission and/or employ a certified Hiphop specialist to answer sensitive kultural questions, and guide businesses, cities and countries through the principles and proper presentations of Hiphop Kulture to the world.

Ninth Overstanding

Every third week in May, Hiphoppas shall be encouraged to remember its ancestors and appreciate the elements and principles and history of Hiphop.

Tenth Overstanding

Hiphop is the name of our collective consciousness. As a conscious way of life we recognize our influence on society, especially on children, and we shall forever keep the rights and welfare of both in mind.

Eleventh Overstanding

Within the collective Hiphop consciousness there are not competing races, tribes, countries, religion, occupations, kultures, nor languages. All are one in consciousness. Hiphop Kulture is one multi-skilled, multi-cultural, multi-racial people.

Twelfth Overstanding

Hiphop Kulture does not intentionally participate in any form of hate, deceit, or theft at any time. At no time shall Hiphop engage in any violent war within itself.

Thirteenth Overstanding

Hiphop Kulture rejects the immature impulse for unwarranted acts of violence, and always seeks diplomatic, non-violent strategies first in the settlement of all disputes. Revolution is preserved as a final solution, when all other means of diplomatic negotiation have failed repeatedly.

Fourteenth Overstanding

Hiphoppas respect nature wherever we are; on this planet as well as on others.

Fifteenth Overstanding

Hiphop holds sacred our duty to contribute to our survival and salvation as a human race on planet Earth. Native American kulture teaches us to respect Mother Earth as our mother.

Sixteenth Overstanding

No one should be a self-proclaimed Hiphop pioneer or "legend" unless they can prove with facts and/or witnesses to their credibility and contributions to Hiphop Kulture.

Seventeenth Overstanding

Hiphop is shown the highest respect when Hiphoppas respect each other. Hiphop Kulture is preserved, nurtured and developed when Hiphoppas preserve, nurture and develop one another.

Eighteenth Overstanding

For the purpose of promoting, interpreting and defending the principles of the Hiphop Declaration of Peace; Hiphop Kulture shall maintain a healthy, caring, fully aware, and wealthy central Hiphop committee. Such committee shall be made up of seven dedicated Hiphoppas invested with the other power to promote, interpret and defend the principles of the Hiphop Declaration of Peace.

Document Two: New York Senate Recognizes November as HIP HOP HISTORY MONTH

LEGISLATIVE RESOLUTION honoring the rich traditions of Hip Hop Culture

WHEREAS, It is the sense of this Legislative Body to pay tribute to those individuals of historic and artistic significance whose creative talents have contributed to the cultural enrichment of our communities and our Nation; and

WHEREAS, The month of November is now recognized by the State of New York as Hip Hop Culture History month; and

WHEREAS, Afrika Bambaattaa, was the first Hip Hop activist, who once said, "Hip Hop Culture was created to be about peace, love, unity and having fun, in order to help people to get away from the negativity that was plaguing our streets"; and

WHEREAS, Even though this negativity still exists, as the culture progresses, Hip Hop Culture plays a big role in the conflict and resolution by encouraging positivity; and

WHEREAS, Hip Hop is made up of Rap, DJ'ing, Break dancing, Up-Rocking, Popping, Locking, Vocal Percussion, and Beat Boxing; and

WHEREAS, The godfather of Hip Hop Culture is Afrika Bambaattaa; and the world's oldest, largest and most respected grass roots Hip Hop organization is the Universal Zulu Nation; and

WHEREAS, Hip Hop Culture is a positive tool for social change; and

WHEREAS, The inception of Hip Hop Culture in the Bronx was during early 1970's; it has been a vehicle for breaking down racial barriers on a world wide level; and

WHEREAS, Hip Hop is a means for overcoming challenges, and a means for teaching awareness and knowledge, inspiration and wisdom; and

WHEREAS, during the 70's Hip Hop was a celebration of life, gradually developing to form a cultural movement as a result of its dynamic energy and momentum; and

WHEREAS, Hip Hop Culture has become, ultimately, a key to uplift the spirit of many; and

WHEREAS, Hip Hop Culture has greatly influenced the entertainment world with its creative contributions in music, dance, art, poetry, and fashion; and

WHEREAS, Hip Hop is the vehicle to deliver innumerable lessons and continues to provide for unity, love, respect, and responsibility; and

WHEREAS, D.J. Afrika Bambaattaa and the Universal Zulu Nation, Cool Herc [known as Kool Herc], Grandmaster Flash, the Cold Crush Brothers, Cool Clyde and Light-nen Lance, Nolie Dee, Maria Davis and Mytika Davis are true inspirations; and

WHEREAS, It is the sense of this Legislative Body, in keeping with its time-honored traditions, to recognize and pay tribute to those organizations which foster ethnic pride and enhance the profile of cultural diversity that strengthens the fabric of the communities of New York State; and

WHEREAS, It is the sense of this Legislative Body that those who enhance the well-being and vitality of their community and has shown a long and sustained commitment to excellence certainly have earned our recognition and applause; now, therefore, be it

RESOLVED, That this Legislative Body pause in its deliberations to honor the rich traditions of Hip Hop Culture; and be it further

RESOLVED, That copies of this Resolution, suitable engrossed, be transmitted to Afrika Bambaataa and all of the participants of the Hip Hop Culture Celebration.

Resolution J6602 Espada adopted December 17, 2002.

Table 7.5   Selected Hip Hop Fashion Lines, 1975–2005

Fashion Line	Owner/Designer	Year Launched
Avirex	Jeff Clyman	1975
Pelle Pelle	Marc Buchanan	1978
Diesel	Renzo Rosso	1978
DKNY (Donna Karan New York)	Donna Karan & Stephen Weiss	1984
Maurice Malone	Maurice Malone	1984
Tommy Hilfiger	Tommy Hilfiger	1984
PNB Nation	Roger McHayle, Isaac Rubinstein, & Kahlil Williams	1987
Karl Kani	Karl Kani (Carl Williams)	1989
Davoucci	Danny Davoudi (President)	1989
Triple 5 Soul	Camella Ehlke (Designer), Troy Morehouse (President)	1989
Cross Colours	Carl Jones	1990
South Pole	Dae Won Khym	1991
Fubu	Carl Brown, J. Alexander, Martin & Keith Perrin	1992
Phat Farm	Russell Simmons	1992
School of Hard Knocks (SOHK)	Gerard Murray	1992
Ecko Unlimited	Marc Ecko	1993
Zoo York	Rodney Smith, Eli Morgan	1993
Damani Dada	Dwayne Lewis & Michael Cherry (Designer)	1995
Mecca USA	Evan Davis, Lando Felix & Tony Shellman (founders but not currently owners)	1995
Enyce	Evan Davis, Lando Felix & Tony Shellman	1996
ARME	Derrick Murray	1997
Johnny Blaze	AST Sportswear & Larry Zimmer	1997
Vokal	Yomi Martin (cofounder/CEO), Nelly (Cornell Haynes), Nick Loftis, Ian Kelly	1997
Wu-wear	Wu-Tang Clan	1997
Bushi	Busta Rhymes	1998
Sean John	P. Diddy (Sean Combs)	1998
Baby Phat	Kimora Lee	1999
Rocawear	Jay-Z & Damon Dash	1999
Akademiks	Donwan & Emmett Harrell	2000
Ruff Ryders Collection	The Ruff Ryders	2000
Cash Money Clothing	Cash Money Millionaires	2001
J-Lo Clothing	Jennifer Lopez	2001
Outkast Clothing Company	Outkast	2001
Snoop Dogg Clothing	Snoop Dogg	2001
Apple Bottom	Nelly	2003
Fetish	Eve	2003
G-Unit Clothing	50 Cent	2003
Ice Wear	Ice-T	2003
Makaveli Clothing	Afeni Shakur	2003
Shady Ltd.	Eminem	2003
Respect ME	Missy Elliott & Adidas	2004
Sedgwick & Cedar	Gessner (Designer), Adam Schatz Ray Riccio, Afrika Bambaataa, Grandmaster Caz, Melle Mel, Chief Rocker Busy Bee & Sha-Rock, DJ Kool Herc	2005

Table 7.6   Selected Hip Hop–Oriented Magazines, 1966–2005

Name	Years of Publication
Blues & Soul	1966 to present
Right On!	1972 to present
Source	1988 to present
Underground Productions	1992 to present
Rap Sheet Magazine	1992 to present
VIBE	1993 to present
Urb	1993 to present
Da Ghetto Tymz	1993 to present
URB	1993 to present
XXL	1997 to present
Blaze	1998–2000
F.E.D.S. (Finally Every Dimension of the Streets)	1998 to present
Pound	1998 to present
Stealth	1999 to present
Don Diva	1999 to present
The Fader	1999 to present
Rap-Up	2000 to present
FELON (Finally Every Level of Neighborhoods)	2001 to present
Complex	2002 to present
Scratch	2004 to present

Note: This list includes print magazines only. Online magazines are not included.

Selected Organizations, Associations, and Programs

his chapter contains an alphabetized, annotated list of Hip Hop–oriented organizations, associations, and programs that are dedicated to the preservation, promulgation, and/or practice of Hip Hop. I have been very selective in choosing which resources to list in an effort to optimize the usefulness of the list to both researchers and readers. No production companies, entertainment companies, marketing or promotions agencies, booking or management agencies, or consulting firms have been included. Furthermore, I have excluded all record labels and talent agencies. Thus, the chapter does not present a comprehensive directory of all Hip Hop–oriented organizations, associations, and programs; rather, it presents a sampling of present initiatives and creative uses of Hip Hop. Many of the groups profiled engage in some sort of educational, community service, youth empowerment, or life skills development capacity. Nevertheless, this chapter is weakened by the lack of availability of current contact information for some of the resources listed, and many of the resources that would otherwise be included are not because the appropriate information could not be secured.

Hip Hop Culture: General

The DJ Project

Jeff Feinman (Project Director)
440 Potrero Avenue
San Francisco, CA 94110
415-487-6714
http://www.thedjproject.com
jeff@theDJproject.com

Based in the desire to promote active participation in education, employment and entrepreneurship, leadership, and community service among youth and young adults, the DJ Project uses Hip Hop to inspire Hip Hop communities. It offers a four-month program for youth in which a guest artist from within the Hip Hop community leads a group of young people in the development, production, and presentation of a recording project, focusing on the business aspects, lyrical content, and context as well as the aesthetics of Hip Hop in the hope that the experience will motivate the participants to aspire to greatness.

The Foundation for the Study of HIPHOP Consciousness

Los Angeles, California
323-281-1412
http://www.thefoundationonline.net
info@thefoundationonline.net

This organization seeks to educate the youth of Los Angeles, California, via Hip Hop–based educational programs in collaboration with the Los Angeles Unified School District. Based in the classroom and centered around several core educational fields of study, including English, history, social science, and art, the community-based foundation aims to help the youth of Los Angeles to improve their academic achievement.

The Greater Philadelphia Hip Hop Alliance

Rashid Duggan (President)
610-457-3493
http://www.gphha.org/
Rashid@gppha.org

Founded by Disco Dave, Funk Wizard Snow, and MC Breeze in 2001, this nonprofit organization aims to unite individuals of the Greater Philadelphia area who are active within Hip Hop Culture and contribute to its preservation. DJs, dancers, graffiti artists, and MCs meet monthly to exchange ideas and concerns and to offer mutual support.

The Hip-Hop Association (H^{2}A)

Martha Diaz (Executive/Creative Director)
215-500-5974
http://www.hiphopassociation.org/
info@hiphopassociation.org

With the slogan "Facilitating, Fostering, & Preserving Hip-Hop Culture," the Hip-Hop Association uses Hip Hop as a tool to promote critical thinking, social change, and unity. Through its International Film Festival, Youth Summit Media, and educational initiatives, the organization has a strong support network of corporations, educators, Hip Hop pioneers, and industry representatives.

Hip Hop Cell Block Project

Virgilio Bravo
718-735-3554
veebravo@hotmail.com

This project presents live Hip Hop performances to New York prison inmates with the aim of using Hip Hop as a tool to inspire dialogue on issues such as identity, empowerment, class, race relations, and numerous other topics. Founded at Rikers Prison by Virgilio Bravo in 1996, the program aids in promoting unity and building relationships among the inmates.

Hip Hop Congress

Reali Robinson IV (President)
http://www.hiphopcongress.com/
1312@1312.org

The Hip Hop Congress's objective is to promote the constructive aspects of Hip Hop Culture to counter the false pictures of Hip Hop associating it strictly with gang violence, drugs, and other negative aspects of inner-city life. The organization, based in local chapters in colleges and high schools around the country, encourages youth to participate in their local communities both socially and creatively through the use of Hip Hop Culture.

Hip Hop Elements

954-977-7886 (phone), 775-249-0062 (fax)
http://www.hiphopelements.com/
webmaster@hiphopelements.com

With its extensive, reputable history, this organization is among the nation's elite when it comes to coordinating and promoting Hip Hop events such as cultural shows, concerts, and educational conferences. Major corporations such as Pepsi, ESPN, and Avirex have supported and sponsored its diverse array of Hip Hop events, such as the annual Hip Hop Elements All-Star Weekend (formerly known as B-Boy Masters Pro-Am) in Miami Beach, Florida.

Hip Hop Project

Kharma Kazi (Chris Rolle), Founder
Art Start
285 West Broadway, Suite 600
New York, NY 10013
800-224-0990 (phone), 212-966-8539 (fax)
http://art-start.org/

Founded in 1999 by Kharma Kazi (Chris Rolle), the Hip Hop Project uses the transformative power of Hip Hop to reach underrepresented youth, providing life skills, leadership development, and experience in the creation of a hip hop album from start to finish. Through a rich curriculum that includes audio production, budgeting and contracts, and other important aspects of creating an album, the youth interact with industry professionals and recording artists to gain skills and confidence.

Hip Hop Summit Action Network

Dr. Benjamin Chavis Muhammad (President and CEO)
http://www.hiphopsummitactionnetwork.org/
info@hsan.org

Founded in 2001, the Hip Hop Summit Action Network (HSAN) seeks to educate youth socially, politically, and culturally through the positive influences of Hip Hop Culture. HSAN provides leadership development programs for youth and encourages many thousands of youth to vote every year through its Hip Hop Team

Vote program. HSAN also actively campaigns against poverty and against all forms of discrimination, racism, violence, police brutality, and numerous other destructive factors that plague the nation's communities.

Hip-Hop Summit Youth Council.   This youth program, founded by activist and author Charles Fisher in 2001 in Queens, provides support and assistance for youth striving to improve their lives while also attempting to improve the overall image of Hip Hop.

Hip-Hop Team Vote.   This area of HSAN is dedicated to educating and encouraging youth to participate in the political process through the vote.

HSAN Collegiate Coalition.   The HSAN Collegiate Coalition was established in September 2003 at Clark Atlanta University in Atlanta, Georgia, and seeks to promote education on college campuses while confronting issues that have a destructive influence on youth in the United States.

HSAN/National Grassroots and Volunteering Office.   The National Grassroots and Volunteering Office (NGVO) is responsible for gathering volunteers (either locally, statewide, or nationally) for the many programs and events that are sponsored by HSAN. Other duties of the NGVO include managing the nationwide membership of the Hip-Hop Team Vote program, communicating with organizations that desire to work with HSAN, and planning and organizing operation strategies for HSAN.

Hip Hop Theater Festival

57 Thames Street, Suite 4B
Brooklyn, NY 11237
718-497-4282 (phone), 718-497-4240 (fax)
http://www.hiphoptheaterfest.com
info@hiphoptheaterfest.org

Aiming to encourage the creation of Hip Hop theater, Danny Hoch founded the Hip Hop Theater Festival in 1999. As a major venue for the production, presentation, collaboration, and development of Hip Hop–related works, the festival caters to an international audience and has presented more than 100 artists from the United States, England, and Canada. All works address critical issues relevant to the Hip Hop communities and serve both an outreach and educational purpose.

The Midnight Forum

Daniel Berry (a.k.a. DINO, Founder and Executive Director)
3426 16th Street, NW #T-1, Washington, DC 20010
202-276-5632 (phone), 202-387-1695 (fax)
http://www.midnightforum.org
TheMidnightForum@yahoo.com

The Midnight Forum, based in Washington, D.C., is a nonprofit organization offering an after-school program and a summer work program geared toward developing young leaders, artists, organizers, and entrepreneurs. Using Hip Hop Culture as a teaching tool, the forum trains youth (ages fourteen to twenty-one) in Hip Hop history, in the elements of Hip Hop, and in various trades related to Hip Hop, such as T-shirt making, record album design, audio production, and life skills development and personal management.

Millennium Education Company of America: Preparing Children for a Whole New World

http://hiphopkids.com/
grammarman11@aol.com

Founded by Charles Herring, Jr., of Monroeville, Pennsylvania, in 1998, the Millennium Education Company of America (MECA) educates children from kindergarten through eighth grade through the use of Hip Hop Culture. Subject matters approached include math, grammar, and black history as well as lessons on safety routines and drug prevention.

National Hip-Hop Political Convention

Baye Adofo Wilson (National Co-chair)
Angela Woodson (National Co-chair)
http://www.hiphopconvention.org
bayewilson@aol.com
adws501@aol.com

The National Hip-Hop Political Convention hosted the monumental, first-ever event by the same name on June 16–19, 2004, at Essex County College, New Jersey Institute of Technology, and Rutgers University. The purpose of the convention was to gather the Hip Hop generation together in order to develop leadership skills, organize a political agenda for the Hip Hop generation, and inspire involvement in local, state, and federal politics.

Project HIP-HOP

Mariama White-Hammond, Executive Director
Boston, MA
617-262-2148
mariama@att.net

Geared toward leadership and life skills development for under-represented youth, Project HIP-HOP (Highways Into the Past–History, Organizing and Power) empowers young people to think and achieve big. Through its numerous programs and initiatives, including the Civil Rights Summer Tour and the *Street Hype* magazine, participants learn of the importance of history and empowerment and the interaction between them.

Project: Think Different

Scherazade Daruvalla King, Founder and Executive Director
14 Beacon Street, Suite 503
Boston, MA 02108
617-557-9200 (phone), 617-971-9492 (fax)
http://www.projectthinkdifferent.org
info@projectthinkdifferent.org

Launched in 2003 and aimed at attacking the negative, violent, misogynistic, and banal media messages, Project: Think Different initiates change by using music, film, and media to engage civic action and dialogue. Hip Hop Culture is prominently used to educate, encourage, and empower people of all ages to be politically active and socially engaged.

Temple of Hiphop

P.O. Box 346
Los Angeles, CA 90028
http://www.templeofhiphop.org/

Founded by Hip Hop legend KRS-One in 1998, the Temple of Hiphop is an international preservation society aimed at promoting, protecting, and preserving Hip Hop. Through the promotion of a Hip Hop lifestyle, the Temple promotes Hip Hop as an agent for world peace and prosperity. The organization is also responsible for the Hiphop Declaration of Peace and the celebration of Hiphop Appreciation Week during the third week in May.

The Universal Zulu Nation

http://www.zulunation.com/
zulus@zulunation.com

The Universal Zulu Nation is one of the most important organizations within Hip Hop Culture. Its Web site offers a unique historical perspective of the evolution and development of Hip Hop Culture by one of its most esteemed innovators, founder Afrika Bambaataa. The site features an abundance of information, including current and archived news, editorials, and other articles, detailed information on the history of Hip Hop Culture and its elements, and biographical information on Bambaataa and his music. Beyond Hip Hop, this site features a variety of informative resources and links on Afrikan-centered beliefs and products.

The University of Hip-Hop

Lavie Raven (Minister of Education)
http://uhiphop.uchicago.edu/docs/
stylekillers@yahoo.com

Formed by Chicago youth from Hubbard High School in 1997, the University of Hip-Hop is a product of self-determination and self-empowerment. The former summer program, with a curriculum focused on developing creativity through the expression of street arts, has developed into an after-school program with local, national, and international branches and networks. The university is grounded in community service, experiential and service learning, and social and political action.

Urban Think Tank Institute

Yvonne Bynoe (Founder/President)
P.O. Box 1476
New York, NY 10185-1476
718-670-3739
http://www.urbanthinktank.org/
UrbanThinkTank@usa.net

Serving as a gathering place and home for those in the Hip Hop generation, the Urban Think Tank Institute encourages open dialogue on issues of political, economic, and cultural importance within minority communities. As the first organization to approach these issues through the Hip Hop generation, Urban Think Tank has had an influence on many later organizations that share similar goals. This nonprofit organization was founded in Brooklyn in June 2000 with the slogan "For the Body of Thinkers in the Hip-Hop Community." *Doula: The Journal of Ram Music and Hip Hop Culture,* launched in September 2000, is produced by the organization on a quarterly schedule.

Words, Beats & Life

Mazi Mutafa (Executive Director)
1327 R Street NW, Suite 23
Washington, DC 20001
202-667-1192
http://www.wblinc.org/

Founded in June 2003 by four University of Maryland alumnae following their success as part of the Black Student Union's sponsored conferences in 2001 and 2002, this organization educates, empowers, encourages, and informs youth and young adults about their value and ability to make a contribution to society. The organization offers a journal *(W B & L Journal);* a DC Urban Arts Academy aimed at providing skills and leadership development in the areas of performing arts, business, and visual arts; and an annual conference featuring educational opportunities and entertainment.

DJing

Battlestyle.org

http://www.battlestyle.org/

Battlestyle.org is an online organization that allows members to share and promote their own original Hip Hop material and communicate with one another via message board forums. Several different forums are provided for specific discussion topics, including a music forum, a turntablism forum, a self-promotion forum, and others. The site also allows members to post their turntable routines and creative works for site visitors to listen to and learn from.

DMC World

P.O. Box 89
Slough Bucks, SL1 8NA
United Kingdom
+44 1628 667124
http://www.dmcworld.com/
webmaster@dmcworld.com

This organization sponsors the World DJ Mixing Championships. Although the competition caters to global DJs of all styles, Hip Hop DJs have dominated the competition since the 1990s. This competition is considered one of the most prestigious for competitive battle DJs.

International Turntablist Federation

ITF Worldwide Headquarters
2200 Cesar Chavez Street
San Francisco, CA 94124
http://www.hip-hop.com/itfusa/
itfworld@hotmail.com

The International Turntablist Federation (ITF) provides information on upcoming turntablist battles and events as well as general information on turntablism. The Web site provides message board forums to promote discussion about DJing and turntablism. One of the ITF's primary goals is to have people around the world acknowledge turntablists as musicians, and turntables as actual musical instruments. The ITF also strives to strengthen, develop, and unify the turntablist community worldwide.

Graffiti

Art Crimes

http://www.artcrimes.com/
info@graffiti.org

Art Crimes is an online gallery showcasing the many different forms and styles of graffiti artwork from around the world. The Web site was established in September 1994 by two photographers, Susan Farrell and Brett Webb, who have collected thousands of graffiti images since then. Known for being the first graffiti site on the Internet, Art Crimes serves to collect and maintain graffiti art in a place where it will not be destroyed and can be viewed by all.

X2 Project–Graffiti Intelligence Interface

P.O. Box 720607
Miami, FL 33172-0011
http://www.x2project.com/
Data@X2Project.com

This organization aims to educate people about graffiti by providing information, photographs, interviews, message board forums, and links. The X2 Project showcases the versatile and wide-ranging use of graffiti art as a vibrant and effective medium and method of communication.

B-Boys/B-Girls

B-Boy Summit

Asia One
http://www.bboysummit.com
asia@bboysummit.com

A four-day, internationally recognized festival, the B-Boy Summit was founded in 1994 to bring together b-boys/b-girls and celebrate the breakdancing aspect of Hip Hop Culture. Over the years, the summit has grown to include DJs, graffiti artists, and MCs. As an organization, the summit sponsors a host of other events and seminars beyond the festival.

The International Urban Dance Masters Association

iudma@dancemaster.com
http://www.dancemaster.com/

This organization is specifically aimed at unifying the various communities of the world via urban dance. It promotes dance as a medium to transcend all generational, cultural, and racial boundaries and attempts to use it as a mechanism for world peace and social change.

MCs

Guerrilla Funk Recordings

P.O. Box 2317
Danville, CA 94526
http://www.guerrillafunk.com/
gat_turner@hotmail.com

More than a musical organization, Guerrilla Funk offers a comprehensive Web site dealing with Hip Hop's most controversial topics, a newsletter with an extensive global subscription base, and press releases and other informative resources for people interested in Hip Hop. Founded by Paris, a politically conscious artist, the company aims to heighten political and economic consciousness within the Hip Hop fold.

Phat Family

http://www.phatfamily.org/

Founded in 1998, this collective of lesbian, gay, bisexual, and transgender (LGBT) DJs, MCs, writers, and b-boys/b-girls aims to provide a supportive network through Phat Family Records. It has a mailing list of more than 250 members and a Web site and sponsors a host of events. Catering to audiences in the United States and Europe, the collective also discusses issues of identity within the music industry and advocates the use of the term Homo Hop.

Rap Coalition

http://www.rapcoalition.org/
rapcoalition@aol.com

Founded by Wendy Day in 1992, the Rap Coalition is a nonprofit organization that unites and educates artists in the rap industry about the music industry while also working to prevent them from being victimized by managers, record labels, and other industry executives and agents. The Rap Coalition has also been responsible for organizing important meetings, summits, and projects, such as a mentoring program where commercial artists lend support and guidance to up-and-coming artists.

Global Hip Hop

United Kingdom

Pedestrian
http://www.pedestrian.info/

Founded in 1997, this UK-based nonprofit organization uses Hip Hop, and more specifically, turntablism, as a teaching/training tool for youth. Geared toward teaching leadership and life skills, the organization has been subcontracted by professional and educational companies to assist with curriculum development and implementation.

Uganda

Uganda Hip-Hop Foundation
http://www.musicuganda.com/hiphopug/
ekongot@hotmail.com

The Uganda Hip-Hop Foundation is a nonprofit organization founded by Ugandan Hip Hop fans to develop Hip Hop Culture in the country and to unite active followers. This organization also serves as a source for Hip Hoppers to share their thoughts on the issues currently surrounding Hip Hop and the urban music industry scene in general. Enriching the lives of youth and accentuating the positive aspects of Ugandan Hip Hop Culture are two primary goals of this growing organization.

Selected Print Resources

his chapter contains an annotated list of print resources for those desiring more in-depth information on Hip Hop Culture and its numerous elements. The resources are arranged by theme and listed in alphabetical order. All of them should be available through local or online bookstores and/or libraries. Biographies, autobiographies, and other resources focusing on specific individuals have been excluded in favor of resources that take a broader view of Hip Hop Culture and history. In addition to books, it includes numerous articles from academic journals, trade magazines, and periodicals. However, readers are urged to explore the Internet as well as to search for online articles related to Hip Hop, which are not included here.

Hip Hop Culture: General

Journals

Doula: Journal of Rap Music and Hip Hop Culture. Brooklyn, NY: Urban Think Tank. Issued quarterly.

The first of its kind, this quarterly journal analyzes how social, political, and economic realities affect rap music, Hip Hop Culture, and the Hip Hop generation through published essays, interviews, reviews, poetry, and the like. Offering Hip Hop intellectuals a forum for stimulating dialogue and engagement, this journal offers a freedom not often associated with academic journals while

A creative collage of Hip Hop–influenced artwork. (iStockphoto.com)

maintaining strict criteria for acceptance and a broad, dedicated subscription list.

WB&L Journal. Washington, DC: Words, Beats and Life.

This journal dedicated to Hip Hop Culture offers a unique presentation of essays, reviews, poetry, and interviews. Each issue has a theme and is centered on a major issue or series of issues. Providing opportunities to both academic and nonacademic scholars and Hip Hop headz, this journal aims to offer a variety of perspectives in the analysis of Hip Hop.

Books

Ayazi-Hashjin, Sherry, and Sule G. Wilson. *Rap and Hip Hop: The Voice of a Generation.* New York: Rosen, 1999.

This book traces the historical chronicle of rap music and Hip Hop Culture through discussion of the movement of music from Africa to America via the slave trade, the importance of the drum in African cultures, and the evolution of African music in America. This text offers a thorough presentation for the young audience for which it is aimed.

Boyd, Todd. *The New H.N.I.C. (Head Niggas in Charge): The Death of Civil Rights and the Reign of Hip Hop.* New York: New York University Press, 2002.

Based in an uncommon analysis of the civil rights era, this book offers an intricate look at how Hip Hop represents the current and future activists within society. Addressing moral, economic, and political issues such as the use of the "N-word," the business savvy and entrepreneurial successes of Russell Simmons and P. Diddy, and Hip Hop's significant influences within politics, this book sheds new light on the universal role of Hip Hop and how it has taken over as a well-grounded means of expression and power.

Chang, Jeff. *Can't Stop Won't Stop: A History of the Hip-Hop Generation.* New York: St. Martin's, 2005.

This book chronicles the extensive history and rapid rise of Hip Hop Culture through an exploration of four foundational elements—Black nationalism, monumental recordings, major events, and the varying uses of Hip Hop as activism—over the past thirty years. Derived through compelling, original interviews with Hip Hop practitioners, gang members, and legendary pioneers such as DJ Kool Herc and Afrika Bambaataa, this educational resource is full of intriguing information for anybody interested in Hip Hop Culture. This mandatory addition to any collection of Hip Hop references is the most up-to-date and comprehensive chronological study of the culture to date.

D, Chuck. *Fight the Power: Rap, Race, and Reality.* New York: Delacorte, 1997.

Addressing such issues as drugs, race relations, the effects of gangsta rap on youth, the negative and antagonistic portrayals of Blacks by Hollywood, and the East Coast versus West Coast conflicts, rapper-turned-author Chuck D provides a detailed observation of the realities that fuel the music industry and ground Hip Hop. Throughout the book, Chuck D attempts to pinpoint some of the many flaws that hinder society from progressing toward peace and unity, in the process creating yet another meaningful case for developing unity among people. This is an exceptional work by one of Hip Hop's greatest MCs.

Dimitriadis, Greg. *Performing Identity/Performing Culture: Hip Hop as Text, Pedagogy, and Lived Practice.* Vol. 1, *Intersections in Communication and Culture.* New York: Peter Lang, 2001.

This tremendously insightful text offers a rare look at how youth use Hip Hop Culture. Based on four years of field work at a Midwestern community center, Dimitriadis offers a theoretical and practical analysis of the intellectual application of Hip Hop Culture among youth in the most practical sense. This is an excellent academic study of how youth learn Hip Hop and what they do with it.

Ehrlich, Gregor, and Dimitri Ehrlich. *Move the Crowd: Voices and Faces of the Hip-Hop Nation.* New York: Pocket Books, 1999.

Filled with full-page color and black-and-white photos of popular Hip Hop artists such as Ice Cube, Flavor Flav, and others, this book captures the phenomenal economic and social successes of Hip Hop, and in particular, rap music, throughout the 1980s and 1990s. Thoughtful quotations from the artists themselves, newspaper headlines, and magazine and newspaper interviews are only a few of the many contributions of this clever chronicle of the success of Hip Hop.

Fernando, S. H., Jr. *The New Beats: Exploring the Music, Culture, and Attitudes of Hip-Hop.* New York: Doubleday, 1994.

Focused on presenting the historical aspects of Hip Hop Culture, Fernando uses interviews that he conducted as his primary source for this chronological account. He discusses the culture as it was in its early days, centering on early fashion trends, language, gangs, early youth culture, graffiti art, breakdancing, and MCing as well as the Jamaican origins of numerous aspects of the culture. Lists of groundbreaking and influential recordings are supplied at the end of each chapter of this extremely informative resource.

Flores, Juan. *From Bomba to Hip-Hop: Puerto Rican Culture and Latino Identity.* New York: Columbia University Press, 2000.

This collection of essays offers Flores's analysis of Puerto Rican contributions to Hip Hop Culture over the years. Challenging the more common presentation of Hip Hop as solely created and developed by African Americans, Flores offers anecdotal and historical evidence to contextualize the Puerto Rican contributions to the culture. This is an excellent addition to any collection of Hip Hop resources, as it brings to life the undermentioned and undervalued contributions of Puerto Ricans and their innovations within Hip Hop.

Forman, Murray. *The 'Hood Comes First: Race, Space and Place in Rap and Hip-Hop.* Middletown, CT: Wesleyan University Press, 2002.

With a primary focus on racial, spatial, and identity formation within rap music and Hip Hop Culture, this book confronts these major issues in an intellectually stimulating manner, providing ample commentary and insightful analysis of the effects of these issues and others within the culture. Covering topics such as the murders of Tupac Shakur and Notorious B.I.G., the development and evolution of Hip Hop, and other crucial moments in Hip Hop history, this book offers a crucial perspective and is a must-have for any collection.

Forman, Murray, and Mark Anthony Neal. *That's the Joint! The Hip-Hop Studies Reader.* New York: Routledge, 2004.

This collection of writings on Hip Hop includes almost twenty-five years' worth of articles, journalistic writings, essays, commentaries, and criticisms that contain a tremendous supply of educational information for all people interested in Hip Hop. Entry topics include the history of Hip Hop, Hip Hop's involvement in national politics, gender issues, and aesthetics, with more than forty written sources in all. This seminal text single-handedly ushered in the term "Hip Hop Studies," promoting the intellectual pursuit of Hip Hop, a move in the right direction.

Fricke, Jim, and Charlie Ahearn. *Yes Yes Y'all: The Experience Music Project Oral History of Hip-Hop's First Decade.* Cambridge, MA: Da Capo, 2002.

Filled with historical references and an amazing collection of almost 200 photographs, posters, and flyers, this book chronicles the first decade of Hip Hop Culture. A substantial amount of the text is based on never-before-seen interviews by over fifty of Hip Hop's legends and pioneers, such as Afrika Bambaataa, Grandmaster Flash, FAB 5 FREDDY, and Grandwizard Theodore. Covering many aspects of the culture, from DJ Kool Herc's renowned parties in the early 1970s to the Sugar Hill Gang's release of "Rapper's Delight" in 1979 and the importance of breakdancing and graffiti art, this book provides a complete account of Hip Hop's illustrious history. This book is essential for any collection of Hip Hop–related reference materials as it is the most comprehensive account of the early years.

George, Nelson. *Hip Hop America.* New York: Viking, 1998.

In this book, George focuses on the growth and maturation, or lack thereof, of Hip Hop Culture in the United States. Involved in the culture since its inception, George writes on topics such as entrepreneurship in Hip Hop; Hip Hop's acceptance into white suburbia; language, fashion, and violence in Hip Hop; and Hip Hop's role in blaxploitation films. With his elaborate perspective on the current state of Hip Hop, George's book is a critical yet careful analysis of the often overlooked realities that exist within the culture.

Green, Jared, ed. *Rap and Hip Hop (Examining Pop Culture).* San Diego: Greenhaven, 2003.

This collection of excerpted essays and articles offers a great starting point for Hip Hop research as it provides various opinions and responses to many aspects of rap music and Hip Hop Culture. Responding to charges of sexism, racism, homophobia, and numerous others, these articles offer critique, criticism, and responses as well as critical analysis. The collection also includes a few studies on the lyrics and popularity of Eminem.

Hager, Steven. *Hip Hop: The Illustrated History of Break Dancing, Rap Music, and Graffiti.* New York: St. Martin's, 1984.

This extremely important and influential text offers rare insight into the evolution and development of Bronx-based Hip Hop Culture. Approaching each of the elements, this text offers clear, concise, and accessible analysis of the early days of Hip Hop. Full of exceptional photographs, it is a must-have in any collection of materials on Hip Hop, as it is one of the first and most impressive offerings written during the early period.

Hoch, Danny. *Jails, Hospitals, and Hip-Hop and Some People.* New York: Villard, 1998.

This unique presentation of Hip Hop–influenced monologues by performance artist Danny Hoch offers a different but extremely effective presentation. Focusing on the diversity in Hip Hop and its power to heal, it is moving and well written, providing accounts of numerous individuals, from the white teenager desiring to be a Black gangsta rapper to the young Puerto Rican bound by crutches yet dreaming of a career in dance.

Jones, K. Maurice. *Say It Loud: The Story of Rap Music.* Brookfield, CT: Millbrook, 1994.

This most impressive text, written for an audience described as "grade 7 and up," offers a simple yet clear analysis of rap music and its African diasporic roots. Full of black-and-white and color pictures as well as song lyrics, this book offers youth a tremendous opportunity to intellectually process the music and culture they experience every day. Anyone who is sensitive to the interests of youth would find it of interest.

Kitwana, Bakari. *The Hip Hop Generation: The Crisis in African American Culture.* New York: Basic Civitas, 2002.

Aimed at discovering solutions to some of the social disparities and challenges faced by Black youth identified by their general passion for Hip Hop, this clever and influential book initiates a conversation long overdue. Described as a manifesto of sorts, this text introduces the Hip Hop generation as individuals born between 1969 and 1984. This is a must-read for anyone daring to approach the political and cultural challenges of the post–civil rights generation.

————. *Why White Kids Love Hip Hop: Wankstas, Wiggas, Wannabes, and the New Reality of Race in America.* New York: Basic Civitas, 2005.

Addressing taboo topics such as "Does Hip Hop really belong to Black kids, or why do White kids love Hip Hop?" Kitwana's text challenges the notions of ownership, identity, and authenticity in Hip Hop. Armed with an understanding of history, society, and the challenges of change, he offers a brilliant entry to some of the most pertinent conversations that youth, young adults, and other citizens of the United States should engage in. This book is highly recommended for anyone aiming to understand the various gray areas and often unspoken thoughts that hinder progress toward racial, class, and generational healing.

Krims, Adam. *Rap Music and the Poetics of Identity.* Cambridge: Cambridge University Press, 2000.

Using music theory as a mode of analysis, this book discusses the compositional elements of rap music in great detail. With in-depth commentary on rap as a genre of music, it is one of only a few works attempting to comment in detail on how the music is put together. The book also offers informative discussions about rap in Holland and rap among the Cree people in Canada.

Light, Alan, ed. *The VIBE History of Hip Hop.* New York: Three Rivers, 1999.

Perhaps one of the most accessible resources on Hip Hop, this exceptional compendium offers an innovative perspective on Hip Hop through topical essays by leading Hip Hop historians, journalists, and activists. Offering 200 photographs, *VIBE* addresses issues such as the role of gender disparities in Hip Hop, money issues, rivalries, and much more. The book explores Hip Hop fashion, movies and videos on Hip Hop, the business side of the culture, and the foundational elements that are part of it and should be of interest to all who have even a slight interest in Hip Hop.

Nelson, Havelock, and Michael Gonzales. *Bring the Noise: A Guide to Rap Music and Hip-Hop Culture.* New York: Harmony, 1991.

Full of facts, biographical sketches, and accounts of major events prior to 1991, this text offers an informative presentation of Hip Hop Culture and the young men and women who developed it.

With its major focus on rap music, the text offers an insightful guide to key and aesthetically pleasing recordings.

Ogg, Alex, and David Upshal. *The Hip Hop Years: A History of Rap.* New York: Fromm International, 2001.

Focused on the rise and success of rap music, this informative book offers a historical and contextual chronicle of the evolution and development of rap music, its highly influential fashion, its language, and record sales. Based on interviews with more than 100 DJs, MCs, critics, and record label executives, the book constitutes an elaborate history of rap music and MCing. Interviewees include DJ Kool Herc, Grandmaster Flash, NWA, Ice-T, Eminem, and Wu-Tang Clan.

Perkins, William Eric, ed. *Droppin' Science: Critical Essays on Rap Music and Hip Hop Culture.* Philadelphia: Temple University Press, 1996.

Composed of a collection of eleven well-researched and well-written essays on Hip Hop, this book discusses often-ignored topics such as the contributions of Latinos and women in Hip Hop as well as the presence of the Black nationalism ideology. With contributions by photographer Ernie Paniccioli and others, this highly educational, thought-provoking book is appropriate for both personal and academic reading.

Perry, Imani. *Prophets of the Hood: Politics and Poetics in Hip Hop.* Durham, NC: Duke University Press, 2004.

Perry's thought-provoking text offers critical commentary on rap music and Hip Hop Culture's ties to the African diaspora through analysis of its use of call and response, reliance on metaphors, and references to the trickster and the outlaw. Perry's lyrical analyses of Ice Cube, Public Enemy, Lil' Kim, Lauryn Hill, and others advance the notion of these MCs as prophets carrying forth the messages of the street via the street's own aesthetic and language. The text offers an exceptional commentary on crime, violence, and misogyny in rap lyrics as well as the effect of these elements on the greater Hip Hop Culture.

Potter, Russell A. *Spectacular Vernaculars: Hip Hop and the Politics of Postmodernism.* Albany: State University of New York, 1995.

This text, cleverly written, approaches Hip Hop's historical and cultural context as an art form within the Black tradition and as a form of resistance to authority. Working through a postmodern analytical framework, the book addresses the appropriation of technology, the importance of material culture, and the phrases and metaphors of Hip Hop language as a response to capitalism. This book is extremely academic in nature, yet it presents an alternative method of analysis and a rare opportunity to contextualize Hip Hop in a nontraditional manner.

Pough, Gwendolyn D. *Check It While I Wreck It: Black Womanhood, Hip-Hop Culture, and the Public Sphere.* Boston: Northeastern University Press, 2004.

This leading text on the goals, creative expressions, and desires of Black women in Hip Hop is extremely timely and exceptionally well researched and written. In addition to addressing the presence of sexism, a misogynistic ideology, and gender-based stereotypes in Hip Hop, Pough positions women such as Queen Latifah, Missy Elliott, and Lil' Kim as extensions of Sojourner Truth and the numerous Black women involved in the struggle for civil rights during the 1950s and 1960s. Merging an examination of Hip Hop with feminist studies and an interest in issues specific to Black women, Pough encourages the use of rap music in the classroom for cultural and educational benefits.

Quinn, Eithne. *"Nuthin' but a 'G' Thang": The Culture and Commerce of Gangsta Rap.* New York: Columbia University Press, 2004.

With the goal of exploring the origins, development, and wide appeal of gangsta rap, Quinn offers a fascinating and clever study, focusing on artists such as Ice Cube, Snoop Dogg, Tupac Shakur, Dr. Dre, and the Geto Boys. Quinn offers her take on the urban crisis faced by young Black men and their response to this crisis via gangsta rap. In addition, she looks at the media's reception and critique of gangsta rap, the reaction of communities most affected by the lyrics, and the character and actions of the gangsta rappers themselves.

Rivera, Raquel Z. *New York Ricans from the Hip Hop Zone.* New York: Palgrave MacMillan, 2003.

Paying tribute to the often underappreciated and unrecognized contributions to Hip Hop from Puerto Ricans, Rivera's book offers an interesting perspective. Acknowledging Rock Steady Crew pioneer Jo-Jo as well as Big Punisher, Angie Martinez, Fat Joe, and others, Rivera aims to revisit the history of Hip Hop Culture, correcting omissions and reclarifying fragments of the chronicle. Part journalistic and part academic in nature, this book is a good read and a definite contribution to Hip Hop scholarship.

Rose, Tricia. *Black Noise: Rap Music and Black Culture in Contemporary America.* Hanover, NH: Wesleyan University Press, 1994.

One of the most cited texts on rap music and Hip Hop Culture and perhaps one of the first published academic studies on the topic, this text offers a unique critical analysis of sexism, identity, and community formation via Black cultural expression. Based on numerous interviews, years of fieldwork, and Rose's own interactions with the music and the culture, this book remains one of the most comprehensive resources on the influence of Hip Hop Culture on society, particularly during the 1980s. This is a must-have for any library or collection with an interest in providing resources on the music and culture of Hip Hop.

Sexton, Adam, ed. *Rap on Rap: Straight Up Talk on Hip Hop Culture.* New York: Dell, 1995.

This collection of essays brings together a unique ensemble of journalists, academicians, practitioners, and other passionate participants in an exploration of the power, message, and urgency of rap music. Authors from Greg Tate to Tricia Rose and from Ice-T to Pat Buchanan present essays, interviews, commentaries, and ranting sessions revealing the tremendous influence that Hip Hop has on society, whether it is appreciated or not.

Shomari, Hashim A. (William A. Lee III). *From the Underground: Hip Hop Culture as an Agent of Social Change.* Fanwood, NJ: X-Factor, 1995.

This study examines important, if not even urgent, aspects of Hip Hop Culture. First, the author establishes that Hip Hop Culture is much broader than just rap music. Next, he presents the political possibilities and downfalls of the culture. Finally, he addresses the effect of the media on Hip Hop Culture and its presentation of the culture to the general society.

Toop, David. *Rap Attack: African Jive to New York Hip Hop.* Boston: South End, 1984.

One of the first intellectual analyses and chronicles of Hip Hop and its African heritage, this text has been extremely influential in Hip Hop studies. Focusing on the South Bronx origins of the culture and based on interviews of pioneers such as Afrika Bambaataa, Grandmaster Flash, Spoonie Gee, Double Trouble, and others, it offers a wealth of information on a time period of Hip Hop that provided the foundation for its later development. This is a must-have in any collection of materials on Hip Hop.

———. *Rap Attack 2: African Rap to Global Hip Hop,* 2d ed. London: Serpent's Tail, 1991.

This second edition of the classic *Rap Attack* brings the material current to its 1991 publication date. It includes the golden years of the 1980s, featuring the rise of groups such as Run-DMC, LL Cool J, the Beastie Boys, and De La Soul.

———. *Rap Attack 3: African Rap to Global Hip Hop.* 3d ed. London: Serpent's Tail, 2000.

This third edition of the classic *Rap Attack* updates the information through the events of 2000. It offers insight on the rise of gangsta rap as well as the fatal shootings of Tupac Shakur and Notorious B.I.G.

Articles and Chapters

Allen, Harry. "Hip-Hop Madness: From Def Jams to Cold Lampin', Rap Music Is OUR Music!" *Essence,* April 1989.

Written by Hip Hop historian and activist Harry Allen, this article accomplishes a number of important tasks. First, Allen asserts Hip Hop as an expression grounded in Black expressive culture and makes a direct connection to the Yoruba people of Nigeria and the Nago people of Benin (formerly Dahomey). Second, Allen compares the present state of Hip Hop at the time of his writing in 1989 to the early years of the culture during the 1970s.

Amber, Jeannine. "Whose Hip-Hop Is This?" *Essence,* June 1997, 150.

This short yet moving piece offers a perspective on the role of violence in Hip Hop during the late 1990s and the effects of the violent murders of Tupac Shakur and Biggie Smalls. The author's personal reflection on the murders of these two influential music icons is widened in scope by her insightful commentary on the effect the murders had within the greater Black community.

Ards, Angela. "Rhyme and Resist: Organizing the Hip-Hop Generation." *The Nation,* July 1999, 11–14+.

This article positions Hip Hop as the next generation of the civil rights movement. Citing the widely celebrated accomplishments of past generations in the struggle for civil rights, the author suggests the use of Hip Hop as a tool for enhanced communication between the generations. She further suggests that young people are replacing the spirituals and freedom songs of the 1950s and 1960s with the rhymes of Tupac Shakur, Busta Rhymes, and the like.

Bradley, Omar N. "Hip Hop Generation: American as Apple Pie." *Billboard,* 18 November 1995, 9.

Addressing the naysayers and haters of Hip Hop who charge that Hip Hop advocates deviant behavior, foul language, and immoral actions, the author of this article strikes back, advocating the view that Hip Hop has transformed energetic, passionate youth, turning them from violent street warriors into creative artists. He suggests that this is a major accomplishment, not only for Hip Hop and the youth in question, but for society as a whole. Further, he cites youth social and political engagement and awareness as the fruits of Hip Hop.

Coker, Cheo H., Tara Roberts, and Dream Hampton. "A Hip-Hop Nation Divided: Is Hip-Hop a Generation's Glory or Proof of Its Decline?" *Essence,* August 1994, 63–64.

This collection of short pieces offers reactions and opinions in response to trends in Hip Hop. From Tara Roberts's commentary on misogynistic lyrics and the conflict between bad lyrics and great beats, to Cheo Coker's suggestion that the media use Hip Hop as a scapegoat, blaming it for the misdeeds even of those who do not listen to hip hop, the articles offer an interesting dialogue on Hip Hop's effect on society and, more important, on issues of Hip Hop identity and ownership.

Fost, Dan. "Reaching the Hip-Hop Generation." *American Demographics* 15 (1993): 15–16.

Offering an analysis of the responses of a population of youth deemed "the Hip Hop generation" to mainstream media messages, this article offers very interesting findings on how this group of youths perceives and processes information. Identifying music and fashion as two influential factors, this study suggests that understanding Hip Hop Culture is critical to understanding the mindset of these young people.

Powell, Kevin. "Hip-Hop Nation 2000." *Essence,* August 1997, 78.

This article offers a candid and intimate presentation of Hip Hop Culture and the Hip Hop generation in the late 1990s. Presented as a collection of thoughts, opinions, and perspectives compiled by Powell, this article is truly a testament to the power of Hip Hop.

Robinson, Ruth Adkins. "Hip-Hop History." *Billboard,* 4 December 1999, 38.

This essay presents a very well-researched synopsis of Hip Hop history, with commentary on changing trends for each decade. The author supplies important information on the influence of the media as well as on social, political, and economic changes in society.

Samuels, Allison, N'Gai Croal, and David Gates. "Battle for the Soul of Hip-Hop: Is Rap—Increasingly Driven by Sex, Violence and Money—Going Too Far? You'd Be Surprised Who Thinks So. The Hip-Hop Elite Squares Off over the Future of Its Music and Videos." *Newsweek,* 9 October 2000, 58–65.

This cover story (with Dr. Dre and Eminem pictured on the cover) includes numerous quotations from leading names in Hip Hop as the team of writers endeavors to address whether rap music and Hip Hop Culture are "going too far." They address the rising prevalence of sex and violence, the passion for money and material culture, and other major issues. This article is full of interesting commentary and includes photographs, as well as a Hip Hop family tree tracing major influences and protégés.

Sherrill, Stephen. "Fear of a Hip Hop Syllabus." *Rolling Stone,* 30 September 1993, 56–58.

This interesting article offers a roundtable of college professors from Brown University, the University of Michigan, and Dartmouth College who discuss incorporating Hip Hop within university curricula. The discussion surrounds which Hip Hop records to include within a course on rap music. Public Enemy, MC Lyte, Salt-n-Pepa, Run-DMC, NWA, and Queen Latifah are all mentioned.

Stapleton, Katina R. "From the Margins to Mainstream: The Political Power of Hip-Hop." *Media, Culture and Society* 20 (1998): 219–234.

This article offers an insightful analysis of Hip Hop's role in inspiring youth political involvement and engagement. The author also comments on the national and international scope of the influence that Hip Hop has, not only on young Blacks but also on the youth of other races and ethnicities worldwide, regardless of gender or class.

Thompson, Robert Farris. "Hip-Hop 101." *Rolling Stone,* 27 March 1986, 95–100.

This article, by a noted anthropologist, traces the roots of Hip Hop Culture to the African continent, positioning Hip Hop as a continuation of numerous African-derived cultural characteristics. The article has been reprinted numerous times and remains one of the most influential short academic treatments of the culture.

DJing

Books

Brewster, Bill, and Frank Broughton. *Last Night a DJ Saved My Life: The History of the Disc Jockey.* New York: Grove, 2000.

This book chronicles the history and role of the DJ in the evolution and development of a few genres of music, with specific attention paid to hip hop and techno. The impressive volume contains interviews with influential DJs, instrumental musicians, critics, and other prominent figures in the music industry, offering a rare insider's perspective. The book is written by music journalists with a passion for dance music and is an extremely informative Hip Hop resource.

Reighley, Kurt B. *Looking for the Perfect Beat: The Art and Culture of the DJ.* New York: Pocket Books, 2000.

This book focuses on the DJ's influence on various popular musical genres, such as hip hop, techno, rock, and house music. Among other topics, this book offers a crash course on some of the greatest DJs and insight into their lives and into how they have affected a generation through their musical innovations. Also included is a basic guide to DJing equipment and techniques.

Schloss, Joseph G. *Making Beats: The Art of Sampling-Based Hip-Hop.* Middletown, CT: Wesleyan University Press, 2004.

Delving into the production of hip hop music with the use of samples, this book discusses the thought processes and procedures of artists who create sample-based music. Throughout the text, Schloss describes the sampling process as a musical art form that has evolved and developed over the years with technological improvements. Based on the author's 2000 doctoral dissertation, this is a rare and impressive academic treatment of an often intellectually taboo topic.

Souvignier, Todd. *The World of DJs and the Turntable Culture.* Milwaukee, WI: Hal Leonard, 2003.

This book offers insight into the history of DJing through interviews with influential DJs, detailed instructions on specific DJing skills, information on how DJ equipment operates, and much more. This is a top-notch educational resource for both aspiring DJs and those who wish to study the history of the art of DJing. Perhaps the closest thing to a textbook or field guide, this text is extremely informative and easy to use.

Articles and Chapters

Berman, Eric. "The Godfathers of Rap." *Rolling Stone,* 23 December 1993, 137+.

This well-researched and well-written article offers a retelling of the early days of rap music with a focus on influential DJs Kool Herc, Afrika Bambaataa, and Grandmaster Flash. Commentary is also presented on Lovebug Starski and the introduction of the term "hip hop."

White, Joseph, and James H. Cones III. "Cool Pose, Rap, Hip-Hop, and the Black Aesthetic." In *Black Man Emerging: Facing the Past and Seizing a Future in America.* New York: W. H. Freeman, 1999, 91–113.

Psychologists Joseph White and James Henry Cones III offer an extremely informative and stimulating analysis of the effects of Hip Hop on Black men. Grounded in numerous case studies and biographical sketches, and sensitive to issues of racism, discrimination, and other forces of oppression, the authors speak to the roles of family, religion, educational opportunity, mentorship, and other external influences in the creation of personal representations of Black masculinity.

Graffiti

Austin, Joe. *Taking the Train: How Graffiti Art Became an Urban Crisis in New York City.* New York: Columbia University Press, 2001.

This book chronicles New York City's graffiti scene from the beginning of the movement in the late 1960s through the numerous battles with Mayor Edward Koch and the Metropolitan Transportation Authority (MTA) during the early 1980s. The evolution and development of the movement is explained, numerous artists are profiled, and an account of graffiti's prominent role in Hip Hop Culture is discussed in detail.

Castleman, Craig. *Getting Up: Subway Graffiti in New York.* Cambridge, MA: MIT Press, 1984.

This author shares the experiences and lives of the graffiti artists who played an instrumental role in developing the graffiti movement in the subways of New York City. The artists' experiences and stories are glimpsed through candid interviews that were conducted by author Craig Castleman, a New Yorker himself.

Chalfant, Henry, and James Prigoff. *Spraycan Art.* New York: Thames and Hudson, 1987.

Featuring spraycan artwork from more than twenty cities around the world, this book chronicles the evolution and development of the art form from its beginnings on subway cars to its acceptance into art galleries. Filled with vibrant photographs, this detailed resource enables readers to relive the history of a once unlawful form of creativity and to experience it firsthand from a leading chronicler and historian of the movement.

Cooper, Martha, and Henry Chalfant. *Subway Art*. New York: Thames and Hudson, 1987.

This brilliant book by two expert photographers offers unique insight into the social and artistic significance of graffiti as a movement and as a part of the greater Hip Hop Culture. Chronicling the origins and history as well as the philosophical approach of the self-acclaimed rebels whose weapon of choice is the spray can, this book also comments on the various styles, techniques, terminology, and collectives of artists within the subway graffiti movement.

Ferrell, Jeff. *Crimes of Style: Urban Graffiti and the Politics of Criminality*. Boston: Northeastern University Press, 1993.

This text addresses the prominence of graffiti as a powerful tool of activism and explores why it has served so well as a foundational element of Hip Hop Culture. Through ethnographic and criminological analysis, Ferrell argues that graffiti is a response to legal and social oppression. The extremely insightful study is based on research conducted in Denver, Colorado, and includes black-and-white photographs.

Murray, James T., and Karla L. Murray. *Broken Windows: Graffiti NYC*. Corte Madera, CA: Gingko, 2002.

This riveting tribute to graffiti offers extensive interviews and numerous photos of "bombs," "pieces," and "throw-ups" by more than 180 artists from the United States, Germany, France, Sweden, Finland, Denmark, Holland, Italy, and Norway. Boasting the largest collection of graffiti by women, this text offers a visual narrative of 1980s' graffiti and its transition from subway trains to large walls. This is an exceptional and widely used presentation of graffiti.

Powers, Stephen. *The Art of Getting Over: Graffiti at the Millennium*. New York: St. Martin's, 1999.

Chronicling the evolution of graffiti art over a thirty-year time period, this book contains interviews with past and present practitioners of the art form, a history of the artistic movement, and photographs of some of the most significant pieces of graffiti that have been done over the years. Powers examines how graffiti art has been able to evolve and develop over the years without succumbing to the lure of the mainstream or being defeated by its arsenal of opponents, such as Mayor Edward Koch and the Metropolitan Transportation Authority.

Rahn, Janice. *Painting without Permission: Hip-Hop Graffiti Subculture.* Westport, CT: Greenwood, 2002.

Aimed at training youth workers and educators, this book offers great practical and theoretical advice. It is an important contribution for those aiming to use Hip Hop to connect with and challenge young people, encouraging the use of graffiti and Hip Hop Culture as an educational tool. Divided into three sections, this text presents interviews with a variety of graffiti artists, takes a look at graffiti as a foundational element of Hip Hop Culture, and explores the notion of graffiti as activism.

Sutherland, Peter, and Revs. *Autograf: New York City's Graffiti Writers.* New York: Powerhouse, 2004.

Featuring exceptional pictures of color and black-and-white graffiti by New York City artists, this text offers a unique portrayal of the social, political, and artistic graffiti movement. The work of artists such as FUTURA, LADY PINK, CYCLE, and CLAW fill this collection of more than 100 portraits, including landscapes. In the format almost of a black book, this collection is an impressive contribution to the study of a foundational element of Hip Hop that is often forgotten.

B-Boys/B-Girls

Although there are numerous texts on b-boying/b-girling, such as *Breakdance: Hip Hop Handbook* by Jairus Green and David Bramwell (Street Style Publications, 2003) and its predecessor *Breakdancing: Mr. Fresh and the Supreme Rockers Show You How* by Mr. Fresh (Avon Books, 1984), these informative contributions are essentially guides on how to do the various moves within the subgenres of Hip Hop dance. Other texts, such as Michael Holman's *Breaking and the New York City Breakers* (Freundlich Books, 1984), although exceptionally informative, are out of print and very difficult to obtain.

MCs

Books

Costello, Mark, and David Foster Wallace. *Signifying Rappers: Rap and Race in the Urban Present.* New York: Ecco, 1990.

Addressing issues such as race and poverty in relation to rap music, this book attempts to explain how the music genre has thrived within the inner-city North Dorchester community of Boston, Massachusetts. It also offers an analysis of rap music as a social, political, economic, and cultural response to society's negative forces. This is an excellent study of a localized Hip Hop scene.

Dee, Kool Moe. *There's a God on the Mic: The True 50 Greatest MCs.* New York: Thunder's Mouth Press, 2003.

In this book, rap legend turned author Kool Moe Dee has compiled a list of the fifty greatest MCs of all time. Using a rating system he developed with seventeen categories, such as lyricism, freestyle ability, live performance ability, originality, flow, and vocabulary, he gives each artist a cumulative score. Explanations for the ratings are supplied as well as impressive color and black-and-white photographs of each artist.

Hip Hop Divas. New York: Harmony, 2001.

Although many of the women who are involved in Hip Hop are overlooked by Hip Hop fans and media alike, they have made tremendous contributions to the culture and continue to do so. This book profiles fifteen female figures who have been instrumental in the evolution and development of Hip Hop over its many years of existence, including Eve, Salt-n-Pepa, Queen Latifah, and Lauryn Hill. Created by the *VIBE* Hip Hop magazine, the book contains photos, essays, and a wealth of information on these exceptional divas of Hip Hop.

Keyes, Cheryl L. *Rap Music and Street Consciousness.* Urbana: University of Illinois Press, 2002.

This extremely informative academic analysis of rap music uses folklore, ethnomusicology, and popular music studies approaches, using a wealth of research, much of which is primary source material. Keyes presents Hip Hop as a cultural movement grounded in social, political, and economic empowerment. She traces rap music from the African continent, through Jamaica, into the South Bronx, and then to all corners of the nation and the international community in the 1980s. This exceptional study offers extensive musical, cultural, and even religious analysis.

Kitwana, Bakari. *The Rap on Gangsta Rap: Who Runs It? Gangsta Rap and Visions of Black Violence.* Chicago: Third World Press, 1995.

This critical review and critique of gangsta rap is infused with charged commentary on the genre as an art form, its relationship to violence and drugs, and its portrayal by the media. Kitwana approaches political, social, and moral issues stemming from the reality of derogatory and often misogynistic lyrics. The commentaries on sexism, gender relations, and racism are exceptionally elucidating.

Miyakawa, Felicia M. *Five Percenter Rap: God Hop's Music, Message, and Black Muslim Mission.* Bloomington: Indiana University Press, 2005.

This academic treatment of the influence of the Five Percent Nation is an exceptional study of the relationship between Hip Hop and religion. With a focus on artists such as Queen Latifah, Wu-Tang Clan, Rakim Allah, Erykah Badu, and others, it explores the merging of the Five Percenter lifestyle and the Hip Hop lifestyle under the influence of many of these same artists. Using rich lyrical analysis, the author introduces a new realm to Hip Hop studies.

Ro, Ronin. *Gangsta: Merchandising the Rhymes of Violence.* New York: St. Martin's, 1996.

This book consists of a collection of articles written by Ronin Ro from 1992 to 1995 that showcase the gangsta rap scenes of New York City and Los Angeles. He discusses rap music's transition from a genre of positive expression and activistic integrity to one where gangsta personas are created and glorified by record companies and media. Ro offers critical commentary on the lyrics that encourage violence, crime, and misogyny and attempts to expose the use of these lyrics by record companies to promote and sell records.

Shaw, William. *Westside: Young Men and Hip Hop in L.A.* New York: Simon and Schuster, 2000.

Set in South Central Los Angeles during the late 1980s, the narrative of this book chronicles the challenges and hardships of seven Black men who hope to one day use their life experiences as opportunities to succeed in the rap music industry. Attempting to follow in the footsteps of their West Coast rap idols—Tupac Shakur, Dr. Dre, and Snoop Dogg—the men seek an escape through music from the violence and crime that plague their neighborhood. This example of literary nonfiction is a great read that illuminates the sweet and bitter clutches of reality.

Small, Michael. *Break It Down: The Inside Story from the New Leaders of Rap.* New York: Citadel, 1992.

Full of photographs, this book offers biographies, interviews, and interesting personal facts about leading rap stars of the 1980s. Including artists' opinions on topics such as racism, violence, crime, and the negative portrayal of Hip Hop in the media, this collection of firsthand accounts is impressive. Salt-n-Pepa, LL Cool J, and KRS-One are just a few of the artists profiled in this reference text.

Articles and Chapters

Bernard-Donals, Michael. "Jazz, Rock 'n' Roll, Rap and Politics." *Journal of Popular Culture* 28, no. 2 (Fall 1994): 127–139.

Discovering the relationship between popular music and politics, this article offers critical analysis of the continuum of popular music, focusing on jazz, rock 'n' roll, and rap. Although each genre intersects with politics differently, this article attempts to draw parallels in addition to approaching external influences such as race and other determinants.

Cocks, Jay, and Stephen Koepp. "Chilling Out on Rap Flash: New City Music Brings Out the Last Word in Wild Style." *Time,* 21 March 1983.

This article captures the rise of Hip Hop Culture during the early 1980s and shows the national influence that the young culture already had by 1983. Referencing the 1982 film *Wild Style* and using Hip Hop jargon while attempting to describe the fashions, the authors display the public's fascination with the highly popular modes of expression called Hip Hop.

King, Aliya S. "More Rappers Hop into the Apparel Business." *Billboard,* 8 May 1999, 49.

This article offers insight into the popular move into the world of fashion by leading MCs. Using fashion as a form of empowerment and economic opportunity, MCs are packaging and marketing their looks to consumers who also tend to be loyal fans. This article speaks of the behind-the-scenes world of this Hip Hop industry.

Ogbar, Jeffrey. "Slouching toward Bork: The Culture Wars and Self-Criticism in Hip Hop Music." *Journal of Black Studies* 30, no. 2 (1999): 164–183.

This article presents the views of many of Hip Hop's major critics and addresses their opposition to the culture. From C. Dolores Tucker to Bob Dole and Robert H. Bork, these opponents find fault with the presence and position of Hip Hop within popular culture. The author also discusses internal criticism within Hip Hop Culture.

Pinn, Anthony. "'How Ya Livin'?': Notes on Rap Music and Social Transformation." *Western Journal of Black Studies* 23, no. 1 (1999): 10–21.

This essay offers an interesting comparative view of Hip Hop and its predecessor, the civil rights movement, exploring how each has used music as an agent of transformation. Grounded in the idea of a continuum, it asserts that Hip Hop is the next manifestation of the civil rights movement, but with new leadership and a different approach. This study positions the changing nature of society relative to social, political, and economic oppression and opportunity as both an asset and a deterrent in the case of Hip Hop.

Safire, William. "The Rap on Hip-Hop." *The New York Times Magazine,* 8 November 1992, 18.

Offering a brief recap of the history of Hip Hop and the evolution of the names and terms most associated with the culture, this article shows the wide appeal of Hip Hop and validates it as an influential art form.

Samuels, David. "The Rap on Rap: The 'Black Music' That Isn't Either." *The New Republic,* 11 November 1991, 24–29.

Extremely critical of the prominent rise of Hip Hop, which in the author's opinion celebrates "ghetto gangsterism" and racism, this article offers an interesting perspective on the controversial topic. Much of the author's commentary concerns the high population of white consumers who are fans of a genre of music dominated by Black performers. Placing rap and Hip Hop within a context dating back to Jamaican toasting, the author seems to be proposing that white consumers have had a tremendous influence on rap music.

Thigpen, David. "Not for Men Only; Women Rappers Are Breaking the Mold with a Message of Their Own." *Time,* 27 May 1991.

This article tells of the rich contributions that women have made to Hip Hop, which are usually overlooked among the well-documented and well-articulated contributions to Hip Hop by men. Focusing on Salt-n-Pepa, Monie Love, and Queen Latifah, the author offers numerous examples of how these and other women fought stereotypes and gender-based discrimination to succeed not only as innovators but as pioneers in Hip Hop Culture.

Journalism/Media

Cepeda, Raquel, ed. *And It Don't Stop: The Best American Hip-Hop Journalism of the Last 25 Years.* New York: Faber and Faber, 2004.

This book is composed of Cepeda's extraordinary collection of the most innovative journalistic articles on Hip Hop since its introduction into mainstream popular culture in the United States. The articles were culled from a variety of sources and provide an immense range of coverage of numerous topics and events. The legacies of Tupac Shakur and Notorious B.I.G. are documented, along with the Sugar Hill Gang's mainstream hit "Rapper's Delight." Featured authors include Toure, Kevin Powell, Harry Allen, Danyel Smith, and Joan Morgan.

Watkins, S. Craig. *Representing: Hip Hop Culture and the Production of Black Cinema.* Chicago: University of Chicago Press, 1998.

Watkins's timely book offers unique commentary and critical analysis of the rise of "ghettocentric films" as a commercially successful subgenre of the motion-picture industry. He carefully deals with the popularity of these films in light of the contradictory treatment of Black youth by general society. *Representing* is an important addition to the body of works revealing the good and bad effects of Hip Hop Culture.

Photographs

Cooper, Martha (photographer), Akim Walta, Zephyr, Charlie Ahearn, FABEL, and Patti Astor. *Hip Hop Files: Photographs, 1979–1984.* New York: Powerhouse, 2004.

The photographs presented in this book document the history and expression of New York's thriving Hip Hop Culture during the early 1980s. The book allows viewers to either reminisce or experience for the first time the early stages of Hip Hop via pictures of the DJs, graffiti artists, b-boys/b-girls, and MCs who were a part of its development. Pioneers included in the book are Afrika Bambaataa, Rock Steady Crew, FAB 5 FREDDY, and numerous others. The book also includes text by Hip Hop innovators such as ZEPHYR, FABEL, and leading Hip Hop chronicler Charlie Ahearn.

Kenner, Rob, and George Pitts. *VX: 10 Years of Vibe Photography.* New York: Vibe, 2003.

This book contains selected photographs that appeared in *VIBE* magazine over the span of a decade (1993–2003). Also included are images that have not been published before, including a collection of outtake pictures. Photographs by Albert Watson, Ellen von Unwerth, David LaChapelle, Baron Claiborne, Melodie McDaniels, and numerous other top-ranked photographers are featured throughout this book, in addition to a foreword by *VIBE* founder Quincy Jones.

Malone, Bonz. *Hip Hop Immortals.* Vol. 1, *The Remix.* New York: Thunder's Mouth, 2003.

The photographs of David LaChapelle, Nitin Vadukul, Jesse Frohman, Christian Witkin, and others that are featured in this book capture the visual essence of Hip Hop. The book contains images of Hip Hop legends such as DJ Kool Herc, Kurtis Blow, Notorious B.I.G., Ice-T, Public Enemy, and numerous others. Both color and black-and-white photographs are included as well as textual commentary by Hip Hop historian Bonz Malone.

Paniccioli, Ernie. *Who Shot Ya? Three Decades of Hip Hop Photography*. New York: Amistad, 2002.

This pictorial showcase presents the photography of the Dean of Hip Hop Photography, Ernie Paniccioli, heralded for over three decades of service to Hip Hop. This work, composed of more than 200 images, includes pictures of Hip Hop greats such as Grandmaster Flash, Tupac Shakur, Notorious B.I.G., Will Smith, Queen Latifah, and plenty more. *Who Shot Ya?* is one of the most important books of Hip Hop photography because it captures the viewpoint of a photographer who has watched Hip Hop evolve and spread.

Powell, Ricky. *Oh Snap! The Rap Photography of Ricky Powell*. New York: St. Martin Griffin, 1998.

Comprising over ten years of photography, this collection of more than eighty publicity shots, ads, and other photos focuses on the rap element of Hip Hop Culture. It includes photos of both old-school and current rap artists, such as Run-DMC, LL Cool J, Public Enemy, Cypress Hill, and Method Man. Most of the images in the book are in color and are accompanied by captions by Hip Hop historian Ricky Powell. This book is a valuable resource for those looking to revisit and/or study the legacy of rap music.

Shabazz, Jamel. *Back in the Days*. New York: Powerhouse, 2001.

This book of photographs showcases the work of photographer Jamel Shabazz, whose photos, taken during the 1980s, capture the Hip Hop scene as it was "back in the days." With essays written by photographer and Hip Hop historian Ernie Paniccioli, this book reflects not only the fashion of Hip Hop Culture throughout the 1980s but also the expressions and attitudes of individuals involved in the scene. Shabazz's photos have been featured in *Source, VIBE,* and other top-ranked magazines. His work offers a critical, photo-based chronicle of issues such as racial justice, economic access, and political equality.

Reference Materials

Bogdanov, Vladimir. *All Music Guide to Hip-Hop: The Definitive Guide to Rap and Hip-Hop*. San Francisco: Backbeat, 2003.

This tremendous resource offers biographical and musical profiles of more than 1,200 artists, ranging from one-hit wonders to multi-award-winning superstars. The guide further provides information on more than 3,100 recordings, ranging from out-of-print and hardly known to multiplatinum releases. Aimed at providing information to seekers of all levels of interest, this resource is also fun to use.

FAB 5 FREDDY (Frederick Braithwaite). *Fresh Fly Flavor: Words and Phrases of the Hip-Hop Generation.* Stamford, CT: Longmeadow, 1992.

This book serves as a dictionary of words and phrases used within Hip Hop Culture. Full of illustrations and photographs of popular culture and Hip Hop icons, this book makes sense out of words that would otherwise be meaningless to many people, particularly those who do not identify with the Hip Hop generation. This is a great resource for those interested in learning the jargon and slang made famous during the 1980s.

Jenkins, Sacha, Elliott Wilson, Chairman Mao, Gabriel Alvarez, and Brent Rollins. *Ego Trip's Book of Rap Lists.* New York: Ego Trip, 1999.

Written by an extraordinary list of top-notch Hip Hop historians and journalists, this text is an impressive resource that condenses a great deal of information in the form of lists. From lyrics to fashion, movies, names, and performances, it is extremely helpful whether you know what you are looking for or not.

Kulkarni, Neil. *Hip Hop: Bring the Noise. The Stories behind the Biggest Songs.* New York: Thunder's Mouth, 2004.

An expansion of the best-selling *Stories behind the Songs* series, this volume is dedicated to revealing the shocking, heartwarming, and brutally honest stories behind the creation of some of Hip Hop's most loved and perhaps most hated songs. Aimed at providing a contrast to the often intellectually condescending media portrayal of Hip Hop artists, this text discovers and reveals the highly political, extremely cleverly constructed, and exceptionally powerful words of fifty of the greatest lyrical contributions to Hip Hop.

McCoy, Judy. *Rap Music in the 1980s: A Reference Guide.* Metuchen, NJ: Scarecrow, 1992.

This excellent resource offers a comprehensive study of rap music resources chronicling the 1980s. It offers a rather exhaustive annotated bibliography of more than 1,000 articles, books, and reviews and a discography of more than 70 entries. All sources relate to rap music and its intersection with mainstream culture, art, politics, and general society. This is a great reference for educators, researchers, and/or students studying the Golden Years of Hip Hop.

Shapiro, Peter. *The Rough Guide to Hip-Hop.* New York: Viking Penguin, 2001.

This guide offers insightful information on DJs, graffiti artists, b-boys/b-girls, MCs, producers, and Hip Hop in general. Including an extensive biography and discography, as well as numerous pictures, the text is small in size but still makes an important contribution to the study of Hip Hop Culture.

Spady, James G., and Joseph D. Eure, eds. *Nation Conscious Rap: AfroAmericanization of Knowledge Series 3.* New York: PC International, 1991.

Spady and Eure have assembled an amazing reference of primary source interviews with the leading names in Hip Hop. Through the lens of Black nationalism, this book presents the social and political realities of Black artists. Answering innovative and sensitive questions, these artists are able to offer a unique look into their own lives and personal journeys. Featured interviewees include KRS-One, Chuck D, Big Daddy Kane, and Q-Tip.

Spady, James G., Charles G. Lee, and H. Samy Alim, eds. *Street Conscious Rap.* Philadelphia: Black History Museum, Umum Loh Publishers, 1999.

This compendium of essays, illustrations, photos, and interviews offers an intimate variety of perspectives on a number of topics, including the intersection of Hip Hop and business, technology, family values, race relations, education, and a host of other intriguing topics. Featuring interviews by Tupac Shakur, Queen Latifah, Chuck D, Common, Eve, and numerous other notables, this book presents a rare view of Hip Hop from the inside out.

Stancell, Steven. *Rap Whoz Who: The World of Rap Music Performers and Promoters.* New York: Schirmer, 1996.

Aimed at capturing the rich and colorful chronicle of Hip Hop in writing, this reference offers information on artists, their lives, their influences, their musical developments, and their stylistic practices as well as insight into their social and political messages. The useful resource also offers short narratives on the music business, the relationship between violence and rap, and the influence of Islam on rap, in addition to a number of great photos.

Stavsky, Lois, I. E. Mozeson, and Dani Reyes Mozeson. *A2Z: The Book of Rap and Hip-Hop Slang.* New York: Boulevard Books, 1995.

This collection of definitions to more than 1,000 words and phrases associated with Hip Hop is an extremely useful aid to the researcher or general reader aiming to decipher the colorful jargon of the culture. From localized nuances to regionalized colloquialisms and national mainstream sayings, it captures the flare and sometimes the flame of a unique, effective, and extremely expressive use of language.

Taylor, Barbara, ed. *The National Rap Directory.* Atlanta: Rising Star Music, 1996.

This book contains a listing of many independent urban music labels and publishers from the 1980s to the mid-1990s. Supplying readers with an address, phone number, fax number, and other contact information for each entry, the directory was updated every year to ensure that the content was as up to date as possible. This directory of more than 1,000 entries also provides articles and tips by music-industry professionals.

Wang, Oliver. *Classic Material: The Hip Hop Album Guide.* Toronto, Canada: ECW Press, 2003.

This book seeks to supply thought-provoking commentary and essays on some of the most influential artists and albums from Hip Hop's past and present. Essays and reviews on Public Enemy, Ice-T, Run-DMC, Tupac Shakur, Jay-Z, and numerous other Hip Hop and popular music icons are written by expert writers whose work has appeared in *Spin, Rolling Stone, Source, VIBE,* and other notable magazines. Over sixty albums are covered in this important work.

Westbrook, Alonzo. *Hip-Hoptionary: A Dictionary of Hip-Hop Termi-nology.* New York: Harlem Moon, 2000.

A lexicon for contemporary urban slang, this reference defines more than 2,500 Hip Hop–related terms, phrases, and colloqui-alisms. The format makes it a tool for quick and easy application. The reference also provides biographies of famous MCs, lists of fashion lines, lists of reference materials, and a list of online dic-tionaries catering to people interested in Hip Hop. The book is di-vided into three sections: slang to English, English to slang, and the lists.

Global Hip Hop

Books

Durand, Alain-Phillipe. *Black, Blanc, Beur: Rap Music and Hip-Hop Culture in the Francophone World.* Lanham, MD: Rowman and Lit-tlefield, 2002.

This collection of essays by a variety of scholars offers an inform-ative look at francophone Hip Hop, exploring the similarities and differences in the appropriation of Hip Hop in French-speaking countries around the world.

Maxwell, Ian. *Phat Beats, Dope Rhymes: Hip Hop Down Under Comin' Upper.* Middletown, CT: Wesleyan University Press, 2003.

This academic work offers a unique perspective on Hip Hop in Sydney, Australia. Written from field notes from August 1992 through October 1994, Maxwell's book offers musical and anthro-pological analysis via a postmodernist cultural studies framework as he deals with identity construction, the creation of a Sydney-based Hip Hop nation, and its relation to the global Hip Hop com-munity. This is a wonderful model of a successful approach to the study on Hip Hop in other parts of the world.

Mitchell, Tony, ed. *Global Noise: Rap and Hip Hop outside the USA.* Middletown, CT: Wesleyan University Press, 2001.

This monumental collection of essays by international scholars explores the various Hip Hop scenes in Canada, Japan, Australia, France, Germany, Bulgaria, Italy, the United Kingdom, Korea, and

New Zealand, in addition to a piece on Islamic Hip Hop. The essays reveal the unique social, political, economic, cultural, and religious situations faced by the youth and how they respond via Hip Hop. This is a tremendous and timely contribution to scholarship on Hip Hop.

Neate, Patrick. *Where You're At: Notes from the Frontline of a Hip-Hop Planet.* New York: Riverhead, 2004.

This exceptional narrative offers an objective presentation of the global nature of Hip Hop through the account of a British novelist who travels to New York, Tokyo (Japan), Rio de Janeiro (Brazil), and Johannesburg (South Africa) in search of Hip Hop expression. His unique ability to not only compare and contrast these expressions but also discover underlying currents in the global Hip Hop movement makes this text an informative and pleasurable read. It would be of interest to anyone who is interested in exploring how Hip Hop has expanded its territory.

Articles and Chapters

Hebdige, Dick. "Rap and Hip Hop: The New York Connection." In *Cut 'N' Mix: Culture, Identity and Caribbean Music.* New York: Methuen, 1987, 136–148.

This chapter traces the connection from Hip Hop's Caribbean origins to its South Bronx implementation. Full of informative research, including interview transcripts, it focuses on Caribbean cultural practices and the DJ Kool Herc.

Selected Nonprint Resources

s a cultural phenomenon, Hip Hop has been affected greatly by the rapid advances in technology that have occurred since the 1970s. This growth is evident not only in the quick transmission and distribution of information but also in the more dynamic audio production and performance practices of the various elements of the culture. This chapter presents an annotated selection of Hip Hop–related documentaries, films, and Web sites. All of the selected works in some way promote, promulgate, and/or present Hip Hop, simultaneously expanding the culture globally and allowing greater access and opportunities for other disenfranchised communities to identify and adapt Hip Hop as their empowering voice.

In the selection of these resources among the thousands of available options, certain criteria were implemented. All the resources that are included display, present, and/or comment on Hip Hop prominently; offer insight and/or valuable commentary on Hip Hop Culture; assist in the analysis and/or understanding of Hip Hop; and offer opportunities to explore and experience the culture and its various elements via media. The attempt here is to let readers know about the most accessible and noteworthy documentaries, films, and Web sites available on Hip Hop. The documentaries and films are available through numerous public and university libraries and in most cases may be purchased on the Internet. Even with these stringent criteria, there are too many resources to publish all of them; thus, I have

A hip hop DJ displays his turntable technique up close. (iStockphoto.com)

excluded all works that are strictly biographical in nature as well as presentations of live concerts or concert-specific recordings. This means that some valuable documentaries are not included, such as *Tupac Shakur: Words Never Die* (Hazard Town, 1997); *Tupac Shakur: Thug Immortal* (Xenon Entertainment Group, 1998); *Tupac Shakur: Before I Wake . . . (*Xenon Pictures, 2001); *Tupac Shakur: Thug Angel* (Image Entertainment, 2002); *Tupac: Resurrection* (Paramount Pictures, 2003), and *2-Pac–4-Ever* (Trinity Home Entertainment, 2003). These films offer insightful commentary not only on the life of the slain Hip Hop icon but also regarding his lasting legacy and leadership within the international Hip Hop community. Films such as *Barbershop* (Cube Vision, 2002), *Barbershop 2: Back in Business* (Cube Vision, 2004), and *Beauty Shop* (Cube Vision, 2005), which are clearly grounded in the aesthetic of Hip Hop, were produced by Ice Cube's production company, and feature numerous Hip Hop artists, were also excluded, along with numerous other worthy films. Web site URLs have all been checked numerous times prior to the printing of this text, but again, these inevitably will change with time.

Documentaries

Hip Hop Culture: General

Bill Moyers—Decoding the Rap: Gangs and Rap Music
Date: 1995
Distributor: Films for the Humanities and Sciences

Media journalist Bill Moyers offers an interesting perspective on the relationship between gang activity and Hip Hop Culture. Emphasizing "gangsta rap" of the early 1990s, Moyers takes the viewer on a tour of Utah's Division of Investigation gang unit led by Sergeant Ron Stallworth. This documentary poignantly addresses the influence of gang life not only on the music, but also on the greater culture of Hip Hop.

Graffiti Rock (and Other Hip Hop Delights)
Date: 2002
Distributor: Music Video Distributors

This compilation of footage from Michael Holman's cable series *Graffiti Rock* that was aired in the 1980s offers a retrospective glimpse into the early years of Hip Hop. Featuring Run-DMC, Kool Moe Dee, FAB 5 FREDDY, Doug E. Fresh, DJ Chill Will, DJ Red Alert, K-Rob, Futura 2000, Jazzy Jay, and many others, this documentary should be viewed by anyone interested in an up-close look at the South Bronx and the origins of Hip Hop.

G(raffiti)V(erité)5: The Sacred Elements of Hip Hop
Date: 2003
Distributor: Bryan World Productions

The fifth of a running five-part series, this film represents a departure for the series from the context of Hip Hop itself and instead focuses on Hip Hop as a learning tool in the classroom. It discusses the therapeutic value of Hip Hop for both student and teacher. This is a must-see for all educators and parents interested in reaching youth.

Hip Hop: A Culture of Influence
Date: 1999
Distributor: Documentary Educational Resources

This documentary offers a wealth of various interviews of artists, critics, fans, and scholars in an attempt to unravel the rapid growth and cultural domination of Hip Hop Culture. It offers commentary on race, sexism, homophobia, commercialization, and other hot issues. Educators will find this documentary worth viewing.

Hip Hop Immortals: We Got Your Kids
Date: 2004
Distributor: Image Entertainment

A complement to the book *Hip Hop Immortals: The Remix* by Bonz Malone (see Chapter 9), this documentary analyzes the rapid growth of Hip Hop from a localized experiment to an international phenomenon. The documentary examines changing trends not only in music but in fashion, language, and aesthetics, as well as the rising appropriation of Hip Hop by major corporations.

Jails, Hospitals & Hip-Hop
Date: 2000
Distributor: Stratosphere Entertainment

Using Hip Hop Culture as the most prevalent component of American urban culture, this film documents the influence of Hip Hop across the United States and the rest of the globe. Using various filming techniques, the filmmakers offer insight into the lives of eight distinctly different characters as they acknowledge, analyze, and address their interaction with Hip Hop.

Material Witness: Race, Identity and the Politics of Gangsta Rap, with Michael Eric Dyson
Date: 1995
Distributor: The Media Educational Foundation

Featuring self-acclaimed Hip Hop intellectual Michael Eric Dyson, this documentary approaches controversial subjects, such as race relations, gangsta rap, identity, gender issues, and many other critical topics within Hip Hop. This is essential viewing for student, teacher, scholar, and parent alike as it challenges, confirms, and clearly presents numerous unspoken and unresolved issues within the culture.

Rap: Looking for the Perfect Beat
Date: 1995
Distributor: Films for the Humanities

Featuring Grandmaster Melle Mel, this documentary offers a unique perspective of the evolution and development of rap music and Hip Hop Culture from the inside out. Full of music video clips and commentary from innovators and others, this work offers insight into the presence of violence, crime, misogyny, and other characteristics of Hip Hop that are often criticized by those both inside and outside of the movement.

Rhyme & Reason
Date: 1997
Distributor: Miramax Films

By many accounts one of the most intriguing and captivating documentaries since its 1997 debut, this work offers insightful commentary by the likes of Heavy D, Ice Cube, Notorious B.I.G., Salt-n-Pepa, and Ice-T. They discuss such topics as the rise in popularity of Hip Hop Culture over the years and the emergence of more regionalized forms of of Hip Hop such as "West Coast," "East Coast," "Southern," and the like.

Soundz of Spirit
Date: 2003
Distributor: Ventura Distribution

Countering the negative portrayal of Hip Hop Culture by popular and critical media, this documentary focuses on the positive aspects and contributions of Hip Hop Culture. Performance clips by Common, Talib Kweli, KRS-One, and others highlight this work.

Straight from the Streets
Date: 1998
Distributor: Ideal Enterprises

Exploring the impact of Hip Hop on urban life, this work addresses and articulates the many contributions of rap music and Hip Hop Culture to the inner city. Some segments, in what is billed as rare and exclusive footage, feature performances by Snoop Doggy Dogg, Ice Cube, Ice-T, and Kurupt. There is also insightful commentary by Minister Louis Farrakhan and Denzel Washington.

Straight Outta Hunter's Point
Date: 2003
Distributor: Zealot Pictures

This documentary displays the use of rap music and Hip Hop Culture as a means of escape from the bitter reality of life in the Hunter's Point Housing Project in San Francisco. It features local artists, including RBL, Posse, JT The Bigga Figga, and others, as well as commentary and analysis of Hip Hop as a "rags to riches" opportunity and the prevalence of crime and violence within the culture.

Wild Style
Date: 1982
Distributor: First Run Features

Heralded as the most important documentary about Hip Hop thus far and slated as one of the first (if not the first) on the subject, this film is an impressive rendering of early Hip Hop history. It captures all four of the foundational elements being accomplished by early innovators and legends. The film remains the most viewed and most cited account of early Hip Hop. Featuring Grandmaster Flash, Busy Bee, Rock Steady Crew, Grand Wizard Theodore, and the Cold Crush Brothers, this depiction recreates the energy, excitement, and seriousness of Hip Hop in its original location by the people who were there.

Word: A Film of the Underground Hip Hop Scene
Date: 2002

Focusing on the practice and performance of the various elements of Hip Hop, this work brings to the forefront the numerous Hip Hop activists who dwell below the popular radar, maintaining the original essence of Hip Hop as much as possible.

DJing

Battle Sounds
Date: 2001

Exploring the substantial role of the DJ in Hip Hop Culture, this documentary presents insightful perspectives on the art of DJing and the rising practice of turntablism, with a focus on battles among DJs and the subculture of the DJ in general. One of its highlights is a captivating interview with Philadelphia-based DJ Jazzy Jeff. The film also features interview clips and performance excerpts from DJ Kid Capri, DJ Cash Money, Grandmixer DST, DJ Premiere, and others.

Scratch
Date: 2001
Distributor: Palm Pictures

Featuring commentary by DJ Jazzy Jay, DJ Stevie Dee, Mixmaster Mike, DJ Q-Bbert, DJ Rob Swift, and numerous others, this work positions the DJ as the founding element of the culture and explores the chronological development of the DJ as a performer. This documentary offers numerous examples of the various ways DJs have expanded upon the legacies of DJs before them.

Graffiti

Bomb the System
Date: 2003
Distributor: Drops Entertainment

An extremely informative depiction of the graffiti scene in New York City, this film offers a tribute to one of the primary elements of Hip Hop Culture with footage taken from its New York City roots. The commentary focuses on the role of crime in graffiti (stealing spray paint, for example), the relationship between graffiti artists and the New York Police Department (including arrests and brutalization), and the local gallery scene. This film is a must-see for graffiti enthusiasts, educators, and students alike.

Style Wars
Date: 1983
Distributor: Public Broadcasting Service (PBS)

One of the earliest (if not the first) documentaries focused solely on the graffiti artist, this film offers tremendous footage of the early New York graffiti scene as well as clips and interviews of legendary artists at work. Highlights include commentary on the drastic measures attempted by the mayor and police to stop the graffiti on New York City subways and other public property.

B-Boys/B-Girls

B-Boy Masters
Date: 2004
Distributor: Music Video Distributors

Capturing the Hip Hop Culture scene in New York City, this documentary presents talented participants of each element who display a high level of competency in many, if not all, of the foundational elements. This is an exceptional view of b-boy/b-girl culture from the New York City perspective.

The Freshest Kids
Date: 2002
Distributor: Image Entertainment Inc.

This documentary is the most comprehensive chronicle of b-boy/b-girl culture to date. Drawing footage, interviews, and clips from early Hip Hop featuring Afrika Bambaataa, DJ Kool Herc, and numerous forgotten legends on through time, this work offers a unique perspective of one of the most underrepresented elements of the culture. Highlights include newer footage and clips of old-school and current b-boys/b-girls in action.

MCs

Back Stage
Date: 2000
Distributor: Dimension Films

Using outtakes and footage from backstage at rap music concerts, this documentary presents the story of the life of a Hip Hop MC. Illuminating the behind-the-scenes activities of Roc-A-Fella and Def Jam artists, the film allows the viewer to experience life on the road from the perspective of the artist.

Beef
Date: 2003
Distributor: Image Entertainment Inc.

The first of a two-part series, this documentary examines the significance of the MC battle to the life and credibility of an MC and as an integral aspect of Hip Hop Culture. Highlights include commentary and excerpts of 50 Cent, Dr. Dre, NWA, and DMX as well as footage of freestyle battles.

Beef II
Date: 2004
Distributor: Image Entertainment Inc.

This sequel to *Beef* presents more battles and rivalries in rap music and Hip Hop Culture. Featuring footage of freestyle battles as well as interviews with Cyprus Hill, 50 Cent, Ice Cube, Sticky Fingaz, and others, this portal into the world of MCing also offers unique commentary on some of the stories behind the battles.

Chuck D's Hip Hop Hall of Fame
Date: 2003
Distributor: Music Video Distribution

Narrated and hosted by the legendary leader of the influential group Public Enemy, Chuck D, this documentary offers an informative perspective of selected old-school MCs. Featuring performance footage by KRS-One and Run-DMC as well as appearances and interviews by Chuck D, Rakim, Ice Cube, Afrika Bambaataa, and numerous others, this work is overflowing with information.

The Darker Side of Black
Date: 1994
Distributor: Filmakers Library

Featuring music video clips and a variety of interviews, this documentary looks at rising levels of violence and gang affiliation within rap music and the effects on Hip Hop Culture. Commenting on controversial issues such as homophobia, misogyny, and the possession and glorification of guns, numerous opinionated critics offer insight, including Professor Cornel West and former Jamaican prime minister Michael Manly.

Lyricist Lounge: Dirty States of America—The Untold Story of Southern Hip-Hop
Date: 2004
Distributor: Image Entertainment

One of only a few documentaries to focus on the southern rap scene and southern components of Hip Hop Culture, this work boasts OutKast, Mystikal, Scarface, and others as "talking heads" on Hip Hop in the region. Featuring numerous interviews and southern rap performance excerpts, this work explores variations in the southern style (Crunk, Bounce, and others) in an attempt to draw a sociopolitical connection to the legacy of the Black South via analysis of its links with slavery, poverty, and the civil rights movement.

East Coast Mix 1: Another Reason to Rhyme
Date: 2000
Distributor: Trinity Home Entertainment

Following the success of *Rhyme and Reason,* director Peter Spirer crafted this unique portal into the lives of Jay-Z, Nas, and Q-Tip. Segments on each artist present a unique perspective of rap music and Hip Hop Culture based on the artists' individual experiences as MCs within the culture. Footage includes Jay-Z in the recording studio, Q-Tip addressing what makes him different from other MCs, and Nas offering a tour of the Queensbridge Housing Projects where he was raised.

Freestyle: The Art of Rhyme
Date: 2000
Distributor: Palm Pictures

This documentary offers an exceptional entrance into the world of freestyling, providing background information on the unwritten rules of the art form, its widely held taboos and traditions, and its impact on Hip Hop Culture. Focusing on the talent, preparation, performance practices, and inherent creativity of the "word-smiths," this glance into freestyling strays from the standard presentation of Hip Hop as a culture overwhelmed by violence, gangs, and crime to highlight the artistic achievements of those who are in the forefront of the movement.

Heroes of Latin Hip Hop
Date: 2002
Distributor: Music Video Distribution

This documentary offers insight into the careers of pioneers Kid Frost, Cypress Hill, and Mellow Man Ace, each of whom has achieved milestones not only within the Latin community but in the Hip Hop movement itself. This work is full of backstage footage and interviews as well as music video and performance clips.

Hip Hop Story: Tha Movie
Date: 2002
Distribution: Ventura Distribution

The first of a three-part series, this film presents the role of numerous MCs in the rapid rise of Hip Hop from a local, community-based expression to a multibillion-dollar industry. Interviews by numerous record-industry executives and artists draw attention to the effect of rap music and Hip Hop Culture on popular culture.

Hip Hop Story 2: Dirty South
Date: 2004
Distributor: Ventura Distribution

The second of a three-part series, this documentary is a unique presentation of southern Hip Hop, exploring the distinct regional flavor of the movement. Bow Wow, Lil' Jon, the Ying Yang Twins, and David Banner serve as "talking heads" in this exploration of Hip Hop in Atlanta, Houston, and Miami.

Hip Hop Story 3: Coast to Coast
Date: 2004
Distributor: Ventura Distribution

The third installment of a three-part series, this film offers a unique look at two generations of MCs. Representatives of the first generation—Jay-Z, Snoop Dogg, 50 Cent, Busta Rhymes, and Ice Cube—reflect on their individual careers, highlighting various successes, while representatives of the next generation—Cassidy, Smoot, Young Gunz, Freeway, and Jin—offer commentary on their individual journeys and the prevalence of contemporary battles that become extremely heated.

Pass the Mic
Date: 2003
Distributor: Image Entertainment Inc.

Critiquing the lack of recognition of the Latin influence on Hip Hop Culture, this documentary offers a revised presentation of Hip Hop Culture from the Latin perspective. Full of interview excerpts and clips from live performance and backstage footage, it spotlights the Latin experience, clearly inspiring the viewer to acknowledge the many Latin contributions to the movement.

The Show
Date: 1995
Distributor: Savoy Pictures

This documentary is full of backstage interviews of artists who comment on the changing industry, the "East Coast–West Coast" rivalry, the use of marijuana, the prevalence of crime, and other critical subjects within Hip Hop Culture. The documentary also recognizes the rich legacies of old-school innovators.

Tha Westside
Date: 2002
Distributor: Image Entertainment

Attending to the lives and careers of major West Coast MCs such as Snoop Dogg, Dr. Dre, and Tupac Shakur, this documentary aims to explore the innovation and influence of the West Coast scene and reveal its effect on national and global Hip Hop Culture.

Additional Elements

Breath Control: The History of the Human Beatbox
Date: 2002
Distributor: Ghost Robot

Featuring legendary innovators Doug E. Fresh, Biz Markie, Rahzel, and others, this documentary offers a historical chronicle of the evolution, development, and presence of beat boxing in Hip Hop Culture. It contains exceptional footage of the art and practice of beat boxing.

Other Films

8 mile
Date: 2002
Distributor: Universal Pictures

Loosely based on the life of Hip Hop mega-star Eminem, this movie offers a unique portrayal of a struggling rapper (played by Eminem) as he attains popularity and prestige on the underground scene. Plagued with racial tension and the pursuit of money, the rapper struggles through life's constant choices using his unique sensibilities gained through his experience with and through Hip Hop.

Beat Street
Date: 1984
Distributor: MGM/UA Home Entertainment

One of the earliest representations of Bronx-based Hip Hop Culture, this film juxtaposes the middle-class experience of college life and the inner-city realities of living in the projects. The movie depicts all of the fundamental elements of Hip Hop and features Grandmaster Melle Mel, Doug E. Fresh, Kool Moe Dee, Kool Herc, Rock Steady Crew, Jazzy Jeff, and many other early innovators.

Belly
Date: 1998
Distributor: Artisan Entertainment

Starring Nas and DMX, this drama is grounded in the Hip Hop experience of Black inner-city youth striving to get out of the ghetto, but burdened by gangs, drugs, crime, and violence. It depicts the role of Black nationalism and the Nation of Islam in providing guidance to lost souls. Nas and hip hop music-video director Hype Williams share writing credits with Anthony Bodden.

Black and White
Date: 2000
Distributor: Columbia TriStar Home Video

This is a film about the making of a documentary that focuses on a group of privileged, high-class teenagers who are intrigued by Hip Hop Culture. Their interest is focused on a former drug kingpin who has recreated himself as a Hip Hop mogul. Issues of identity, money, sex, and drugs are all addressed in this unique depiction of the behind-the-scenes making of a fictional documentary.

Body Rock
Date: 1984
Distributor: New World Pictures

When a young b-boy, Chilly D, exchanges his life on the local scene for the glamorous life of a popular superstar, he leaves behind his crew, the Body Rocks, his girlfriend, and his mother. This film shows the reality that plagues numerous Hip Hop stars as they live the "rags to riches" story yet struggle with identity.

Boyz N the Hood
Date: 1991
Distributor: Criterion Collection

One of the most noted Hip Hop–influenced films of the early 1990s, this picture vividly depicts the streets and the culture from which West Coast gangsta rap arose. Starring Ice Cube, it enters the realm of drugs, violence, crime, and many of the other vices associated with street gangs.

Breakin'
Date: 1984
Distributor: MGM

One of the earliest depictions of the California-based influences on Hip Hop Culture, this film offers a unique presentation of West Coast funk styles (that is, poppin', locking, and so on) by prominent dancers of the local and regional street-dance scene.

Breakin' 2: Electric Boogaloo
Date: 1984
Distributor: TriStar Pictures

This sequel to *Breakin'* depicts the use of street dancing as a tool for social and political change, drawing on the sounds, styles, and aesthetics of the West Coast to portray another side of early Hip Hop history.

Brown Sugar
Date: 2002
Distributor: 20th Century Fox

Poised as an ode to Hip Hop, this unique film takes a look at the rap music industry and its effect on Hip Hop Culture from the perspectives of a record-industry executive, a music critic, and an aspiring artist.

Carmen: A Hip Hopera
Date: 2001
Distributor: MTV Films

Starring Lil' Bow Wow, Mos Def, Jermaine Dupri, and Beyoncé Knowles and narrated by Da Brat, this film aims to present Bizet's *Carmen* to the Hip Hop nation. Featuring rap music, Hip Hop fashion and aesthetics, and the four elements of Hip Hop, this presentation is clearly an attempt to have a new generation experience one of history's great works.

CB4
Date: 1993
Distributor: Universal Pictures

This satirical comedy tells the story of a suburban MC who believes he has what it takes to be a rap superstar and forms the group CB4. His rise to fame within the rap music industry is typical in some ways of real-life success stories. Ice Cube, Flava Flav, and Ice-T are featured in the film.

Corrupt
Date: 1999
Distributor: Sterling Home Entertainment

Featuring Silkk the Shocker and Ice-T, this drama presents the story of a gang truce amid the drug culture of the streets. Plagued by the desire to exit the inner city, MJ tries to strategize and plot his way out of the "hood." Hip Hop Culture is clearly displayed in this film.

Don't Be a Menace to South Central while Drinking Your Juice in the Hood
Date: 1996
Distributor: Miramax Films

Using parody and satire to comment on and subtly critique the stereotypical presentation of Hip Hop and contemporary Hip Hop Culture itself, this film follows the trials, tribulations, and triumphs of a fictional character named Ashtray in a south-central Los Angeles inner city. Characterized as a "hood" movie, this film, like numerous others, has stereotypical inner-city settings.

Tha Eastsidaz
Date: 2000
Distributor: Xenon Entertainment Group

This film focuses on gang life and features a slate of West Coast artists. It presents the politics of gang warfare and retaliation as well as the effects of gang culture on the community. Highly influenced by Hip Hop Culture, this movie portrays young people struggling to "make good" out of a bad situation.

Fear of a Black Hat
Date: 1994
Distributor: Avatar Productions

Using satire and parody, this self-acclaimed "mock-u-mentary" offers subtle criticism of the usual portrayal of rap music and greater Hip Hop Culture by popular media. Through comedy, the film offers unique perspectives on commercialization, commoditization, and identity as well as on the hyper-indulgent lifestyles of rap stars.

Friday
Date: 1995
Distributor: New Line Home Video

One of the most popular in a list of "hood" films, this movie stars Ice Cube (and is cowritten by DJ Pooh) in a comical depiction of two lifelong friends who find themselves in a constant string of crises. Hip Hop Culture is prevalent throughout. See *Friday After Next* and *Next Friday.*

Friday After Next
Date: 2002
Distributor: New Line Cinema

This third installment in the *Friday* series is yet another example of the "hood" film. Focusing on marijuana, money, and "gettin' over" as part of Hip Hop Culture, this film does not stray far from the general sentiments of the first two.

Higher Learning
Date: 1995
Distributor: Columbia Pictures

The third installment of director John Singleton's trilogy about life in south-central Los Angeles (after *Boyz 'N the Hood* and *Poetic Justice*), this film depicts the various dilemmas faced by three college freshmen who find themselves in the midst of racial, sexual, and class warfare. Hip Hop on the university scene is a major focus.

Hot Boyz
Date: 1999
Distributor: Artisan Entertainment

Written, directed, and produced by Master P (No Limit Films), this movie is about a young rap star who starts his own gang. Featuring Silkk the Shocker, C-Murder, Snoop Dogg, and Master P, it offers an inside perspective of the relationship between Hip Hop and gangs while also commenting on territorialism, the politics of gang warfare, and the internal struggles of a person who is trying to do good in a bad situation.

House Party
Date: 1990
Distributor: New Line Cinema

The first of a three-part series, this film features the rap duo Kid 'N Play as two high-schoolers planning a house party. The comedy offers an interesting presentation of high-school cliques and a Hip Hop–inspired commentary on racial profiling, gang intimidation, and parent–child relationships.

House Party 2
Date: 1991
Distributor: New Line Cinema

This sequel to *House Party* travels a path that is similar to the plot of the original film—this time, Kid 'n Play plan and execute a pajama house party. Full of Hip Hop influences indicative of the early 1990s, it presents the adventures of a misguided high-school senior who consistently succumbs to peer-pressure, frequently prioritizes fun over school work, and routinely disobeys his absentee parents' orders.

House Party 3
Date: 1994
Distributor: New Line Cinema

Again focusing on the importance of the house party scene during the 1990s, this third film in the series is about the planning and execution of the ultimate bachelor party. As in the first two parts, comedy is used to comment on and critique social situations that young Hip Hoppers faced in the mid-1990s.

How High
Date: 2001
Distributor: Universal Pictures

Featuring the duo Method Man and Redman, this comedy about the effects of smoking marijuana is riddled with references from Hip Hop Culture and deals with the intersection of Hip Hop and the Ivory Tower.

Juice
Date: 1992
Distributor: Paramount Home Video

Starring Tupac Shakur, this film is a portrayal of four Harlem friends who aim to take on the neighborhood and eventually each other in order to attain "juice," or street credibility. It focuses on the rough terrain of the inner city. The effects and influence of Hip Hop Culture flow through both the soundtrack and the movie as a whole.

Krush Groove
Date: 1985
Distributor: Warner Brothers

This film offers a unique look at the early days of Def Jam Records. Featuring Run-DMC, Kurtis Blow, the Fat Boys, and other early innovators, it portrays the Hip Hop Culture of the 1980s, and especially the rise of Russell Simmons.

Next Friday
Date: 2000
Distributor: New Line Cinema

This sequel to *Friday* moves the inner-city comedy to the suburbs as the characters in their typical fashion deal with living the inner-city lifestyle outside of the inner city. The movie also marks the entrée of Hip Hop artists into the motion-picture arena as writers, producers, and directors.

Play'd: A Hip Hop Story
Date: 2002
Distributor: Artisan Entertainment

Sparks fly when an East Coast rapper leaves home en route to the West Coast after signing with a major label. The East Coast versus West Coast rivalry takes center stage in this film. Loosely based on numerous accounts of the rivalry between Tupac Shakur and Notorious B.I.G., it exposes some of the controversy surrounding the media-based presentation of their interactions.

Poetic Justice
Date: 1993
Distributor: Columbia Pictures

The second picture in John Singleton's trilogy on life in south-central Los Angeles, this film tells of a dramatic love story between a young woman who is mourning the recent loss of a boyfriend who was killed in gang violence and a streetwise homeboy played by Tupac Shakur. Dealing with daily issues of inner-city teens, such as peer pressure, gang violence, teenage pregnancy, drugs, and acceptance, the film highlights the fashions, aesthetics, and general attitudes of Hip Hop Culture.

Rappin'
Date: 1985
Distributor: Cannon Pictures

This story of Hip Hop activism features John Hood, a young b-boy who tries to save his grandmother's building from demolition by competing in a rap contest; if he wins, the cash prize would provide the funds he needs to help. The film presents Hip Hop as a rich forum of expression used by perceived ostracized and underprivileged young people.

Save the Last Dance
Date: 2001
Distributor: Paramount Pictures

This film presents the story of a young white aspiring ballerina who ventures to Chicago's South Side and meets a young black street dancer. He introduces her to Hip Hop Culture and the reality of interracial dating. The language, dance, fashion, and music of Hip Hop Culture are foundational to the film.

Slam
Date: 1998
Distributor: Trimark Pictures

Focusing on gang culture, this film is about a young rapper who uses his talent to address social, political, cultural, and economic issues facing his inner-city neighborhood. He struggles through one bad situation after another by relying on his unique survival sensibilities and his artistic talent.

Soul Plane
Date: 2004
Distributor: MGM Home Entertainment

This outrageous comedy offers a hyper-stereotypical portrayal of Hip Hop Culture, yet it clearly articulates many of the issues challenged by those both inside and outside the culture. Featuring Snoop Dogg and Method Man as actors, and using Snoop Dogg's music, this film has money, sex, and drugs at the heart of its plot.

State Property
Date: 2002
Distributor: Lions Gate Films

Starring Memphis Bleek and the Roc-A-Fella crew, this film, produced by Roc-A-Fella Films, takes an in-depth look at gang culture and the rivalries, violence, retaliation, and killing that it often entails. This dramatization of supposedly actual events becomes a rags-to-riches story gone bad when greed takes over. Viewers may equate the context and content of the film to lyrics prevalent in East Coast gangsta rap, which is slightly different from those of West Coast gangsta rap.

State Property II
Date: 2005
Distributor: Lions Gate Films

This sequel to *State Property,* directed by Roc-A-Fella's Damon Dash, is a continuation of the original film in both content and context, but this time the story follows the lives of three undisputedly notorious gangsters. Starring Damon Dash, Noreaga, and Beanie Sigel, it depicts gang rivalry, deception, peer pressure, deceit, and greed, one perception of what life is like in the Hip Hop–influenced inner city.

Survival of the Illest
Date: 2004
Distributor: Lions Gate Films House Entertainment

This story about hustlers, thugs, crooks, and the negative vices experienced on the streets of the "Dirty South" stars Scarface, E-40, and Big Moe. Drawing on the representation of the southern Hip Hop scene presented in many rap lyrics, this film portrays the relationship between gang life and the pursuit of street credibility and money.

Thicker Than Water'
Date: 1999
Distributor: Palm Pictures

Starring Fat Joe and Mack 10, and with appearances by Big Pun and Ice Cube as two thugs with talent and a desire to be rappers, this film examines the intersection of Hip Hop Culture and the world of drugs. The two main characters struggle through one decision after another in pursuit of money to purchase their own equipment for a recording studio.

Tougher Than Leather
Date: 1988
Distributor: New Line Cinema

Featuring Run-DMC, the story behind this New York–based film shows how easy it is to get caught up in bad activities and bad decisions when it seems like you are on top of the world. Filmed on the site of the early Hip Hop scene and featuring the music of many early Hip Hop innovators, the film offers one of the last portrayals of Hip Hop's heyday.

Turn It Up
Date: 2000
Distributor: New Line Cinema

This film tells the story of a talented rapper who is faced with deciding between loyalty to his family or loyalty to a childhood friend who, through illegal means, has provided him with a way to attain the future in the Hip Hop industry that he so passionately desires to pursue. Based loosely on a real story and starring Pras (Fugees) and Ja Rule, this film offers a perspective on the real struggles of many artists who are determined to pursue Hip Hop as a mechanism for having a better life.

The Wash
Date: 2001
Distributor: Lions Gate Films

Written and directed by DJ Pooh and starring Dr. Dre, Snoop Dogg, Xzibit, Ludacris, and Eminem, this film brings to life the 1970s movie *Car Wash* via Hip Hop. Full of comical antics, it not only portrays Hip Hop Culture but also uses real-life struggles as the root of many of the jokes.

Wave Twisters
Date: 2001
Distributor: Music Video Distributors

The first animated Hip Hop film and the first film relying solely on scratch music for sound, this film offers a creative storyline of a team of oral hygienists determined to save Hip Hop Culture. Featuring the writing and the scratching of DJ Q-Bert, this is a must-see.

Whiteboys
Date: 1999
Distributor: Fox Searchlight Pictures

This film portrays a white Iowa resident who does his best to present himself as a Black person via his talk, walk, dress, and activities. Grounded in stereotypes, this film examines various perspectives on what it means to be Black and what it means to be a part of Hip Hop Culture. The movie features Snoop Dogg, Fat Joe, dead prez, Slick Rick, and Doug E. Fresh.

You Got Served
Date: 2004
Distributor: Columbia TriStar

This is a film about the world of street dance as exemplified by the circuit surrounding Mr. Rad's Warehouse in Los Angeles. When a suburban group invades the turf of already warring crews, enemies become partners in order to retain control and dominance in their neighborhood. Contemporary Hip Hop street dance is the focus of this film.

Web Sites

The 411 Online
http://www.the411online.com

Featuring current and archived Hip Hop–oriented news, album reviews, and album release information, this site also offers current
and archived artist interviews. The archives of magazine interviews span from 1994 to 1997, whereas online interviews range
from 1998 to 2005. The site contains links to audio clips, reviews,
articles, photographs, and news and video clips for specific artists.

50mm Los Angeles.com
http://50mmlosangeles.com

Dedicated to graffiti in Los Angeles, this site features photographs
of graffiti throughout the city by many known and unknown writers, taggers, and bombers. In addition, it provides links, events,
and a discussion forum dedicated solely to graffiti.

All Hip Hop.com
http://www.allhiphop.com

One of the premier Hip Hop news sites and providers, All Hip
Hop.com, through daily e-mails, keeps enthusiasts up to date on
current and breaking news within Hip Hop. Featuring interviews,
reviews, multimedia links, and editorials, it serves as a major
source of information for other online and offline print magazines, radio, newspaper, and television outlets.

Battlesounds
http://www.battlesounds.com

This supplement to the documentary of the same name offers
clips from the film as well as background information on the
making and development of the film. Historical and technical
background information on turntablism is also included.

B-Boys.com
http://www.b-boys.com

With the goal of building a positive online Hip Hop community,
this site contains an extensive timeline of Hip Hop history
(1973–2001), numerous discussion forums, and other important
information relative to Hip Hop's growth and development over

its thirty-plus years. Special focus is placed on b-boy communities both in the United States (primarily New York City) and the United Kingdom, with photos and information. The site also offers an annotated listing of "Old School Hip Hop Tapes" from 1978 to 1983.

Davey D's Hip Hop Corner
http://www.daveyd.com

This prominent, popular, and extremely consistent site offers a variety of articles, editorials, news reports, album release information, and album reviews as well as in-depth interviews with early Hip Hop innovators and current popular artists. Although Davey D, an active radio/print journalist and Hip Hop activist, writes much of the content of the site, various artists, some unknown and some very renowned, also post writings to the site.

Global Hip Hop
http://www.globalhiphop.com

Although posed as a site focusing on global Hip Hop, this site focuses largely on artists prominent in the United States. Featuring news on current Hip Hop–related events and happenings, album reviews, interviews of artists, and an online store offering music and apparel, this site is very informative for both novice and expert Hip Hop headz.

Graff Inc.
http://www.graffinc.com

This site features an extensive list of prominent and lesser known graffiti artists as well as clips of pieces, bombs, murals, and a host of other photos. It also offers a message board forum where enthusiasts and novices can explore the world of graffiti through conversation about various topics of interest and issues facing artists and their fans.

Graffiti Grapher: Cartesian and Polar Coordinate Geometry in Graffiti Culture
http://www.ccd.rpi.edu/Eglash/csdt/subcult/grafitti/index.htm

Placing graffiti properly as one of the four foundational elements of Hip Hop Culture, this site offers a historical analysis of the evolution and development of graffiti both prior to and within its role in Hip Hop Culture. The site also offers explanations of different methods and styles of graffiti art.

The HipHop Cipher: Reloaded
http://www.thehiphopcipher.com

This site offers artist biographies, album reviews and release information, and news updates on current and future Hip Hop–related events. Links to music-video clips are also included.

Hip Hop Directory
http://www.hiphop-directory.com

This clearinghouse of information offers an enormous number of links to Hip Hop–related Web sites, such as the sites of individual MCs and DJs, sites featuring movie and documentary trailers, merchandise sites, and e-zines. This site also offers a host of discussion-board forums on Hip Hop–related topics.

HipHopDX.com
http://www.hiphopdx.com

This site offers current and archived album reviews as well as information on future releases. It also posts current news on or about Hip Hop–related events and occurrences as well as message board forums on a variety of topics that are accessible to visitors.

HipHopFoundry
http://hiphopfoundry.com/index.php

In addition to Hip Hop–related news and interviews, this site offers biographical information on selected artists as well as reviews of selected albums. Contact information is available for Hip Hop–oriented clothing lines and there are numerous opportunities to engage in online dialogue through the many message board forums hosted on the site.

Hip Hop Galaxy
http://www.hiphopgalaxy.com

Dedicated to Hip Hop Culture, this site focuses on the MC and rap music. Offering artist biographies, information on recent and future album releases, reviews, and current news, this site contains a wealth of information. In addition, it supplies links to numerous Hip Hop–oriented articles as well as to online music and apparel stores.

Hip Hop Havoc
http://www.hiphophavoc.com

A clearinghouse of information, this site offers up-to-date news from the world of Hip Hop, information about events within Hip Hop, interviews of influential artists, and news of album releases, including DJ mix tapes and CDs. The site also offers an online store for merchandise and apparel.

Hip Hop Ladies.com
http://www.hiphop-ladies.com

This site offers up-to-date news and information on the ladies of Hip Hop. Featuring interviews on the presence and influence of women in Hip Hop worldwide and numerous opportunities for open discussion on complementary topics, this site is very useful and informative.

Hip Hop Network
http://www.hiphop-network.com

As a clearinghouse of information relative to the Hip Hop community, this site offers links to articles on Hip Hop and general Hip Hop news stories as well as information on the four foundational elements. The site utilizes streaming audio and video and provides a rich resource to both novice and aficionado.

Hip Hop Research Portal
http://www.hiphopportal.net

Developed by a Case Western Reserve University librarian, Tiffeni Fontno, this monumental and innovative searchable database serves as a centralized repository for the collection and retrieval of numerous resources for the study of Hip Hop Culture. International in scope and with resources dating back to 1975, the collection offers access to monographs, periodicals, theses and dissertations, bibliographies, discographies, and audiovisual materials as well as encyclopedias and dictionaries on Hip Hop.

ILLHILL.com
http://www.illhill.com

This site provides daily news updates on Hip Hop–related events and occurrences, artist interviews, editorials, album reviews, links to a wide variety of articles, and discussion board forums.

It also offers routine giveaways, sweepstakes, and Hip Hop–related contests.

Jam 2 Dis
http://www.jam2dis.com

One of the many Web sites specializing in DJs and mix CDs, this site also supplies information on the greater Hip Hop Culture. It offers historical background on the four foundational elements as well as independent chat rooms for each. Music lovers may also purchase mix tapes and CDs, rap CDs, and a host of other examples of Hip Hop genres and styles through the site.

Mrwiggles.biz
http://www.mrwiggleshiphop.net/index.htm

A tremendous resource on Hip Hop Culture by one of its leading b-boys, this site features an extensive timeline of major events and important occasions in Hip Hop (1940–2003). Its unique offering is Mr. Wiggles's own personal recollections of his involvement in various phases and stages of Hip Hop. He includes an extremely informative presentation on the development of the b-boy and a breakdown of the various types and styles of dance associated with b-boying. The site also features discussion forums and links to numerous articles.

New York City Graffiti @ 149st
http://www.at149st.com/index.html

This site features an extensive history of graffiti art, a list of graffiti artists and crews along with biographical information, and links to some of their work. It includes a glossary of terms identified with graffiti and Hip Hop. An interesting addition to the site is a section dedicated to the role and influence of women in graffiti.

Okay Player
http://www.okayplayer.com

This online community features a collective of artists with common ideologies and similar approaches to Hip Hop. In addition to general Hip Hop–related news, the site offers links to personal information about individual artists. Message board forums are also provided for numerous threads of discussion.

OldSchoolHipHop.com
http://www.oldschoolhiphop.com/index.html

Dedicated to keeping the legacy of old-school Hip Hop Culture alive, this site offers insightful information on the first few decades of Hip Hop in the form of biographical sketches of various artists; articles, reviews, and editorials by various artists; and an annotated list of albums noting their influences on old-school and contemporary Hip Hop Culture. The site also offers plot summary reviews and commentary on documentaries and movies related to the early days of Hip Hop.

Rap Basement
http://www.rapbasement.com

With regularly updated news stories, tour information, release dates, message boards, and chat rooms, this site connects Hip Hop fans to one another around the world. It also offers audio, video, and photo downloads as well as interviews and movie and game reviews. Links to artists' Web sites are also included.

Rapstation.com
http://www.rapstation.com

Although it focuses on the MC, this site offers a wealth of information on Hip Hop Culture in general as well. It includes interviews, information on current events, and message board forums on numerous topics and would be useful for Hip Hop enthusiasts as well as for those seeking to learn the basics.

Raptism.com
http://www.raptism.com

Containing album reviews, exclusive interviews, and current Hip Hop–related news, this site offers a portal for both the Hip Hop head and the novice to explore the vast domain of Hip Hop Culture. Containing multimedia clips of various music videos as well as discussion board forums on prominent topics and issues related to Hip Hop, this site attempts to bridge the gap between local, regional, and national boundaries through Internet-based connections.

Skratchamental.com
http://www.skratchamental.com

This informative site offers a wealth of information on turntablism. In addition to historical and background technical information, it includes tips on basic and advanced turntable techniques as well as information on hardware and turntable gear. It also has a number of discussion forums.

SOHH.com
http://www.sohh.com

Containing Hip Hop–related news and articles, this site highlights the most current news and must-read articles within feature sections. It includes thousands of topics for online discussion within the message board forum section.

SoundSlam
http://www.soundslam.com/main.php

Focused on Hip Hop Culture, this clearinghouse of information offers current news and interviews, album reviews, and short biographical sketches that are supplemented by streaming audio and video clips. Furthermore, this site offers a variety of articles written by different authors dealing with numerous hot topics related to current and past issues in Hip Hop.

Styluswars
http://www.styluswars.com

Dedicated to the DJ and turntablist, this site offers biographical information, interviews, and recent and archived information on album releases by DJs and turntablists. It also includes a list of upcoming events as well as ample opportunity for feedback and discussion via message board forums.

Subway Outlaws
http://www.subwayoutlaws.com

Focused on subway graffiti in New York City, this site discusses the history of subway art and supplies personal narratives of known and unknown artists. It also has an image gallery of burners, throw-ups, tags, and canvases, many by legends of subway graffiti art, as well as some works from outside of New York.

Appendix A

Thirty Influential Hip Hop Albums

he DJ initiated Hip Hop Culture. With turntables, 12-inch records (singles), and a crew of graffiti writers, dancers, and eventually MCs, the DJ was the centerpiece of Hip Hop. The release of Run-DMC's album *Run-DMC* (Profile, 1984) sparked a lasting change in the soundscape of Hip Hop because it led the way for albums to replace singles in commercial popularity in the genre. The songs on albums were connected by a concept or underlying message that flowed from one song to the next. These themes were sometimes obvious to the listener and sometimes more subtle. In addition, songs were often bridged by interludes and creative transitions. The hip hop album brought prestige not only to the recording artist but also to the producer, whose responsibilities included packaging the records into an album in an organized and aesthetically pleasing manner.

The thirty albums listed here all influenced and continue to influence Hip Hop. I have not simply chosen the most popular albums of the day or the albums that created the most media response but instead selected albums that engage the listener with social, political, economic, and/or cultural critique, discussion, or commentary. Each album selected effectively approaches the current state of society and/or Hip Hop at the time of its release. Each also has had a transcendental effect—that is, it has been able to reach beyond the various constituencies of Hip Hop and speak to a much broader audience. Furthermore, each album selected has served as a model or a platform to inspire and influence subsequent artists. These thirty influential hip hop albums reveal the importance and influence of music to the broader culture, as many of them in some way reflect or affect new trends and representations of elements of Hip Hop beyond the DJ or MC. Finally, no compilation albums are included. These selections are the "must-haves" in any collection (private, public library, school or university library, digital music library, etc.). They are presented in chronological order by release date.

It is important to note that the last entry is dated 2001. This does not suggest that albums released subsequent to 2001 are not influential; rather, it acknowledges the fact that the influence of an album is best recognized by its rippling effect through time, after all of the media hype has subsided. Furthermore, it acknowledges the technical advances of digital downloading, which, in effect, entice consumers to return to purchasing individual records (singles) instead of complete albums.

Run-DMC. *Raising Hell.* Profile, 1986.

Deemed by Russell Simmons the "first b-boy album," *Raising Hell* captured the pinnacle of Run-DMC's musical career. With the expert coproduction of Rick Rubin and featuring singles such as "My Adidas," "You Be Illin'," and "Peter Piper," this album stands as a classic among communities of DJs, graffiti artists, b-boys/b-girls, and MCs. The collaboration with Steven Tyler and Joe Perry of Aerosmith, "Walk This Way," remains in a league of its own as a prime example of the rich fusion of hip hop and rock and an exemplar of how hip hop expanded its fan base.

Boogie Down Productions. *Criminal Minded.* Sugar Hill, 1987.

This pioneering hard-core rap album features previously unspoken tales of life in the inner city from an extremely raw and gritty perspective. Singles such as "South Bronx" and "The Bridge Is Over" reveal KRS-One's battling skills, while "9mm Goes Bang" and "P Is Free" reveal his polished rhyming skills and rare ability to display versatility in presentation. This is the only BDP album featuring DJ Scott La Rock, and judging from his presentation here, it is certain he would have quickly soared among the ranks of the greatest DJs if it were not for his senseless murder in 1987.

Eric B. & Rakim. *Paid in Full.* 4th & Broadway, 1987.

Responsible for ushering in a new era of Hip Hop, this album not only raised expectations for MCs but also showcased the power of the dynamic duo Eric B. and Rakim. Singles such as "Eric B. for

President," "I Know You Got Soul," and "I Ain't No Joke" display both Rakim's unmatched rhyming skills and Eric B.'s mastery at DJing and production. Nearly twenty years later, this monumental album remains as captivating, stimulating, and appealing as it was when released.

Jungle Brothers. *Straight out of the Jungle.* Warlock, 1988.

A call to socially conscious and morally responsible action, this debut album from participants in the Native Tongues Posse opened the door to the musical union of jazz and hip hop. Grounded in Black nationalism, the Jungle Brothers created a place for the expression of various forms of pride within Hip Hop Culture. Singles such as "Jimbrowski," "Here We Go," and "I'll Have You" signaled the times and the sounds of the late 1980s.

Public Enemy. *It Takes a Nation of Millions to Hold Us Back.* Def Jam, 1988.

No other Hip Hop album to date has combined the kind of rage, anger, chaos, and protest that this album expresses with as much passion, hope, empowerment, and sociopolitical commentary and critique. And no other Hip Hop group has startled, challenged, and stimulated its audience as much as Public Enemy while influencing, invoking, and imploring an entire generation. This album and its numerous singles stand as a testament to the power of expression through the art of music.

Stetsasonic. *In Full Gear.* Tommy Boy, 1988.

Versatility remains the theme of one of Hip Hop's original bands. This double album offers seventeen singles with various approaches to Hip Hop, ranging from human beat-boxing to R&B-influenced hip hop, to jazz-influenced hip hop, to dancehall reggae–influenced hip hop, and rock-influenced hip hop, to mention a few. This classic album offers the best in sampling technology as well as "live" band performance.

Ultramagnetic MCs. *Critical Breakdown.* Next Plateau, 1988.

This debut album from the former members of the New York City Breakers and b-boy group People's Choice offers an early glimpse at what would later be referred to as underground Hip Hop. Full of unconventional beats, rhymes, and production techniques, the album rose to great prominence without necessarily competing with other mainstream acts of the day. Featuring the single "Ego Trippin'" and a host of other rap classics, the album and the crew remain exemplars of the diverse expressions of Hip Hop.

3rd Bass. *The Cactus Album.* Def Jam, 1989.

Featuring singles such as "The Gas Face," Steppin' to the A.M.," and "Brooklyn Queens," this album cut across racial lines with the hard-hitting New York style prominent during the golden years of Hip Hop. Full of hot beats and clever rhymes, the album captured the hearts and ears of Hip Hoppers across the country. The production on this album (by Prince Paul and Bomb Squad) is beyond impressive.

Beastie Boys. *Paul's Boutique.* Capitol, 1989.

Although the work of this unique trio is often labeled as pop instead of the hip hop that it is, the Beastie Boys expanded their range with this album. Offering a lesson in how to use the sounds of jazz, rock, folk, blues, and other genres through the expert use of a sampler, this album is full of aggressive, energetic, and fun singles exhibiting classic Beastie Boy antics and humor.

De La Soul. *3 Feet High and Rising.* Tommy Boy, 1989.

Introducing the Daisy (Da Inna Sound Y'all) Age in Hip Hop, this recording offers an innovative approach to hip hop through the sounds of pop, disco, soul, and country. The extremely creative wordsmiths perform more than twenty singles tied together by the motif of a game show skit. Featuring singles such as "The Magic Number," "Ghetto Thang," and "Jenifa Taught Me (Derwin's Revenge)," the album represented a positive alternative to the rising hard-core and militant rap of the period.

A Tribe Called Quest. *The Low End Theory.* Jive, 1991.

The most popular group from the Native Tongues Posse, A Tribe Called Quest expanded the fusion of jazz and hip hop, not stopping with simply incorporating jazz sounds but infusing the jazz sentiment into their hip hop explorations. Featuring singles such as "Excursion," "Verses from the Abstract," and "Check the Rhyme," the album offers some of the smoothest, most fluid rhymes of the era, matched only by the masterful musical backdrop. This album established the historical, musical, and cultural link between jazz and hip hop.

Cypress Hill. *Cypress Hill.* Ruffhouse, 1991.

Only a few groups have the kind of indescribable, mystical sound that can sonically captivate all listeners far and wide. Cypress Hill got onto this short list with this album, which ushered numerous rock and alternative fans into the Hip Hop fold. Often imitated yet rarely matched, this group of Latin artists not only mastered the beats and rhymes but the presentation as well.

Ice-T. *O.G. Original Gangster.* Sire, 1991.

Ice-T's most influential album offers the first major look at West Coast gangsta rap and the raw, violent, sexist sounds that it contained—sounds that were full of rage yet real and true to their subject. The album has influenced numerous artists and groups since its release. On this album, Ice-T also debuted his band Body Count on one of the singles. This monumental album opened the floodgates for gangsta rap, a subgenre that would soon overwhelm the mainstream appearance of rap music.

Main Source. *Breaking Atoms.* Wild Pitch, 1991.

One of the few albums whose legacy was diminished by its placement on an unstable record label, Main Source's *Breaking Atoms* is one of the greatest albums never heard by most. Featuring the recorded debuts of Akinyele and Nas and showcasing one of the all-time best group recordings, "Live at the Barbeque," this classic album offers unspeakable production and extraordinary beats and rhymes. Anyone possessing this album is likely a true aficionado of hip hop.

Das EFX. *Dead Serious.* East West, 1992.

The futuristic band name "Das EFX" is an indicator of the extremely different sounds and expressions offered on this unique album, which exhibits a style of rhyming based on angular and aggressive rhythms. The impact of this new style was widely felt both in music and dance. The album's longevity on radio was extremely influential as Hip Hop continued to develop into its second decade.

Dr. Dre. *The Chronic.* Death Row, 1992.

Introducing the Parliament-Funkadelic-inspired G-Funk sound of the West Coast, this album changed the nature of hip hop production and offered a lesson on how to package a hit album. Showcasing the underappreciated talents of Dr. Dre, it features singles such as "Nuthin' but a 'G' Thang," "Dre Day," and "Let Me Ride," offering a unique look at life in Los Angeles from the perspective of a street hustler (otherwise known as a "G"). This album single-handedly moved the dominant locus of hip hop from New York City to Los Angeles.

Gang Starr. *Daily Operation.* Chrysalis, 1992.

From opening to closing, this album offers the best of the underground Hip Hop sound of the period. The extremely tight rhymes of Guru mixed with the extraordinary production of Premier are reflected not only on the popular singles "Soliloquy of Chaos" and "DWYCK" but throughout the entire album. Able to present hardcore lyrics and jazz-influenced expression, these non–New York natives nevertheless offer the powerful, piercing sounds of New York.

Pete Rock & CL Smooth. *Mecca and the Soul Brother.* Elektra/Asylum, 1992.

Offering an unprecedented eighty minutes of hit singles, this album is a tremendous exploration of skill and creative expression. The hard-hitting, powerful presentation of the duo continues to be emulated by artists over a decade later. Full of social, political, and moral commentary over some extremely well-produced tracks, this is eighty minutes of listening well spent.

Wu-Tang Clan. *Enter the Wu-Tang (36 Chambers).* Loud, 1993.

This debut album of one of the most influential groups of the 1990s offers an introduction to the hard-core sounds of a unique collective and to the outstanding production talents of their visionary leader, RZA. It includes the hit singles "C.R.E.A.M." and "Can It Be All So Simple" among a host of other memorable tracks. This album returned hip hop to New York from the West Coast, paving the way for the rise and dominance of Notorious B.I.G., Jay-Z, Nas, and others.

Nas. *Illmatic.* Columbia, 1994.

At a time when the phrase "keepin' it real" was often said but rarely realized, this album kept it real in the realest sense of the word. Full of verbal wit, rhythmic dexterity, and well-produced tracks, this debut solo album put Nas not only on the list of hip hop greats but instantly close to the top of that list. Featuring tracks such as "N.Y. State of Mind," "Halftime," and "It Ain't Hard to Tell," this album proved there was no question as to Nas's potency, position, or ability to speak the truth.

Notorious B.I.G. *Ready to Die.* Bad Boy, 1994.

In this album, a collection of tales from one of Hip Hop's greatest storytellers, Notorious B.I.G.'s use of voice, style, and presence offers a hard-core gangsta twist, while his attention to detail and ability to keep a listener enthralled from beginning to end is old school. The album captures the hunger of a skilled MC who would quickly rise to great acclaim and fall even quicker to a senseless death. Featuring singles such as "Ready to Die," "Juicy," and "Big Poppa," this album reinvented the East Coast hard-core gangsta style of rap that remains in vogue a decade after this crucial recording.

Mobb Deep. *The Infamous.* Loud, 1995.

One of the most convincing and compelling East Coast gangsta albums to date, this album is exemplary in concept, vision, and execution. Featuring singles such as "Survival of the Fittest," "Eye for an Eye (Your Beef Is Mines)," and "Shook Ones, Pt. 2," this album has a raw, gritty, dark sound that became characteristic of the period. The in-your-face presentation may not be user friendly, but it certainly has influenced a host of contemporary artists and groups.

The Fugees. *The Score.* Ruffhouse, 1996.

This second album from a uniquely talented group ignited a new era of alternative hip hop to challenge the sounds and sentiments of the gangsta-influenced and sex-ridden rap of the period. Offering singles such as "Ready or Not," "Fu-Gee-La," and "Killing Me Softly with His Song," the eclectic group expresses a socially conscious message unparalleled during the period. This monumental recording not only left a mark on Hip Hop but offered a tremendous contribution to the music industry in the name of Hip Hop.

Tupac Shakur. *All Eyez on Me.* Death Row, 1996.

Whether it was the rawness, the passion, the rhymes, the beats, or all of the above, this album touched the hearts and lives of many who acknowledge Tupac as a popular-culture icon and legend among legends. This rare double disc CD of all new material, featuring twenty-seven singles, showcases his unique contribution. The rhymes are untouchable, as are the beats, but neither compares at all to the messages conveyed by this extremely gifted individual.

Missy Elliott. *Supa Dupa Fly*. Goldmind/Elektra, 1997.

This album impacted Hip Hop, R&B, and alternative music as well as urban radio and music videos. Most important, it challenged Hip Hop Culture to deal with its rapid gender discrimination as Missy Elliott quickly rose as one of its most prominent female superstars. With creative and production partner Timbaland, Missy Elliott changed the nature of Hip Hop with the sound, look, and feel of this album and challenged the way it is presented and perceived. Featuring singles "Hit 'Em Wit da Hee," "Beep Me 911," and "The Rain (Supa Dupa Fly)," she introduced a new style of hip hop that has been followed, emulated, and in many ways expanded upon.

Lauryn Hill. *The Miseducation of Lauryn Hill*. Ruffhouse, 1998.

Displaying the diversity and versatility of Hip Hop, this album offers a personal perspective on life through social, political, and cultural critique. The collection of tremendously effective songs, ranging from R&B-influenced to reggae-influenced and pop-influenced material, displays Hill's superstar talent. Although some critics would describe this work as something other than hip hop, it is evident through song, performance, aesthetic, and intent that although it may not be stereotypical, it certainly is Hip Hop.

Mos Def & Talib Kweli. *Mos Def & Talib Kweli Are Black Star*. Rawkus, 1998.

Aiming to restore pride, purpose, and posture to Hip Hop, Mos Def and Talib Kweli together exemplify the gray space between underground and mainstream. Featuring singles such as "K.O.S. (Determination)," "Definition," "Respiration," and "Brown Skin Lady," the album offers a unique look at what Hip Hop could mean to the world if it were not all castigated as violent, sexist, and immoral. This album changed the perception of the division between underground and mainstream, as these "underground" artists became extremely "mainstream" personalities.

Jurassic 5. *Quality Control.* Interscope, 2000.

By one of the most innovative and influential underground groups of the twenty-first century, this album offers impressive rhyming over the excellent production from Nu-Mark and Cut Chemist. Providing an alternative to the pop- or gangsta-influenced sounds of much of the hip hop of the period, it displays a respect and passion for old-school hip hop that is refreshing. This album and its creators stand as yet another example of how artists and groups from the underground are forced into the mainstream by their proud and well-pleased fans.

OutKast. *Stankonia.* LaFace, 2000.

Featuring hit singles such as "Ms. Jackson" and "B.O.B.," this album contains some of the most memorable hooks and clever production techniques to date. The album offers uniquely critical commentary on numerous real-life issues in addition to party favorites. Elevating the contributions of the South to Hip Hop, this album remains a giant among giants.

Jay-Z. *The Blueprint.* Uptown/Universal, 2001.

This album offers the best of one of Hip Hop's moguls, whose business savvy and high-class lifestyle do not discount his ability to offer hard-core, streetwise beats and rhymes. Feature singles such as "U Don't Know" and "The Ruler's Back" only scratch the surface of the enormous contribution of this album. Though the album is often considered pop by many critics, here Jay-Z once and for all showcases his verbal prowess as he delivers some of the most impressive lyrics ever heard on vinyl.

Appendix B

Fifty Influential Hip Hop Records (Singles)

ip Hop Culture began with DJs playing records. The DJs inspired the graffiti artists and motivated the dancers to show their stuff, and everyone in the vicinity became an MC, ready to take a turn rhyming over the record. This chapter lists and comments on fifty of the most influential hip hop records (singles) recorded over the past thirty-plus years of the monumental culture.

Those listed are not simply the most popular songs of Hip Hop, however; instead, the fifty recordings were selected according to specific criteria designed to favor the songs that were most influential in Hip Hop. Each song selected engages the listener with social, political, economic, and/or cultural critique, discussion, or commentary. Each one effectively approaches the current state of society and/or Hip Hop at the time of its release. Each has had a transcendental effect in that it was able to reach beyond the various constituencies of Hip Hop to speak to a much broader audience. And each has served as a model or platform to inspire and influence subsequent artists. These fifty songs thus represent the great influence that music has had in Hip Hop Culture. Many of them in some way reflect trends and representations of elements of Hip Hop or have affected those trends. Songs on this list do not necessarily appear on the album list in the previous appendix—under the criteria used, qualifying as a top single did not guarantee qualification for the album that single appears on, and vice versa. These selections are the "must-haves" in any collection (private, public library, school or university library, digital music library, etc.). Each record selected clearly displays some variation or combination of extreme flow, hot beats, or amazing production, in addition to critical content, and each has left an imprint on Hip Hop for years to come. The songs are presented in chronological order by album release date.

The last entry is dated 2002. This does not suggest that subsequent records are not influential; rather, it recognizes that it is important to allow the test of time to be a final criterion of a record's influence. These fifty recordings have stood the test of time and are just as current and influential as they were at the time of release.

Songs that were released as singles are listed by artist or group, song title, recording company, and year of release; for songs that appeared on an album, the album title is also included in italics.

Sugarhill Gang. "Rapper's Delight." Sugar Hill, 1979.

This important recording single-handedly introduced the world to the creative expression of Hip Hop, although it does not serve as the best definitive example of the early sounds of the culture.

Kurtis Blow. "The Breaks." *Kurtis Blow.* Mercury, 1980.

One of the first widely celebrated inner-city anthems, this classic recording was widely accepted by the R&B and pop audiences, indirectly spreading the influence of Hip Hop beyond its local enclave.

Grandmaster Flash & the Furious Five. "The Adventures of Grandmaster Flash on the Wheels of Steel." *The Message.* Sugar Hill, 1981.

A historic record of sorts, this recording showcased not only the unmatched skills of Grandmaster Flash on the turntables but also the numerous genres of music that influenced and assisted in the creation and development of Hip Hop owing to their presence on records.

Whodini. "Magic's Wand." Jive, 1982.

Recognized as the first rap record to feature an accompanying music video, this comical presentation of name checks and references to the burgeoning Hip Hop movement sparked a new trend in the presentation and performance of rap music.

Grandmaster Flash & the Furious Five. "The Message." Sugar Hill, 1982.

Boasting a hook that remains current and consistently cited twenty years later, this record introduced socially conscious message rap, taking a slight detour from the prominent styles of party music most noted during the early years of Hip Hop.

Afrika Bambaataa. "Planet Rock." *Planet Rock—The Album.* Tommy Boy, 1982.

This record not only debuted the new sounds of Bambaataa's electro-funk, utilizing synthesizers, samplers, and a host of technology not previously associated with hip hop, but also remains one of the most sampled records within Hip Hop to date.

Run-DMC. "It's Like That"/"Sucker M.C.'s." *Run-D.M.C.* Profile, 1983.

Never before had a rap group created a record so well put together that the group members actually finished each others' lines. This record, with hard drum- and bass-oriented rhythms produced by the DJ, ushered in a new style and presentation of rap music.

UTFO. "Roxanne, Roxanne." Select, 1984.

This record sparked over 100 responses to the braggadocios prowess exemplified by the fictitious character, Roxanne. The response records immediately created a new urban legend in the form of Roxanne as female MCs across the country recorded their own versions of Roxanne stories. The record remains not only an enduring example of well-produced music but the subject of one of Hip Hop's often-told stories.

Doug E. Fresh & Get Fresh Crew. "The Show/La-Di-Da-Di." *The Show/La Di Da Di.* Reality, 1985.

This record has been remade, reworked, sampled, and resampled by numerous groups over the past twenty years, but none capture the inventiveness and charismatic performance of the original, which is considered a classic in Hip Hop.

Schoolly D. "P.S.K. What Does It Mean?" *Schoolly D.* Jive, 1986.

Acclaimed as the first gangsta rap record, this rare introduction into gang activity and the gang lifestyle inspired the rise of gangsta rap.

Public Enemy. "Black Steel in the Hour of Chaos." *It Takes a Nation of Millions to Hold Us Back.* Def Jam, 1988.

Containing some of the most recited lyrics of the late 1980s, this record offered a unique lesson to Public Enemy's contemporaries and subsequent artists in how to inspire and empower common everyday Black folk (directly) and all folks (indirectly) to aim for self-empowerment and self-determination.

Slick Rick the Ruler. "Children's Story." *The Great Adventures of Slick Rick.* Def Jam, 1988.

One of the earliest examples of Hip Hop storytelling by the greatest Hip Hop storyteller, this graphic telling of a tragic story resonates with anyone who has had a rebellious streak regardless of gender, race, or class. It showcases the power of Hip Hop to unify and call to action.

Jazzy Jeff & the Fresh Prince. "Parent's Just Don't Understand." *He's the DJ, I'm the Rapper.* Jive, 1988.

This record introduced more young people to Hip Hop than any other record to date due to its prominence on MTV and its legendary status as the lead song on the first rap album to win numerous prestigious awards.

Kid 'n Play. "Rollin' with Kid 'n Play." *2 Hype.* Select, 1988.

Kid 'n Play is known for its members' innovative presentation of fashion and dance. Their hit record not only ushered in a new style of fashion, from clothing to haircuts, but also a new form and style of b-boying/b-girling that drew from various outdated dance styles but refreshed them with the Hip Hop flare.

EPMD. "You Gots to Chill." *Strictly Business.* Priority, 1988.

This extremely popular record enjoyed an immense reception from listeners across the country and great success on urban radio, making it one of the most celebrated party jams of the late 1980s.

Young MC. "Busta Move." *Stone Cold Rhymin'.* Delicious Vinyl/Rhino, 1989.

This clever record, full of pop riffs, ignited a long list of hip hop crossover records that offered an entrée to the genre for audiences that did not have access to the often hard-core sounds of Hip Hop during this period.

NWA. "F*** Tha Police." *Straight Outta Compton.* Priority, 1989.

Speaking the words that infuriated thousands of the nation's police officers, yet deemed the group worthy of accolades as "heroes" by millions of citizens, NWA proved the potential for music to serve as a tool for speaking out against misconduct by law enforcement with this record. The effect was revolutionary for youth in the inner city and ironically within the nation's suburban areas as well.

Queen Latifah. "Ladies First." *All Hail the Queen.* Tommy Boy, 1989.

This landmark recording exerted the presence of an extremely skilled female MC. Queen Latifah shocked the world as she delivered lyrics with force and power, often citing her well-received feminist ideology.

East-West All-Stars. "Self Destruction." Jive, 1989.

Motivated by a death that occurred at a rap concert, with this recording the East-West All-Stars launched the Stop the Violence Movement. They ultimately raised half a million dollars for the National Urban League in an effort to assist in dealing with urban and gang-related violence.

Tone Loc. "Wild Thing." *Loc-ed After Dark.* Delicious Vinyl/Rhino, 1989.

This extremely popular radio and dance-club record sold more than 2 million copies, a rare feat for a record, thanks to its non-threatening and comical storyline by the deep-voiced Tone Loc.

MC Hammer. "U Can't Touch This." *Please Hammer, Don't Hurt 'Em.* Capitol, 1990.

This classic record, which catered to numerous audiences outside of Hip Hop as well as within the genre, brought great acclaim and notoriety to one of Hip Hop's greatest and most recognized entertainers.

Geto Boys. "My Mind's Playing Tricks on Me." *We Can't Be Stopped.* Rap-A-Lot, 1991.

Noted as one of the most effective recorded musical portrayals of inner-city life, this record remains a model for contemporary artists. It has often been imitated in the years since its release.

Ice-T (with Body Count). "Cop Killer." *Body Count.* Sire, 1992.

The most controversial rap record in the history of Hip Hop, inciting responses from Capitol Hill and the White House, this record achieved close to immortal status for Ice-T as an MC and made him an instant legend on the street.

Ice Cube. "It Was a Good Day." *The Predator.* Priority, 1992.

With a host of hits, this record offers some of Ice Cube's most innovative lyrics and perhaps one of his most appealing total packages. It catered to a wide Hip Hop audience.

Kriss Kross. "Jump." *Totally Krossed Out.* Ruffhouse, 1992.

Amid all of the negative content and violent presentations of Hip Hop that appeared during this period, this unique record by a fashionable and extremely innovative duo offered a powerful party tune that catered to all audiences.

The Disposable Heroes of Hip-Hoprisy. "Language of Violence." *Hypocrisy Is the Greatest Luxury.* 4th & Broadway, 1992.

This monumental record attacked the homophobia that is often displayed in Hip Hop lyrics, performance practice, and music videos while also critiquing other forms of prejudice championed by prominent MCs.

Dr. Dre. "Nuthin' but a "G" Thang." *The Chronic.* Death Row, 1992.

This revolutionary record introduced the world to the G-funk sound, which dominated Hip Hop for the next few years, and moved the dominant seat of power from New York to California.

Pharcyde. "Passing Me By." *Bizarre Ride II the Pharcyde.* Delicious Vinyl/Rhino, 1992.

With a catchy tune, extraordinary production, and a captivating vibe, this record offers listeners a sad soliloquy of romance gone awry.

Arrested Development. "Tennessee." *3 Years, 5 Months & 2 Days in the Life of. . . .* Chrysalis, 1992.

This personal and highly spiritual testimony by one of Hip Hop's revolutionary alternative groups offered an escape from the violent and misogynistic lyrics of prevalent gangsta rappers of the period.

Pete Rock & C. L. Smooth. "They Reminisce Over You (T.R.O.Y.)." *Mecca and the Soul Brother.* Elektra/Asylum, 1992.

This tribute to dancer Trouble T-Roy, whose accidental death shocked the Hip Hop community, offers a unique, emotional presentation from a period suffused with violent, nonemotional rhymes.

A Tribe Called Quest. "Award Tour." *Midnight Marauders.* Jive, 1993.

Using a catchy hook and a smooth delivery, this record met with a level of success that attests to the worldwide audience that both the group and Hip Hop had earned by the mid-1990s.

Digable Planets. "Rebirth of Slick (Cool Like Dat)." *Reachin' (A New Refutation of Time and Space).* Pendulum, 1993.

This smooth, fluid record offered a refreshing sound within Hip Hop as the group incorporated the sound and essence of jazz within a unique commentary on the creative continuum of Black popular culture.

MC Lyte. "Ruff Neck." *Ain't No Other.* First Priority, 1993.

This classic inner-city anthem offers one of the most impressive deliveries of hip hop and quickly became one of the most renowned party hits of the 1990s.

Wu-Tang Clan. "C.R.E.A.M. (Cash Rules Everything Around Me)." *Enter the Wu-Tang (36 Chambers).* Loud/RCA, 1994.

This instant classic party and dance record introduced the revolutionary and extremely creative sounds of the Wu-Tang Clan while also topping numerous charts around the world.

Common. "I Used to Love H.E.R." *Resurrection*. Relativity, 1994.

A unique commentary on the rapid decline of Hip Hop, masked as a critique of a romantic affair, this record is a critical analysis of the effects of the overwhelmingly violent and overly sexist lyrics within hip hop of the period.

Notorious B.I.G. "Juicy." *Ready to Die.* Bad Boy, 1994.

Undoubtedly one of the most widely known and recited records of the 1990s, this chart-topper launched the international career of one of Hip Hop's most highly regarded and most skilled MCs.

Warren G. "Regulate." *Regulate . . . G Funk Era.* Def Jam, 1994.

Grounded by extremely tight production and the crooning of Nate Dogg, this record became an all-time favorite for many. Its constant urban radio air play helped it to become not only well known but an international hit.

Bone Thugs-n-Harmony. "Crossroad." *E. 1999 Eternal.* Ruthless, 1995.

Written in memory of record executive and rapper Easy-E, this track, depicting a spiritual journey, sold over 4 million copies in the United States alone.

Coolio. "Gangsta's Paradise." *Gangsta's Paradise.* Tommy Boy, 1995.

Coolio's dark and dreary rap about the utopian gangsta lifestyle was one of the most celebrated records of the year, climbing numerous charts and selling an abundance of records.

Mobb Deep. "Shook Ones Pt. 2." *The Infamous.* Loud/RCA, 1995.

Mixing the most incredible musical tracks with unmatched delivery of exceptional lyrics, this record stands unparalleled even by the greatest of MCs.

Marley Marl. "Symphony Vol.1." *Marley Marl's House of Hits.* Cold Chillin', 1995.

One of the most acclaimed and widely recited collaborative recordings of a collective of MCs, this record features the expert work of Masta Ace, Craig G., Kool G. Rap, and Big Daddy Kane.

2Pac. "Hit em Up." *Death Row Greatest Hits.* Death Row, 1996.

This record, one among numerous options from this widely celebrated popular-culture icon and Hip Hop legend, reveals the urgency and power that made 2Pac (Tupac Shakur) the undisputed voice of an entire generation and one of the dominant voices of all time within Hip Hop.

Nas. "If I Ruled the World (Imagine That)." *It Was Written.* Columbia, 1996.

Featuring the singing of award-winning artist Lauryn Hill, this record offers a unique message of hope and achieved great acclaim through its appeal to people of all walks of life.

Company Flow. "The Fire in Which You Burn." *Funcrusher Plus.* Rawkus/MCA, 1997.

One of the great displays of competitive yet complementary group rhyming, this record features the Juggaknots in a clear display of verbal prowess and rhythmic dexterity.

Missy Elliott. "The Rain." *Supa Dupa Fly.* Goldmind/Elektra, 1997.

Perhaps the most innovative presentation of Hip Hop to date, this record offers a unique rhyming scheme, a unique musical track, and a unique accompanying music video, all by an extremely unique artist.

DMX. "Ruff Ryders Anthem." *It's Dark and Hell Is Hot.* Def Jam, 1998.

Showcasing DMX's rough and gritty yet polished rhyming flow, this record offers a unique style of MCing that has been emulated by peers and contemporaries.

Nelly. "Country Grammer." *Country Grammar.* Universal, 2000.

Single-handedly placing St. Louis, Missouri, on the Hip Hop radar, this clever commentary on country grammar displayed the weight of the role that public appeal and well-placed media exposure play in attaining prestige and recognition.

Nelly. "Air Force Ones." *Nellyville.* Universal, 2002.

An example of a song used as a commercial for a product, this recording assisted in revolutionizing the relationship between Hip Hop and big business, forming a bond between the two that appears, for the time being, to be inseparable.

50 Cent. "In Da Club." *Get Rich or Die Tryin'.* Shady/Aftermath/Interscope, 2002.

This urban radio and dance-club hit spent the greater part of a year as the symbolic and media-recognized sound of Hip Hop both in the United States and abroad.

Eminem. "Lose Yourself." *8 Mile.* Interscope, 2002.

This chart-topping hit landed an audience just about everywhere in the world with its captivating beat and lyrics, which continue to be recited by folks of all ages, races, genders, and classes.

Glossary

African diaspora   The spreading of various African cultural characteristics throughout the world, both directly (via migration) and indirectly (via slavery).

Afrikan   The spelling used by many, including the Temple of Hiphop, to symbolize the nonexistence of the letter "C" in many African languages. The use of the letter "K" offers a subtle protest against Western cultural domination.

Afro   A tightly curled, round hairstyle made popular by Black Americans during the 1960s and 1970s.

Afrocentric   Term used to imply a connection to African heritage or to the African diaspora.

Album   A collection of recordings compiled and released as a single work. Complete CDs are also called albums.

All-city   Descriptive term for graffiti art on major subway lines that travel around the city.

All-country   Descriptive term for graffiti art on a major railroad freight line that travels around the country.

Alliteration   A literary device using the same or similar consonants at the beginning of a string of words that is used in hip hop and rap music.

American Forces Network (AFN)
A worldwide broadcasting mechanism of U.S.-based television and radio, primarily targeted toward overseas servicemen and women, provided by the U.S. Department of Defense. AFN introduced hip hop music and Hip Hop Culture to many around the globe through U.S.-based sitcoms and radio programming.

Apache line
One of numerous methods of gang initiation. In the Apache line, an initiate must walk a certain distance in a straight line while gang members on both sides actively beat the initiate.

Back spinning
The DJ technique of spinning a record counterclockwise.

Baggin'
One of numerous terms used to describe talking about someone in a negative way, either to their face or behind their back.

Bata
A group of three double-ended drums used in the rituals of the Lucumi (Yoruba) cult in Cuba, as well as in more contemporary forms of Cuban music and dance.

Battle
A competition between DJs, graffiti artists, b-boys/b-girls, or MCs and their peers. The competition can be formal for a prize, but most often it is informal for no prize other than pride.

Battling
The act of competing in a battle.

B-boy/b-girl
The dance-oriented participants in Hip Hop Culture; however, the term is now also used to describe practitioners of Hip Hop Culture in general.

Beat box
An electronic device used to program drum and other percussion sounds, most often used by producers and/or DJs.

Beat juggling
The method of creating a piece of music by organizing existing drumbeats with a mixer and two turntables.

Beats
Most often used to describe an instrumental recording of rhythms used by MCs to rap over. The term is also used to describe drum-based patterns.

Bebop
The fast-paced and often complex, usually improvisational subgenre of jazz prominent in the 1940s.

Bed-stuy
One of the many nicknames for the Bedford-Stuyvesant neighborhood of Brooklyn, New York.

Beef
A conflict or problem between individuals or groups of people.

Black arts movement
The artistic movement complementary to the Black power movement that used artistic expression to convey the social, political, economic, and cultural desires of many Blacks during the 1960s.

Black books
The sketch/idea notebooks carried around and used by graffiti artists to plan and practice future works.

Black expressive culture
The artistic expression of descendants of the African diaspora, most generally located in the United States. Music, all formats of fine art, dance, and literature are included as well as speech and gesture, fashion, performance practice, and athleticism.

Black Panther Party
Originally named the Black Panther Party for Self-Defense, this progressive political organization, founded by Huey P. Newton along with Bobby Seale, pursued equality, justice, and freedom for Blacks during the 1960s.

Black power
A political term first used by writer Robert F. Williams during the 1950s and 1960s to describe the social organization of Black people to further themselves in the understanding of Black culture and to emphasize their influence and progress within society.

Black power movement   A social, political, economic, and cultural movement during the 1960s that aimed to move aggressively toward equality and justice for Blacks.

Black Spades   One of the most revered Bronx-based street gangs. They were formerly known as the Savage Seven.

Blaxploitation   A film genre during the 1970s in which predominantly Black actors and actresses portrayed stereotypical roles, often including great amounts of violence, crime, drugs, and prostitution.

Bling bling   The prominence and often the possession of jewelry and other forms of visible material possessions.

Boasting   Verbal praises or brags about skills, personal attributes, possessions, and the like.

Bombin'   The act of tagging or doing a "throw up" or a "piece" in graffiti art.

Boogaloo   A funk-oriented street dance developed on the West Coast during the 1970s that influenced numerous b-boys/b-girls.

Boogie Down   One of many nicknames for Bronx, New York.

Boombox   A portable audio system, often containing one or two cassette players and two sizable built-in speakers.

Bootleg   An illegal or counterfeit duplicate, often of musical recordings.

Boy band   An all-male group assembled by audition and by an outside force other than the performing artists themselves.

Break (break beats)   The instrumental portion of a song focusing primarily on the percussion. DJ Kool Herc was the first to use and popularize the break beats of songs by playing them continuously using two of the same record on two turntables.

Breakin' A particular type of dance style, most often performed during the break of a song (hence the name of the dance) by the b-boys/b-girls. Dance is one of the four foundational elements of Hip Hop Culture.

Broadway show tune A genre of music composed specifically for live theater.

Campbell-lock The nickname for the funk-oriented street-dance style developed by Don Campbell during the 1970s and made popular by many b-boys/b-girls.

Cappin' One of numerous terms used to describe talking about someone in negative terms, either to their face or behind their back.

Catch on A funk-oriented street dance developed on the West Coast during the 1970s that influenced numerous b-boys/b-girls.

Cholos A Mexican gangster.

Civil rights movement An ongoing social and political movement by Blacks in their quest for equal rights and equal access to justice. The height of the movement was from 1945 through 1970.

COINTELPRO An acronym for the Counter Intelligence Program used by the Federal Bureau of Investigation to combat dissident political organizations. Many have alluded to the fact that local police units have used similar force as was used in FBI COINTELPRO investigations, such as police surveillance, harassment, and peculiar treatment of subjects soley due to their involvement in Hip Hop Culture.

Cult flick A film that sparks a following of people who have an intimate connection with the characters or plot of the film and who tend to watch the film over and over again.

Cutting

One of numerous techniques used by DJs when mixing records between two turntables.

Danzón

A traditional Cuban dance form developed in the 1930s and 1940s.

DAT

An acronym for digital audiotape.

DJ

Short for "disc jockey"; a person who plays records (or CDs) at parties, clubs, on the radio, or for competition. DJing is one of four foundational elements of Hip Hop Culture.

Dope

Illegal narcotics.

Double-dutch jump rope

A complex style of jump roping using two ropes simultaneously and featuring acrobatic movements and sung children's rhymes.

Dreads

Short for dreadlocks, a hairstyle featuring long, thick braids and popularized by Rastafarians.

Electro-funk

A genre of music based on electronic and sampled sounds. It was influenced by the European group Kraftwerk, but developed and popularized by Afrika Bambaataa.

Electronica

A variety of electronic-influenced music, whether dance-oriented or for casual listening.

FBI

Acronym for the Federal Bureau of Investigation, a federal police force and principal investigative unit of the U.S. Department of Justice.

Fifth element

An element of Hip Hop Culture beyond the foundational four elements (see Chapter 2). For some, the fifth element is human beat boxing; for others, it is the idea of "Knowledge, wisdom, and overstanding" promoted by Afrika Bambaataa.

Five Percent Nation	A Black American social and religious movement founded in Harlem in the 1960s by Clarence 13X. The Five Percent Nation is also known as the Nation of Gods and Earths.
Flow	A continuous delivery of rhymes by an MC.
Funk	A music genre of the 1960s and 1970s championed by James Brown and others who influenced the early sounds of Hip Hop.
Gangbanger	An individual who is part of a street gang; often associated with the use of violence and guns.
Gangsta	A practitioner of gangsta rap music. The term can also refer to a member of a street gang.
Gangsta rap	The hard-core music influenced by the actions and lifestyles of gangstas.
Gold record	An award and designation by the Recording Industry Association of America (RIAA) in recognition of more than 500,000 units sold.
Graffiti	A form of artistic expression with a lengthy history. Its connection to Hip Hop Culture occurs as inner-city youth, particularly in New York, used the form of expression, often on public property, to articulate their needs, wants, and desires to a population of adults who would not listen to them. Early on, graffiti was considered one of the four foundational elements of the Hip Hop Culture. Graffiti is typically done on large surfaces such as walls, trains, and the like.
Grandmaster	A term borrowed from martial arts symbolizing the highest level of competence or achievement.
Grandmixer	A term based on the martial arts term "grandmaster" symbolizing the highest

level of competence or achievement, yet specifically used to acknowledge a DJ who specializes in mixing.

Grandwizard   A term based on the martial arts term "grandmaster" symbolizing the highest level of competence or achievement.

Griot   A name most often associated with the West African poet/musician who carries and reveals the local history of a community through oral tradition. The term has been borrowed by other cultures, including Black Americans to speak of individuals who retain the legacy and heritage of local, regional, and cultural communities through oral tradition.

Guagua   A Cuban percussion block or traditional Cuban stick pattern.

Habaneros   Residents of Havana, Cuba.

Hater   A person who expresses dislike or disdain for something with no reasoning.

Hip hop   The musical expression of Hip Hop Culture. Although it is often differentiated from rap music, it is similar to rap in its use of DJs, MCs, and producers. Usually lowercase (hip hop).

Hip Hop Culture   Hip Hop Culture began with four foundational elements used by inner city youth, first in New York's boroughs, to express themselves. Built on the elements of DJ, MC, graffiti, and dance (including breakin', popin', and others), Hip Cop Culture has continued as a global movement still retaining the importance of social conscious and political, economic, and cultural engagement.

Hip Hop generation   The term used to describe a generation of young people born between 1965 and 1984.

Hip Hop head	A Hip Hop enthusiast or aficionado.
Hiphop	Term used by KRS-One and the Temple of Hiphop to distinguish the cultural and activist aspects of the culture rather than just the musical genre. They close it up as one word but often capitalize it.
Homeboy	A male associate or friend from the neighborhood.
Homegirl	A female associate or friend from the neighborhood.
'Hood	Short for "neighborhood"; most often refers to an inner-city, impoverished community.
Hoodie	A sweatshirt with a hood. During the 1980s and early 1990s hoodies were a common part of Hip Hop fashion, prior to the rise of Hip Hop specialty fashion lines.
House music	A specific type of electronic dance music prominent during the early to mid-1980s.
Human beat box	An individual who performs percussion vocally, emulating the sounds of kick drums, snares, hi-hats, scratching, and other sound effects to develop patterns that can be rapped or sung over. Certain human beat boxers also mimic the sounds of instruments such as the bass and brass horns.
Indie record label	A small or independent record label not associated with or owned by a major corporation or parent company.
Inner city	The poorer, less prestigious areas within a major city.
Ivory tower	The highest level of intellectual pursuit, most often a prestigious institution of higher learning or an isolated enclave of invited intellects.
J Hip Hop	Japanese underground Hip Hop.
J rap	Japanese mainstream Hip Hop.

Jam

A party.

Jonesin'

Talking about someone usually in a negataive way, either to their face or behind their back. The term also can mean a craving.

Knickers

Men's baggy trousers worn by West Coast street dancers during the 1970s.

Kulture

A term popularized by KRS-One and the Temple of Hiphop alluding to the absence of the letter "C" in many African languages.

Latchkey kids

The growing population of children who return from school to a home of limited supervision, if any, due to the work schedule of their parent(s).

Lay-ups

The area set aside to store trains or freight cars when not in use. Some lay-ups are under tunnels, elevated, or in large yards. Lay-ups served as prime locations for graffiti.

Locking

A funk-oriented style of street dance developed on the West Coast during the 1970s.

Machismo

An exaggerated sense of masculinity.

Mambo

The dance and rhythmic pattern produced by the fusion of traditional Cuban rhythms and jazz that was developed during the 1950s.

MC

A master of ceremony, or "emcee." The term also describes a foundational element of Hip Hop Culture.

Metropolitan Transportation Authority (MTA)

A public-benefit corporation chartered by the state of New York and responsible for buses, subways, railways, bridges, tunnels, and most, if not all, other public transportation opportunities and facilities.

Misogyny

An exaggerated aversion to women or hate of women.

Mix tapes/CDs A compilation of songs (often compiled by a DJ) that is usually composed of previously unreleased rap songs or remixes of existing songs.

Mogul A wealthy and extremely powerful person.

MP3 A digital format of audio data used to transmit song files or sound waves over the Internet.

Multiplatinum record An award and designation by the Recording Industry Association of America (RIAA) in recognition of 2 million or more units sold.

NAACP Acronym for the National Association for the Advancement of Colored People, a civil rights organization founded in 1909 on behalf of Black people.

Old school The style of Hip Hop (particularly rap music) dating back to the 1970s and lasting through the mid-1980s.

Onomatopoeia A literary device using words that imitate the sounds they describe that is used in hip hop and rap music.

Overstanding A term coined by Afrika Bambaataa, borrowing from the Rastafarian principle of nonconformity. For Bambaataa, "under" implied negative energy, whereas "over" has a positive connotation.

PA system Short for public address system, a combination of a power amp and speakers used for amplification.

Parents Music Resource Center (PMRC) A committee of several wives of prominent congressmen and White House staff formed in 1985 to educate parents on the abundance of negative influences in popular music. The group sought the censorship and rating of commercially distributed music.

Piece	Short for "masterpiece"; used to describe graffiti that is larger than a tag, often accomplished in multiple colors.
Piecin'	In graffiti art, the action of doing a "piece."
Platinum record	An award and designation by the Recording Industry Association of America (RIAA) in recognition of over 1 million units sold.
Playing the dozens	One of numerous phrases and terms used to describe talking about someone in negative terms, either to their face or behind their back.
Poppin'	A funk-oriented style of street dance developed on the West Coast during the 1970s.
Posse	A group of associates.
Producer	In the music industry, the person directly responsible for the overall concept of a recording. In hip hop and rap, most often the producer creates the outline or framework that the MC, DJ, and other participants will work from.
Pun	A literary device used to produce a comical play on words that is used in hip hop and rap music.
Quick-mix theory	A system developed by Grandmaster Flash in which he marked breaks on records and used a set of headphones to preview the breaks before mixing them live through the loudspeakers.
Rap	Rhythmic speaking or rhyming, either to a beat (that is, a recorded track, human beat box, and the like) or a cappella.
Rap music	The music of Hip Hop Culture. Traditionally, rap music consisted of the combined talents and creativity of both an MC and a DJ, but most current rap music does not involve a DJ. This genre of music consists of many local and regional styles as well as

different philosophical approaches and includes gangsta rap, East Coast rap, West Coast rap, southern rap, and conscious rap, to name a few.

Rapero   A Cuban rapper or MC.

Rappin'   The act of speaking rhythmically over music or other rhythmic accompaniment such as hand claps, beat boxing, and the like.

Rastafarian   A religious movement founded by working-class and poor Jamaicans during the 1930s stressing nonconformity and a high reverence for Haile Selassie, the former emperor of Ethiopia.

Record (single)   A gramophone record with a single song on one side (A-side) and another song on the opposite side (B-side).

Rumba   A traditional Cuban dance, drumming style, and song form.

Running the mill One of the numerous methods of gang recruitment where an initiate must walk a certain distance in a straight line while gang members on both sides actively beat the initiate.

Russian roulette A prominent gang initiation practice where the initiate places a round in a revolver, spins the cylinder, and fires the revolver at himself at close range, displaying the ability to conquer fear.

Sampling   Taking excerpts of prerecorded music and using them in a new work.

Scratch   DJing technique discovered by Grandwizard Theodore in which sounds and effects are created through the manual manipulation of a record while it spins on a turntable.

Scratchin'   A technique used by DJs and turntablists that involves moving a record back and forth while it is being played on a turntable to produce a unique sound.

Shout-out   A DJ name checking, or calling out one's name, over the microphone in a public place or on a recording.

Skullie   A small cotton or knit hat.

Slum lord   A landlord who does not maintain a safe, well-kept property but instead allows the property to fall below safety and health code standards, to the neglect of their tenants.

Smurf   A French b-boy/b-girl.

Son   A traditional Cuban dance, drumming style, and song form.

Stepin'/Steppin'   A funk-oriented style of street dance developed on the West Coast during the 1970s.

Stickin'   A funk-oriented style of street dance developed on the West Coast during the 1970s.

Tag   A graffiti artist's or writer's signature. A tag is usually composed of a few characters that are usually written or drawn the same way every time.

Taggin'   Producing a tag, most often with spray paint or markers.

Techno   A popular form of electronic dance music prominent during the 1980s.

Throw up   A quick execution of graffiti of any size. Often more than one color is used. In some areas, a "throw up" implies the use of bubble letters.

Thug   A street tough and often streetwise person.

Thuglife   The often misunderstood and misperceived acronym offered by Tupac Shakur for "The Hate U Gave Little Infants F***s Everyone."

Also a code of conduct presented to West Coast gangstas by Tupac and Mutulu Shakur during a 1992 truce.

Toast The Jamaican art of talking over instrumental tracks, often to incite people to dance and participate.

Turf Gang or personal territory.

Turntable A phonograph used by a DJ or turntablist.

Turntable Jahz The creative term used by the Invisibl Skratch Piklz to describe their jazz-influenced approach to turntablism, offering a tribute to the improvisational aspects and the overall jazz aesthetic.

Turntablism The practice of performing on turntables as musical instruments popularized in the 1990s with groups such as the Beat Junkies, Invisibl Skratch Piklz, X-Ecutioners, and others.

Turntablist Someone who uses the turntable as a musical instrument and has a mastery of some fundamental DJing techniques.

12-inch A record (single) as opposed to an album. In some cases the "12-inch" will contain various versions of the same song, often called "remixes."

Underground Local, regional, and perhaps national (due to technology) environments where Hip Hop remains below the radar of the media and mainstream public awareness and is not highly commercialized. The underground most often exposes the four foundational elements as well as additional, more recent elements.

Walkman A pocket-sized cassette player, often combined with a radio. Instead of a loudspeaker, the Walkman uses a lightweight earphone for personal use.

Wigger   A pejorative term used to describe a White kid who mimics the stereotypical presentation of language, fashion, and mannerisms of Black kids from the ghetto.

Wild style   A complex yet personalized style of graffiti.

Writer   A person who does graffiti most often in the form of a "tag" or "throw up."

Index